The Greek
Concept of Nature

D1712825

SUNY series in Ancient Greek Philosophy

Anthony Preus, editor

The Greek
Concept of Nature

Gerard Naddaf

State University of New York Press

Published by
State University of New York Press, Albany

For information, contact State University of New York Press, Albany, NY
www.sunypress.edu

Production by Michael Haggett
Marketing by Michael Campochiaro

Library of Congress Cataloging-in-Publication Data

Naddaf, Gerard, 1950–
    The Greek concept of nature / Gerard Naddaf.
    p. cm. — (SUNY series in ancient Greek philosophy)
    Includes bibliographical references and index.
    ISBN 0-7914-6373-7
    1. Philosophy of nature—History. 2. Philosophy, Ancient. I. Title. II. Series.
B185.N325 2004
113'.0938—dc22
                                                                    2004006772

10 9 8 7 6 5 4 3 2 1

For Emily and Alexander

Contents

Preface

In 1992, I published a book entitled: *L'origine et l'évolution du concept grec de "physis."* It met with a generally favorable reception among reviewers, and over the years, I received encouragement to produce an English edition of the work. It seems that the idea of nature in ancient Greece fascinates scholars in a variety of different fields.

While the present volume, *The Greek Concept of Nature,* retains the germ that initiated the 1992 work, it is not a simple translation of the earlier volume. There has been a considerable development. This is due primarily to further reflection on the subject—albeit also with the engagement with new scholarship. This development with new ideas will be even more evident in the two subsequent volumes: *Plato and the Peri Phuseōs Tradition* and *Living in Conformity with Nature.* The focus of the latter will be Aristotle and the Hellenistic Tradition, which was not initially treated in the 1992 work.

I would like to express my gratitude to Luc Brisson, Pierre Hadot, Robert Hahn, Pierre Pellegrin, Tony Preus, Tom Robinson, and the late Mathias Baltes and Trevor Saunders for their encouragement. I would also like to thank Benoît Castelnérac, Alex Livingston, and Richard Allen for their editorial assistance. And, of course, SUNY Press for their tolerance for my delinquent manuscript.

Translations from the Greek are my own unless otherwise indicated. After some reflection, I decided to employ transliterated Greek throughout, in place of Greek characters. I have transliterated the η and ω by ē and ō. The iota subscripts are indicated at the end of the long vowel, for example: ῳ gives ōi. In order to lighten the text, I have not reproduced the accents. In my view, this makes the work more accessible to an audience that includes readers who are not specialists in the field.

Finally, I would like to thank the Social Sciences and Humanities Research Council of Canada and York University for their generous support.

ABBREVIATIONS

DK   H. Diels and W. Kranz, *Die Fragmente der Vorsokratiker,* 6th ed., Berlin: Weidmann, 1951.

KRS   G. S. Kirk, J. E. Raven, and M. Schofield, *The Presocratic Philosophers,* 2nd ed., Cambridge: Cambridge University Press, 1983.

Introduction

The Greek notion of *phusis,* usually translated as nature (from the Latin *natura*), has been decisive both for the early history of philosophy and for its subsequent development. In fact, it is often said that the Greeks discovered "nature." But what did the earliest philosophers actually have in mind when they spoke of *phusis?* There is a formidable amount of controversy on the subject. This investigation attempts to reconstruct from a historical perspective the origin and evolution of this concept.

The impetus behind this study (and the general thesis it proposes) originated many years ago in an analysis of book 10 of Plato's *Laws.* In this work (which will be the subject of a separate volume), Plato criticizes those who wrote works in prose or in verse of the *peri phuseōs* type. Plato's primary reproach is that the authors of these works never admitted the notion of intention (implied by *technē*) as the explanatory principle behind the order that governs the universe. This refusal, in Plato's eyes, is at the basis of the "atheism" of his time. In order to understand the true meaning of the doctrine of Plato's adversaries, I felt that it was necessary to reconstruct the entire movement of thought that led to the problem that Plato was attempting to resolve.

When one closely examines the contents of these works entitled *Peri phuseōs,* it is clear their primary aim is to explain how the *present* order of things was established. This, in fact, clearly follows from Plato's own analysis in *Laws* 10. These works propose a theory to explain the origin (and development) of the world, humanity, and the city/society. The structure of these works (even before undertaking a linguistic analysis of the word *phusis*) leads one to conclude that for the first philosophers or pre-Socratics as we conventionally call them, the word *phusis* in this context means the origin and growth of the universe as a totality. And since humanity and the society in which they reside are also part of this totality explanations of the origin and development of humanity and society must necessarily follow an explanation of the world.

In *Laws* 10, Hesiod is also among the accused. The reason is that according to Hesiod's account in the *Theogony,* the gods originate *after* the universe. More precisely, according to Hesiod's theogonic account, gods are derived

1

from primordial entities (Chaos, Gaia, Eros, Tartaros, etc.), whereas for Plato, if one does not postulate a divinity present from the beginning and independent of the material on which it works, it is impossible to attribute the order that governs the universe to an intelligence.

When one closely analyses Hesiod's theogonic account, it is possible to discern the same three part schema that is discernable in the pre-Socratic accounts of the *peri phuseōs* type: namely a cosmogony, an anthropogony, and a politogony. In reality, this three part schema is intimately connected with the form of a cosmogonic myth which, in turn, is closely connected with the mythico-ritual scenario of the periodic renewal of the world. The aim is to provide an explanation for the *present* social and natural order and a guarantee that these orders will remain as they are. In fact, in a cosmogonical myth, both cosmic evolution and cosmic order are modeled on, and expressed in terms of, the socio-political structure or life of the community.

In a certain sense, this myth explains and guarantees a "way of life" for the social group. This brings us to another interesting feature of accounts of the *peri phuseōs* type. It is still somewhat commonplace to associate the pre-Socratic conception of philosophy with complete "disinterested" inquiry or speculation (evidenced somewhat in Aristotle's generic *phusiologoi* to qualify these individuals). But a keen interest in politics appears to have been the *norm* among these early philosophers. In fact, it is possible that their respective *historia* (investigation or inquiry) may have been politically motivated. The word *historia* and/or *phusis* or more precisely *historia peri phuseōs,* may have been the newly minted phraseology to express the new rational approach to a way of life in conformity with the new political realities and the new comprehensive view of how the world, man and society originated and developed.

There is, in fact, an interesting parallel and continuity between political engagement and cosmological theory and by extension a way of life in all the pre-Socratic *historia* of the *peri phuseōs* type and their mythical antecedents. However, our own investigation covers a wide framework and could also be considered as a more general history of early Greek philosophy. Indeed, there is a correlation between accounts of the *peri phuseōs* type and the word *philosophia* which may also have been newly minted. Thus according to Heraclitus (DK22B35) "lovers of wisdom ought very much to be inquirers into many things" *(chrē gar eu mala pollōn historas philosophous andras einai),*[1] and there is no doubt, as we will see, that the pre-Socratics investigated a wide range of *interrelated* things.[2]

If a detailed analysis of book 10 of Plato's *Laws* was the impetus behind this investigation, the method which guided it is grounded in a clarification of the word *phusis.* This linguistic analysis constitutes the departure point for all the subsequent research, historical, philosophical, spiritual, and even archeological. Here is a brief overview of what follows.

The primary aim of chapter 1 is to understand the general meaning of the word *phusis*. The chapter thus begins with a linguistic analysis of the word *phusis*. It follows from this analysis that the fundamental and etymological meaning of the term *phusis* is that of "growth" and as an action noun ending in *-sis, phusis* means the whole process of growth of a thing from birth to maturity. I then examine the one and only occurrence of the word in Homer which is not only compatible with this analysis, but the general context in which it appears, an analysis of the properties of a magical plant in an encounter between gods and humans, can also serve as an example (something scholars have failed to notice), for what one could (or should) expect to find in the prephilosophical/rational use of the word. When we turn to the first occurrence of the word in a pre-Socratic, Heraclitus DK22B1, it is clear that *phusis* means not only the *essential character* of a thing, but also how a/the thing originates and develops and thus continues to regulate its nature. In sum, *phusis* must be understood dynamically as the "real constitution" of a thing as it is realized from beginning to end with all of its properties. This in fact is the meaning that one finds nearly every time that the term *phusis* is employed in the writings of the pre-Socratics. It is never employed in the sense of something static, although the accent may be on either the *phusis* as origin, the *phusis* as process, or the *phusis* as result. All three, of course, are comprised in the original meaning of the word *phusis*.

Did the pre-Socratics beginning with the Ionians also understand *phusis* in a comprehensive sense, that is, to designate not just a particular thing, but *all* things? I argue that they did and this, in fact, is what must be understood by the expression *historia peri phuseōs,* that is, an investigation into the nature of things. There is, in fact, a good deal of consensus on this point. However, scholars diverge considerably on the meaning of *phusis* in the expression *historia peri phuseōs*. After an analysis of the expression *Peri phuseōs* as the title of a work, different scholarly interpretations of the word *phusis* in the expressions *peri phuseōs* and *historia peri phuseōs* are examined. There are, in the main, four different interpretations: (1) *phusis* in the sense of primordial matter; (2) *phusis* in the sense of process; (3) *phusis* in the sense of primordial matter and process; and (4) *phusis* in the sense of the origin, process, and result.

In light of the linguistic analysis of the word *phusis,* I argue for the fourth interpretation. In sum, the term *phusis,* in the comprehensive sense, refers to the origin and the growth of the universe from beginning to end. In conjunction with this, I examine three series of texts, including a number of Hippocratic medical texts, which, in my view, demonstrate (1) this notion of *phusis;* (2) the relation between this notion and the method in vogue with the pre-Socratics; and (3) the relation between the generation of the *kosmos* and the expression *peri phuseōs* or *historia peri phuseōs*.

What follows from these texts is that the pre-Socratics understood by the expression, *historia peri phuseōs,* a true history of the universe, from its origins to the present, and this history certainly included the origin of mankind. However, I argue that the *historia* included more than this. In my view, the *historia* was about how the present order of things was established and thus included the origin and development of human culture and/or society. This is precisely what we find in Plato's detailed description of accounts of the *peri phuseōs* type in book 10 of the *Laws* which is included in these texts. Moreover, this is consistent with the general account and structure of cosmogonical myths. Their aim is also to explain how the present natural *and* social order emerged from beginning to end. This is subject of chapter 2.

In chapter 2, I begin with an analysis of myth and, in particular, a cosmogonic myth. A myth is considered to be a true story that relates *how* something real came into existence. Because myth wants to bring about the truth it proclaims, events that occurred *ab origine* are reenacted in ritual, that is, demonstrative acts that are perceived as having been performed at the beginning of time by gods or ancestors. This is also the case with the cosmogonic myth, providing both an explanation for the present social and natural order and a guarantee the present orders of nature and society will remain as they are. In a cosmogonical myth both cosmic evolution and cosmic order are modeled on and expressed in terms of the socio-political structure or life of the community. From this perspective, the society in which ancient humanity resides is the logical starting point. Thus, in order to explain how the present social order came into being, the cosmogonic myth must necessarily begin with the birth of the world (a cosmogony), then recount the birth of mankind (an anthropogony), and finally relate the birth of society (a sociogony or politogony). For ancient peoples, society comes into existence without a real past in the sense it only reflects the result of a series of events that took place *in illo tempore,* that is, before the "chronological" time of the people who narrate the myth.

I examine an excellent example of such a cosmogonic myth: the great creation epic, the *Enuma Elish.* This myth narrates how the sovereign god Marduk established the present order of things. The *Enuma Elish* begins with a description of the primordial reality (or chaos). It then describes the birth and evolution of the *present* order of things (natural and social), a universe that exhibits law and order. This is the result of a combat between Tiamat and Marduk, or more precisely, between two generations of gods representing disorder and order respectively. Following this, we can easily follow the birth of humankind (and its reason for being) and the type and structure of society in which humans will reside. The *Enuma Elish,* like all cosmogonic myths, which relate how the world was delivered from regression and chaos, was reiterated and re-actualized each year in the capital city during the New Year festival. A series of rites re-actualized the battle which had taken place *in illo tempore* between Marduk (represented by the king) and Tiamat (the Dragon symbolizing the primordial ocean). The victory of god and his cosmogonic work assured once again the regularity of nature's rhythms and the good state of society in its entirety. The ceremony was attended by the social elite who renewed their oath of allegiance to the king, just as the gods swore an oath to Marduk when he was elected king. They would have listened with reverence to the sacred epic, and its recital and reenactment would have persuaded them how an "ideal state" should be organized and why their loyal support should be unequivocal.

Following this, I examine Hesiod's *Theogony* which is another prime example of a cosmogonical myth. The *Theogony*, a hymn in honor of Zeus, explains how the god, after a series of socio-political power struggles, defeats his enemies and dispenses, as the new ruler, privileges and obligations among the immortals, thus establishing and guaranteeing the permanence of the present order of things. I begin, however, with some important preliminary remarks including Hesiod as an historical figure, his relation with the alphabet, and, most important, how his reference to the Lelantine war reinforces the thesis that the *Theogony* is essentially "conservative," since it tends to praise and support the aristocracy—indeed, it gives the aristocracy a mythical justification, since it anchors the institution in a cosmogonical myth. I then analyze the overall structure of the *Theogony* beginning with the cosmogony strictly speaking and show how this myth has the same three part schema that one finds in the *Enuma Elish* creation story. In conjunction with this, I show that Hesiod's *Theogony* explains the origin of the organizational structure and code of values of the gods and by extension, the heroes and nobles of Hesiod's time.

I then show the most notable difference between the cosmogonic myth presented by Hesiod and that of the *Enuma Elish:* the absence of ritual. Indeed, even if Hesiod's *Theogony* offers an explanation of the origin and the evolution of the world and proposes an exemplary socio-political model of "existence" for mankind within the world order established by Zeus, what is striking about Hesiod's account is that, in it, the periodic renewal of the world, humanity, and society is no longer necessary. In fact, the manner in which the cosmogony is represented in Hesiod's *Theogony* strongly suggests that the renewal ritual no longer has a reason for being. A comparison of the roles played by Zeus and by Marduk in their respective cosmogonies clearly demonstrates this. Unlike Marduk, Zeus does not intervene in the natural order of things. He is simply at the origin of a new socio-political order. This may explain why Hesiod's theogonic text unfolds in a perfectly linear and irreversible way. Unlike Marduk, Zeus does not recreate what is already in place: the physical universe as we know it. I attribute this novelty in Hesiod to the collapse of the Mycenean civilization. There is no doubt, however, that Hesiod's *Theogony* would have been performed (and thus ritualized, so to speak) before an audience. Further, there is no doubt that it was addressed to an aristocratic elite and that it was meant to enhance, if anything, their value system: a Homeric and thus a conservative value system at least by the then current standards.

I then turn to the *Works and Days* which presents, in my view, a very different position. While it does contain several traditional myths that convey messages that the social group could have considered as having been transmitted by its ancestors, in many respects it is advocating a new type of social reform, a new type of general *aretē*. Indeed, in the *Works and Days*, Hesiod contests the Homeric conception of *aretē* and offers another in its place. No longer the possession of nobles and heros, the *aretē*-norm now belongs to another class of men. The *panaristos*, the complete man, is the successful farmer, and *aretē* now signifies the qualities that enable a person to prosper and avoid famine.

In the *Works and Days* as in the *Theogony*, the kings are again at center stage; however, the description offered by Hesiod in the former is radically different from the latter. Hesiod directly challenges the kings of Thespies with an astonishing amount of free speech. In the *Works and Days*, the kings are unequivocally characterized as greedy and their verdicts as corrupt. In the *Theogony*, receiving gifts in exchange for delivering judgments is a right of a mediator or king, and Hesiod painted there a rather flattering picture of the custom. In the *Works and Days*, Hesiod is clearly vexed by the system of gifts. He doubts that the verdict or *dikē* will be straight, and he suggests that he has firsthand knowledge of this. In Hesiod's eyes, this system of justice must be replaced at any cost, for it clearly has a legal force. If one considers that the *Works and Days* unequivocally argues that the justice system of the *basileis* must be replaced with a more objective (if not codified) notion of justice (and since it must have been "performed" on a regular basis), it must have had a lasting and subversive effect on subsequent generations. From this perspective, Hesiod is certainly a catalyst for western political paideia; indeed, an advocate and initiator of a new revolutionary way of thinking which will influence political ideals and their corresponding cosmological models.

In chapter 3, I examine the first rational account of the *peri phuseōs* type, that of Anaximander of Miletus (610–546 BCE). In this chapter, I argue that the present order of things for Anaximander comprises not only the physical world strictly speaking but also the socio-political world in which the investigator/author resided. From this perspective, I concur somewhat with W. A. Heidel, for whom the aim of Anaximander's book *Peri phuseōs* was "to sketch the life-history of the cosmos from the moment of its emergence from infinitude to the author's own time." This is precisely what Hesiod is attempting to do in the *Theogony*. He sought to explain how Zeus established the present order of things, natural and social. This is the aim of a cosmogonical myth in general, and Anaximander is clearly attempting to accomplish the same end. This is why he must begin with a cosmogony and then go on to an anthropogony and finally to a politogony. However, his approach, as I attempt to show, is radically different since his explanation is not only naturalistic, but he clearly and distinctly separates all three developments.

I begin my study of Anaximander's *historia* with an analysis of the origin and development of his cosmological model. This necessitates beginning with an analysis of his chronological starting point, that is, *phusis* as *archē*, and why he choose *to apeiron* to qualify this entity. I then examine his cosmogony, noting the similarities and differences with its mythical antecedents. The central idea is that the cosmos grows, like a living being, from a seed or germ. This germ contains the two primary opposites hot and cold. Once the separation of the mutually hostile opposites commences, the natural operation of their reciprocal power accounts for all natural change.

Following this I give a detailed examination of Anaximander's famous cosmological model which places an immobile earth at the *center* of a celestial sphere surrounded by three concentric rings which contain the heavenly bodies. The examination shows that Anaximander conceived his universe or cosmological model according to a mathematical or geometrical plan which reflects a propensity for both *geometrical* equality and symmetry following the series 3. Although this conclusion has been adopted by the vast majority of commentators there is considerable disagreement on the origin and significance of the numbers and consequently about the origin of the cosmological model. I examine the four main hypotheses: (1) the numbers are the result of a sacred or mythical inspiration; (2) the numbers are the result of an astronomical inspiration; (3) the numbers (at least the 3 to 1 ratio) are the result of an architectural or technical inspiration; and (4) the numbers are a result of a political inspiration. I attempt to show that the political hypothesis is the only valid one, but for reasons that had not been hitherto evoked. I argue that the numbers that translate the sizes and distances of the heavenly bodies in relation to the earth correspond in some way or other to the three social groups of which the *polis* of Anaximander's time was composed: the aristocracy, the (new) middle class and the peasantry (or poor). Anaximander's cosmological model reflects what he saw as the only possible way of ridding the *polis* of the political dissention of his time: *isonomia*. In the final analysis, what we have is a sort of reciprocal relation between the microcosm of the city and the macrocosm of the universe.

The explanation that Anaximander gives us of the origin of humanity and of the other living beings (not mentioned by the poets or in mythical accounts) is, as in the case of his cosmology, the first naturalistic explanation in this domain. As one might expect, his explanation is entirely consistent with his cosmological system. Indeed, the same natural processes are at work. Living beings emerge from a sort of primeval moisture or slime which is activated by the heat of the sun after the initial formation of the universe. Based on the testimonia it seems safe to say that Anaximander argued that in the beginning members of the human species were born from a different animal species that was capable of nourishing them until such time as they could support themselves. Moreover, *man* no longer has the temporal and logical priority over *woman* that he possessed in the mythical accounts of the Greeks. Finally, since human beings have a real beginning in time, the origin of humanity and society are no longer represented as coeval; that is, human beings will no longer be seen as coming into existence within the context of a fully functioning society as it was the case in mythical accounts.

The most important obstacle we encounter in coming to terms with Anaximander's view on the origin and evolution of society is, of course, a lack of testimonia. Nonetheless, there is some non-Peripatician doxographical evidence which is not contested by commentators. These attest to Anaximander as a mapmaker and geographer. I show that geography and history are, in fact, inseparable at this point in time. Indeed, according to Strabo they are both closely connected with politics and cosmology and he cites Anaximander on the authority of Eratosthenes as a prime example if not the initiator of this. I argue meanwhile that Anaximander was no armchair philosopher. He formulated his theory through investigation and discovery; he travelled extensively, notably to Egypt via Naucratis. In this regard, I attempt to show that Egypt, or, more precisely, the Nile Delta, was seen as the cradle of civilization and, in certain respects, as the center of the universe. I argue that there is a good deal of circumstantial evidence for this, but the argument must be read as a whole. Some of the evidence will corroborate Martin Bernal's claims regarding the relation between Greece and Egypt, albeit for different reasons. It is all part of what one author has called the Egyptian mirage in ancient Greece.

In chapter 4, I attempt to show that most of the pre-Socratics wrote a work of the *peri phuseōs* type and that their respective *historia* followed the same three part schema that one finds in Anaximander and the cosmogonical myths that preceded him. I examine them in more or less the conventional chronological order: Xenophanes, Pythagoras and the Pythagoreans, Heraclitus, Parmenides, Empedocles, Anaxagoras and the Atomists: Leucippus and Democritus. In each instance, I begin with a synopsis of the historical and political milieu in which the philosopher resided. I attempt to show that each philosopher was an active participant in the social and political milieu in which they resided and often well beyond its confines, contrary to what most contemporary scholars seem to suggest. In conjunction with this, they all seem to have advocated the rule of law and all seem to have been strong proponents of democracy or its nascent equivalent, *isonomia* and this, despite the fact that they all came from wealthy and/or aristocratic backgrounds. Moreover, they all saw a reciprocal relation between microcosm and macrocosm and, in various degrees, they all argued that political theory and practise (indeed the general structure of the state) should be grounded in cosmology.

I also attempt to connect the philosophers with one another since it is abundantly clear that they were all well aware of their respective works which was prompted to a large degree through the written word and the facility of travel by sea. Indeed, it is clear that the awareness of their respective *historia* and their own distinctive cultural milieux, travels, temper, spirit of *agōn,* fostered the originality of the respective *historia.* Moreover, they were all preoccupied with the pursuit of *alētheia* (truth) rather than *kleos* (glory) whence the importance of anchoring their *historia* in a *logos* or a reasoned argument.

Despite references to *theos,* their universal systems are explained in terms of natural causes as is the origin of human beings. It is the fact that human beings are given a real beginning in time that drives, in my view, their respective views on the origin of civilization. However, I also attempt, within the limits of space, to account for a number of specific features in their respective *historia,* including views on the nature of the soul, knowledge, wealth, morality, harmony, justice, virtue, law, and divinity. It was indeed the fact that the divinity was to be eventually entirely eliminated from the functioning of the universe that prompted Plato to write his own *historia* of the *peri phuseōs* type for the consequences of this, in his eyes, were responsible for the nihilistic attitude toward morality and the state. This will be addressed in the second volume.

1

The Meaning of *Peri Phuseōs*

Prologue

There is no doubt the Greek notion of *phusis* (usually translated as nature from the latin *natura*), has been decisive both for the early history of philosphy and for its subsequent development. In fact, it is often said the Greeks discovered "nature." But what did the earliest philosophers actually have in mind when they spoke of *phusis?* There is a great deal of discussion on the subject. In this opening chapter, this question begins with a linguistical analysis of the word, then examines the first (and only) occurrence of the word in Homer, the first use of the term by a pre-Socratic, and finally examines in detail the use of the term in the famous expression (and possible book title), *peri phuseōs*. The aim here is to help us understand not only what the earliest thinkers understood by *phusis,* but also how they conceived nature and why they developed the distinctive cosmologies we are familar with.

The Etymology of *Phusis*

In ancient Greek, an action noun and its result can be derived from every type of verb by means of the suffix *-sis* (Holt 1941, 46). According to Benveniste (1948, 80), the general meaning of words ending in *-sis* is "the abstract notion of the process conceived as an objective realization," that is to say "one expresses by *-sis* the notion as being outside the subject, and in this sense objective and established as accomplished from the fact that it is objective" (1948, 85). In other words, contrary to action nouns ending in *-tus,* when the word ending in -*tus* always refers to the same subject as the verbal form (i.e., *pausethai mnēstuos,* "to cease courting"), nouns ending in -*sis* are in syntactic liaison with transitive/factive or operative verbs (to make, to place, etc.). The verb takes the word ending in -*sis* for its object. Thus, the verb indicates (Benveniste 1948, 82) "the concrete actualization of the notion conceived on the noetic plan as effective and objective" (i.e., *dote brōsin:* to give something to eat; or *zētēsin poieisthai:* to realize an inquiry). As an action noun ending in -*sis,* Benveniste defines *phusis* as the (completed) realization of a becoming—that is to say, the nature [of a thing] as it is realized, with all its properties.[1]

Since the root holds a precise meaning, it logically suffices to find the root of the verb stem, from which the term *phusis* is derived, to discover its precise meaning. *Phusis* is derived from the verb *phuō-phuomai.* In ancient Greek, the *phuō* family has a number of particular characteristics. While it is easier to analyze the formation of the present starting from the Indo-European root **bhū-,* everything happens as if the group *phuō-phuomai* were derived from the root **bhŭ-.* Indeed, the nominal *phusis* as well as the present *phuō-phuomai,* has a short *ŭ,* while the root, **bhū-*bhŭ-,* has a long *ū.* The reason for the supposition that **bhū-* is the original root is because the primary meaning of the ancient root **bhū-* is to grow, to produce, to develop (Chantraine 1968–80, 4:123). Just as in the active transitive, *phuō* has the meaning "to grow, to produce, to bring forth, to beget"[2] and, in the middle passive and intransitive forms of *phuomai,* the meaning "to grow, to spring up, to come into being, to grow on, to attach to." Moreover, Homeric Greek knows no other meanings than "to grow, to produce," (in particular, in the context of vegetation), and in addition, these meanings are the only ones found in a number of other Indo-European languages besides Greek: in Armenian *busanim,* "I grow," *boys,* "plant"; in Albanian *bïin,* "to germinate," *bimë,* "plant;" not to mention the Slavic languages, which have representatives of a *bhū-lo-* meaning "plant." (Burger 1925,1; Chantraine 1968–80, 4:123). Again, although the group composed of the old aorist *ephun* (skr. *abūt*) and the perfect *pephuka* (skr. *babhŭva*) evolved and took on the meaning of "becoming"—such that the root could be employed to complete the system of **a, es-,* "to exist, to be"[3]—its etymological meaning of "growth" still persists in Homer.[4]

If one considers that all the compounds of the term *phusis*[5] and its corresponding verb *phuō-phuomai* conserve the primary meaning of "growth, growing" throughout antiquity (and, in particular, in the context of vegetation), then it seems clear the fundamental and etymological meaning of the term *phusis* is that of growth, even if the meaning of the term evolved.[6] It therefore follows from a linguistic analysis of the word that, as an action noun ending in -*sis, phusis* means the whole process of growth of a thing from birth to maturity.

Phusis in the Odyssey

In book 10 of the *Odyssey*, the wily hero Odysseus relates the adventures of his wanderings to the Phaeacians, an idealized human community. However, Odysseus' adventures have nothing to do with the heroic antagonists of the *Iliad* but rather with giants, witches, sea-monsters, and the like—supernatural beings which inhabit the world of the irrational and the magical. Odysseus begins his tale by describing how he just barely escaped from the island of the Laestrygonians with his own ship and comrades while the other eleven ships in the fleet were destroyed and their crews killed and devoured by man-eating giants. He then finds himself and his crew on the island of Aeaea, the isle of the fair-tressed goddess Circe, aunt of the infamous enchantress Medea and of the Minotaur, daughter of Helios and Perse and granddaughter of Oceanus, one of the primordial entities in Greek cosmogonical myth.[7] Circe is a witch who turns people into animals—a widely diffused theme in folktales—and this is the initial fate of several of Odysseus' comrades. While on a reconnaissance mission, they arrive at Circe's enchanted palace in a forest. They are invited in and offered a potion mixed with what is described as "baneful drugs" (*pharmaka lugra*, 10.236). They drink the potion and forget their native land. Subsequently, they are struck with a *rhabdos* (10.238) or "magic wand" and turned into swine—although they retain their wits (*nous*, 10.240).

Upon hearing of their disappearance but not yet aware of their fate, Odysseus sets out in pursuit of his companions. While heading up the road, he is stopped by the god Hermes who instructs him in all of Circe's "deadly wiles" (*olophōia dēnea*, 289). The god tells Odysseus what he must do when Circe tries to bewitch him. Hermes gives Odysseus a plant, a *pharmakon esthlon* (10.287; 292) or "effective drug" which will prevent him from being transformed into a pig (10.287–92). The plant is an effective antidote to Circe's *pharmakon lugron*.[8] It stops change and provides protection against Circe's powers (10.287–92). But for the plant to work, Odysseus must in some sense understand its *phusis*. Thus, after drawing the *pharmakon* from the ground and giving it to Odysseus, Hermes proceeds to show/explain/reveal its *phusis* to him: *kai moi phusin autou edeixe* (10. 303). The plant is described as having a black root and a white flower (304). Moreover, it is said to be called *mōlu* or moly by the gods and is hard to dig (305) albeit not for gods for whom all things are possible (306). This is the one and only occurrence of the word *phusis* in the Homeric corpus. Indeed, it is the first occurrence of the term prior to its use by a pre-Socratic philosopher.

At first glance, the term *phusis* seems to be employed synonymously with *eidos, morphē,* or *phuē* (all of which are found in Homer), insofar as the moly plant is identified by its form.[9] It seems Homer could have written *kai moi eidos (morphē; phuē) autou edeixe*. However, that Homer does not employ the terms *eidos, morphē* or *phuē* suggests the possibility that the term *phusis* means something quite different from "form" or "exterior aspect." As already indicated, Emile Benveniste, as part of his analysis of nouns in *-sis,* suggests that in its appearance in Homer *phusis* can be defined as "the (completed) realization of a becoming" and thus as "the nature [of the thing] as it is realized, with all its properties."[10] In other words, while *eidos, morphē* and *phuē* designate the form or the physical constitution of a thing, *phusis* designates the process by which the object becomes what it is.

Many commentators claim Hermes only shows the natural form of the plant to Odysseus and there is no reference to growth or process in this example.[11] However, as Alfred Heubeck correctly notes, "*deiknunai* may mean not only showing something visible, but also giving instruction."[12] It is quite possible, then, that Hermes explains—and must explain—the whole *phusis* of the potent herb *(pharmakon)* to Odysseus in order to save him from Circe's spells. This would mean Hermes reveals both the external (black root,[13] milk white flower, etc.) and internal (that is, hidden) properties of the plant to Odysseus, even though Homer only explicitly refers to the external properties (10.287–92). This notion of hiddenness will be fundamental to Heraclitus' idea of *phusis.*[14] Meanwhile, since the moly plant is characterized as a "divine" plant and thus revealed in "divine" language,[15] there is no reason why Hermes, who possesses such knowledge, would not have explained the divine origin (that is, origin myth) of the plant in order to enable Odysseus to understand how and why it acquired its current powers.[16] After all, the gods generally do things and/or create things for a reason, and the secret is only revealed when the origin of the thing is known.[17] Moreover, this understanding of what Hermes says to Odysseus corresponds with Benveniste's etymological analysis. In order to be able to ward off magic, Odysseus needs more than simple possession of the moly plant when he confronts Circe.[18] To make use of the plant's magical power, it is likely Odysseus must understand why the gods created it, an understanding that requires that he comprehend its *phusis*—that is, the whole process of the growth of the moly plant from beginning to end.[19]

The First Pre-Socratic Occurrence of *Phusis*

Is there a relation between the etymology and the proposed Homeric meaning of the term *phusis* and the way it is used by the pre-Socratics? In my view, there is real semantic continuity here. Consider the first appearance of the term in a pre-Socratic work. Heraclitus states that although men do not or will not understand what his words reveal he will nonetheless engage in "distinguishing each thing according to its nature *(phusis)* and explaining how it is" (*kata phusin diaireōn hekaston kai phazōn hokōs echei,* DK22B1). In this fragment, the fundamental meaning of *phusis*—the nature of a thing as it is realized with all of its properities from beginning to end, or the whole process of growth of a thing from birth to maturity—is not in doubt.

Heraclitus states that to explain or reveal *(phrazein)*[20] the present state of a thing (perhaps to name it correctly!) requires an analysis of the nature *(phusis)* of the thing, that is, an analysis of how it originated and developed.[21] As Kahn notes, "This expression of Heraclitus suggests that, in contemporary prose, the term *phusis* had become specialized to indicate the *essential character* of a thing *as well as* [my italics] the process by which it arose."[22] In sum, to know the real constitution of a thing (what makes it behave and appear as it does) entails a knowledge of the processes that regulate its nature, and these processes are the same processes that were behind the origin of the present order of things.[23] In the final analysis, if Heraclitus wanted to accent the structure of the thing, he could have employed either the word *logos* or the word *kosmos,* that is, "distinguish each thing according to its *logos* or *kosmos*."[24]

Phusis must be understood dynamically as the real constitution of a thing as it is realized from beginning to end with all of its properties. This is the meaning one finds nearly every time the term *phusis* is employed in the writings of the pre-Socratics.[25] It is never employed in the sense of something static, although the accent may be on either the *phusis* as origin, the *phusis* as process, or the *phusis* as result. All three, of course, are comprised in the original meaning of the word *phusis*.

The Comprehensive Meaning of *Phusis*.

Although *phusis* is absent from the writings of early Ionians, that is, the first philosophic writings, it is unanimously accepted today, as it was in antiquity, that the concept of *phusis* was a creation of Ionian science. It was a creation to the extent the word permitted the Ionians to present a new conception of the world in which natural causes were substituted for mythical ones.[26] However, scholars are far from unanimous on what the pre-Socratics, beginning with the early Ionians, really understood by this term in a comprehensive sense, that is, as it must be understood in the expression *historia peri phuseōs*: an investigation into the nature of things. Indeed, some argue that although the early Ionians may be said to have invented the concept of nature *(phusis),* they had no single word for nature, that is, nature as an "all-inclusive system ordered by immanent law."[27] In my view, the early Ionians did indeed have a comprehensive vision of nature and this vision was reflected in the term *phusis*. In fact, a comprehensive vision of nature is not incompatible with the Homeric notion of the word *phusis* although this does not suggest that Homer in any way invented, influenced, or even understood the meaning *phusis* was later to take. What matters is that already in Homer, *phusis* designates the whole process of growth of a thing from its birth to its maturity.

Before examining the meaning of the term *phusis* in the expression *historia peri phuseōs,* something must be said about the expression *Peri phuseōs* as the title of a work.

Peri Phuseōs as the Title of a Work

Although it is clear that the title *Peri phuseōs* was employed indiscriminately by writers of the Alexandrian period to characterise the works of almost all the pre-Socratics beginning with the early Ionians, that is, the Milesians, contemporary scholars disagree on precisely when a title was, in fact, first employed by a pre-Socratic. While no one argues Milesians themselves actually employed the title *Peri phuseōs,* Heidel (1910, 81) contends that "philosophical works were familiarly quoted as bearing the title *Peri phuseōs* sometimes *before* [my italics] the close of the fifth century." West (1971, 9) appears no less convinced. According to him, instead of *"Hērakleitos Blosōnos Ephesios tade legei: tou de logou eontos aiei ktl.,"* a text of Heraclitus would have started with: *"HĒRAKLEITOU PERI PHUSEŌS. tou de logou toude ktl."* This also appears to be Burnet's position when he states that the ancient philosophers themselves did not use titles (I assume, as we now employ them), but that the name of the writer and the title of the text composed the first sentence of the work, as one can observe in the work of Herodotus.[28] Guthrie (1971, 194), for his part, claims it is safe to say Parmenides employed this title.[29] Guthrie bases his contention on Gorgias' parody of the title, *On Nature,* with his own title: *On the Non-existent or on Nature (Peri tou mē ontos ē Peri phuseōs).* Others, such as Verdenius (1947, 272) and Kahn (1960/1993, 6n2), cite the Hippocratic treatise *On Ancient Medicine* 20 *(Empedoklēs ē alloi hoi peri phuseōs gegraphasin)* to support their claim that a title was employed at least from the time of Empedocles (that is, from the middle of the fifth century).[30] Others, such as Leisegang (*RE* 20–1, 1135) and Schmalzriedt (1970), appear to contend that the use of the title began later, in the fifth century.[31] Finally, there are some such as Lloyd (1979, 34 n119) and Huffmann (1993, 93–96) who appear noncommital although they do not appear to contest that the pre-Socratics wrote about the nature of things *(peri phuseōs).*

In the final analysis, it is not important where the title was placed, or if there even was a title, since the vast majority of commentators, both ancient and modern, concur that the primary goal of the written works of the pre-Socratics was to provide a *historia peri phuseōs.* What is important is (1) who was the first author to write his opinions *peri phuseōs* and thus to initiate and endorse the new scientific tradition and (2) what the famous expressions *peri phuseōs* and *historia peri phuseōs* mean in this context. On the first point, I concur with Kahn (1960/1993, 7) that it was undoubtably Anaximander of Miletus, "It was he who first wrote down his views *peri phuseōs,* and thereby established a new literary form—the first in which prose was employed—which was to serve as the written basis for the new scientific tradition."[32] In what follows, I focus on the second point, that is, to determine just what the pre-Socratics understood by the word *phusis,* particularly in the expressions *peri phuseōs* and *historia peri phuseōs.*

Interpretations of the Meaning of *Phusis* in the Expression *Peri Phuseōs*

In the main there are four different interpretations of what the pre-Socratic physicists understood by the term *phusis* in the expression *peri phuseōs* or *historia peri phuseōs*. These interpret *phusis:*

1. in the sense of primordial matter
2. in the sense of process
3. in the sense of primordial matter and process
4. in the sense of the origin, process and result.[33]

Phusis in the Sense of Primordial Matter

The first interpretation was proposed by John Burnet. According to Burnet (1945, 10–11; see also 1914, 21), from the outset *phusis* meant the permanent and primary substance out of which something was made and the early Ionians were seeking the one *phusis* of all things.[34] Consequently, the expression *peri phuseōs* could be translated as "concerning the primary substance." The notion of becoming (or process) inherent to the substance is secondary for Burnet. He bases his interpretation on a passage from Plato and on another passage from Aristotle. According to Burnet, both employ *phusis* in the sense of "primordial substance" when discussing ancient philosophy (Burnet, 1930/1945, 11n.11).

The passage from Plato to which Burnet refers is found at *Laws*10.892c2: *phusin boulontai legein tēn peri ta prōta.* For Burnet, the word *genesis* in this passage signifies: *to ex hou,* "that from which." This also appears to be A.E. Taylor's interpretation.[35] He translates this passage in his edition of the *Laws:* "by *nature* they mean what was there to begin with." Now in *Laws* 10.891c2–3, Plato explicitly states atheistic materialists understand by nature *(phusis)* the four primary elements (earth, air, fire, and water) of all things *(tōn* *prōtōn).*[36] This statement may have been behind Burnet's and Taylor's interpretation of *Laws* 10.892c2. However, Plato understands by *genesis* (and thus *phusis*) here the "productive force" connected with the first elements (that is, what commands or directs them). He wants to show that if the universe were generated (as the materialists affirm), then it was *psuchē* (or soul) rather than the four inanimate elements that initiated the process. Therefore *psuchē* has more of a right to be called *phusis*. The soul commands and the body obeys.

The text from Aristotle is found in *Physics* 2.193a21: *Dioper hoi men pur, hoi de gēn, hoi d'aera phasin, hoi de hudōr, hoi d'enia toutōn, hoi de panta tauta tēn phusin einai tēn tōn ontōn.* "And this is why some have said that it was earth that constituted the nature of things, some fire, some air, some water, and some several and some all of these elemental substances." Nevertheless, it is not a secret to anyone that Aristotle interpreted the Milesians from the point of view of his own theory of four causes: material, efficient, formal, and final.[37] That is why Aristotle remarks in the *Metaphysics,* when he is searching for the predecessors of the material principal or cause, "Most of the first to philosophize [or the earliest philosophers] were concerned with only the material principles of all things." (*Tōn de prōtōn philosophēsantōn hoi pleistoi tas en hulēs eidei monas ōiēthēsan archas einai pantōn: Meta.* 1. 983 b 7–9). This is strange if one considers that what immediately follows this sentence defines this cause, or material principal, both as the constituent principle *and* the primary "generator."[38]

Phusis in the Sense of Process

The second interpretation of the meaning of *phusis* belongs to O. Gigon (1935, 101) who argues, "Ich möchte *phusis* im primitivisten Sinn (Synonym mit *genesis*) verstehen und interpretieren." In this interpretation, pre-Socratics put the emphasis on the process, and its the primordial substance which becomes secondary.

The position that *genesis* is a synonym for *phusis* is not without foundation even if the two terms are derived from different roots. Indeed, this is not the crux of the problem, since no one would deny that the notion of growth for the Greeks implied both life and motion. The problem is rather the following: whatever the importance given to the notion of process (including "growth" in the sense of a principle or law intrinsic to nature), it cannot be understood to mean an absolute principle or *archē*—which was fundamental for the pre-Socratics.[39]

Furthermore, since the notion of *phusis* as process can be understood in the sense of the law or principle intrinsic to the idea of nature, that is, as designating what is responsible for the behaviour of such and such a thing, R.G.

Collingwood (1945, 43) can be included as adhering to this interpretation when he writes: "Nature, for them [the Ionian philosophers], never meant the world or the things which go to make up the world, but something inhering in these things which made them behave as they did."

Phusis in the Sense of Primordial Matter *and* Process

The third interpretation is upheld by W. Jaeger (1947, 20).[40] Jaeger finds support for his thesis, at least in part, from the study of two passages of Homer's *Iliad* where it is said Ocean is the genesis of all gods and of all things: *Ōkeanon te, theōn genesin* (*Iliad* 14.201); and *Ōkeanou, hosper genesis pantessi tetuktai* (*Iliad* 14. 246). In these passages, according to Jaeger, *genesis* encompasses the same double meaning as *phusis,* and, as a result, "To say Ocean is the *genesis* of everything is virtually the same as calling it the *phusis* of everything" (Jaeger 1947, 20).

What he understands by this double meaning is, on the one hand, "the process of growth and emergence" and on the other, "that from which they *(ta onta)* have grown, and from which their growth is constantly renewed," in other words, its source or origin.

The interpretation of L. Lachier (1972, 667) blends well with Jaeger's when he writes, "le sens fondamental [of the word phusis] est l'idée d'une existence qui se produit ou du moins se détermine elle-même, en tout ou en partie, sans avoir besoin d'une cause étrangère."[41]

Now both Lachier and Jaeger are correct if *phusis* is understood as a synonym of the verb *phuomai* (to begin to grow) and if we agree with the old adage that it is inconceivable something can come from nothing. In this way, the double meaning is possible. Nevertheless, in the passages of Homer cited above, *genesis* implies a meaning Jaeger seems to have missed, namely, the "result" of this "productive power." Indeed, as Benveniste (1948, 76) correctly notes, Ocean gave birth to all beings, that is, to "a completed, accomplished 'birth'" ("une 'naissance' effective, réalisée"). From this perspective, the word *genesis* would cover the same triple meaning as the word *phusis* in Homer's works.

Jaeger also states *genesis* is a synonym of *phusis*. However, since the term *phusis* is absent from the first philosophical writings, how can it be argued with any certainty that *phusis* is synonymous with *genesis?* The answer is found in Aristotle's *Metaphysics* (1.983b7–984a4), where these same passages of Homer are quoted precisely to explain what certain writers (in particular, Plato) believe—namely, that "by having presented Ocean and Tethys as authors of the world's generation" *(Ōkeanon te gar kai Tēthon epoiēsan tēs geneseōs pateras),* Homer shares Thales' opinion on what constitutes *phusis*. The fact Aristotle does not agree with them is of little importance here. What is important is that certain authors argue that for both Homer and Thales, water is equivalent to the term *phusis* insofar as it is the principle *(archē)* or the first cause *(prōtē aitia)* of all things, and it is this element which generated the completed realities *(onta)*.

Phusis in the Sense of Origin, Process, and Result

According to the fourth interpretation, which is that of Heidel, Kahn and Barnes as well as my own,[42] the term *phusis* in the expression *peri phuseōs* or *historia peri phuseōs* comprises three things: (1) the absolute *archē,* that is, the element or cause that is both the primary constituent and the primary generator of all things; (2) the process of growth strictly speaking; and (3) the outcome, product, or result of this process. In brief, it means the whole process of the growth of a thing, from its birth or commencement, to its maturity. More precisely, the term *phusis,* in the expression *peri phuseōs* or *historia peri phuseōs,* refers, at a minimum, to the origin and the growth of the universe from beginning to end. Indeed, the pre-Socratics, with whom this expression originated, were interested (at least initially) in a cosmogony in the literal sense of the word. They were not interested in a description of the universe as it is but in a history of the universe; in an explanation of its origin (*phusis* as absolute *archē*), of the stages of its evolution (*phusis* as process of growth), and finally of its result, the *kosmos* as we know it (*phusis* as the result).

In this regard, it is interesting to note such a cosmogony involves not one, but two departure points: a chronological and a logical. The chronological or temporal starting point is called chaos in the modern sense of the term: to wit, the state of confusion existing before creation. The logical starting point, on the other hand, is the *kosmos* itself, that is, the natural world conceived as a structured whole in which each constituent part has a place. Indeed, people have always sought to know how the present order of things originated from the primordial chaos.[43]

Presently, I would like to examine three series of texts which, in my view, demonstrate (1) this notion of *phusis;* (2) the relation between this notion and the method in vogue with the pre-Socratics; and (3) the relation between the generation of the *kosmos* and the expression *peri phuseōs* or *historia peri phuseōs.*

Several Concrete Examples Illustrating Such a Notion

An example which provides a good illustration of the first notion is found in Hippocratic works which focus on embryology. In order to treat the problem of generation, the author calls upon either empirical research, or analogies, or both. Thus, in the treatise *The Seed,* which forms a whole with the treatise *The Nature of the Child,* the author begins by informing us that the sperm (or seed)[44] comes from the entire body (ch. 1) of each parent (chap. 6–8),[45] after which he describes the evolution of the child's body inside its mother's womb. Chapters 22–27 contain a long digression where the author establishes an analogy between the growth of plants and the growth of embryos such that the womb *(mētra)* is to the embryo *(embruon)* what the earth *(gē)* is to the plant *(phumenon)* that lives in it. He concludes: "if you review what I have said, you will find that from beginning to end *(ex archēs es telos)* the process of growth *(tēn phusin)* in plants and in humans is exactly the same." (trans. I.M. Lonie)

In chapter 29, the author explains that his method is based both on the observation of facts and on analogy

> If you take twenty or more eggs and place them to hatch under two or more fowls, and on each day, starting from the second right up until the day on which the egg is hatched, you take one egg, break it open and examine it, you will find that everything is as I described it—making allowance of course for the degree to which one can compare the growth of a chicken *(ornithos phusin)* to that of a human being *(anthrōpou phusei)*." In sum, "you will find that the growth of the infant *(tēn phusin tou paidiou)* is from the beginning to the end *(mechris es telos)* exactly as I have described it in my discourse.

The meaning of the expressions *ex archēs es telos* and *mechris es telos* are clear. When it comes to enquiring into the *phusis* of something, it is the whole process from beginning to end which is understood. In the case of the embryo, the author is not concerned with "the way it is" but "how did it come into existence" and "of what basic elements is it composed." This explains Aristotle's pertinent remark with respect to his predecessors; to wit: they enquired into "how each being naturally came to exist rather than how it is" *(pōs hekaston gignesthai pephuke mallon hē pōs estin).*[46] Indeed, what counts for Aristotle is not the unformed embryo but the *ousia* or essence of a thing "for the genesis is for the sake of the essence *(ousia),* not the essence *(ousia)* for the sake of the genesis" *(Parts of Animals* 1.640 a 18–19). This is why he criticizes Empedocles directly after this passage because Empedocles argues that the characteristics proper to each animal are the result of accidental events, which occurred during their development. For Empedocles, the essence or form is not in the beginning, as it is for Aristotle. Indeed, for both Hippocratic physicians and pre-Socratic philosophers the process is something real, that is, it has a real history and is defined in relation to its material source. For Aristotle, it is a simple circular process in which the end of a cycle is the beginning of another cycle. The reason for this is that once a being is born it must create a being similar to itself to participate in the eternal and the divine as much as possible.[47]

Notion and Method in Vogue with the Pre-Socratics

To define the relation between the notion of *phusis* and the method in vogue with the pre-Socratics, it is necessary to examine the texts which deal with the relation between medicine and the philosophy of nature. Medicine studies the composition of the body to better analyze the causes of sickness and their remedies. Since the composition of the body is contiguous with the problem of growth, this in turn raises those of generation and of production. Considering the period in question it is not surprising the primary concerns of the physicians overlapped those of the physicists. On the one hand, both claim the *phusis* of man and the *phusis* of the *kosmos* are the same. On the other hand, both look for the causes of life and death and by extension of health and sickness.[48] Of course, physicians and philosophers did not all agree on the relation itself, and the controversy that it generated in the Hippocratic camp provides valuable insights into the methods in vogue with the pre-Socratics as well as clarifications on the meaning of *historia peri phuseōs*.

Consider the two following texts, which illustrate what we have just said. The first text is from the author of *Regimen* I, who writes:

> I maintain that he who intends to write correctly concerning the regimen of man must first know and discern the nature of man in general *(pantos phusin anthrōpou)*, that is know from what things he is orginially composed *(gnōnai men apo tinōn sunesthēken ex archēs)*, and discern by what parts he is controlled *(diagōnai de hupo tinōn mereōn kekratētai)* for if he does not know that primary constitution *(tēn ex archēs suntastin)*, he will be incapable of knowing their results *(ta hup'ekeinōn gignomena)*, and if he does not discern what dominates in the body, he will be incapable of providing the patient with a treatment. *(Regimen* I.2.1)

Later the author adds that the physician should also know what occurs in the whole universe *(holos kosmos)* such as the seasons of the year, the changes in the winds, and even the rising and setting of the stars in order to guard against the changes and excesses from which diseases come to men *(Regimen* I.2.2).[49]

The second text is from the author of the *Ancient Medicine* who supports the antithesis of this:

> I think I have discussed this subject sufficiently, but there are some physicians and philosophers[50] who maintain that no one can understand the sci-

ence of medicine unless he knows what man is *(hoti estin anthrōpos);* that anyone who proposes to treat men for their illnesses must first learn of such things. Their discourse then tends to philosophy as may be seen in such writings of Empedocles and all others who have ever written about nature *(peri phusios);* they discuss the origins of man *(ex archēs hoti estin anthrōpos),* how he was initially formed *(kai hopōs egeneto prōton)* and of what elements he was constituted *(ka hoppothen sunepagē).* It is my opinion that all which has been written by physicians and philosophers on nature *(peri phusios)* has more to do with painting than medicine. I do not believe that any clear knowledge of nature *(peri phusios)* can be obtained from any source other than a study of medicine and then only through a thorough mastery of the science.[51] (trans. J. Chadwick and W.N. Mann with minor changes)

Let's examine the two texts more closely while placing them in the context of their respective treatise. The first text claims the principles of medicine are subject to an investigation of nature in general *(peri phuseōs historia).* In sum, its author argues that to treat effectively the regimen of man, a knowledge of the nature *(phusis)* of man in general is necessary. This entails two things: (1) a knowledge of the fundamental constituents from which man was composed at creation, in order to know of their effects; (2) a discernment of the elements which predominate in order to furnish an effective treatment to the patient.

As such, the author of *Regimen* I claims first that the constituents of all things, including man, are water and fire (I.3.4); and second that the structure of the body is composed in such a way that it imitates the structure of the universe: "fire structured everything *(panta diakosmēsato)* in the body the way it is, to make it an imitation of the universe *(apomimēsin tou holou),* matching the little organs with the large and the large with the small." (I.10.1)[52] This remark comes after the author has described the formation of the human foetus, which he sees as similar to the structure of the universe. In fact, an interest in embryology can be discerned among all the philosophers to whom this author frequently alludes.[53]

The relation between embryology and cosmogony is certainly not new. According to the doxographical tradition, Anaximander seems to have conceived his cosmogony along similiar lines when he makes an analogy between the seed of animals and the development of the embryo—albeit his description is purely natural. This is also the case for certain Pythagorean authors, which is not surprising if one considers the meaning and importance of the term *kosmos* in their philosophy (see Huffman 1993, 97–99; 219–220). In fact, the mythical image of a universal egg from which the world emerged establishes to what degree such a notion could be primitive. As G. E. R. Lloyd (1966, 176) so aptly demonstrates, reasoning by analogy, which consists of concluding from the existence of certain resemblances observed between two objects the existence of other resemblances, is a mode of reasoning that, in a certain manner, is common to all people regardless of the period.

According to the author of the treatise *Regimen* I, an anthropology entails an anthropogony, just as a cosmology entails a cosmogony. Since the anthropogony is (to a certain degree) the completion of the cosmogony it is reasonable to assume a cosmogony is equally part of the curriculum as we shall see with the treatise, *On Fleshes (Peri sarkōn).* The reason the author of *Regimen* I wants to know the fundamental constituents from which the *phusis* of man and the universe are made implies a form of mysticism common to all people since the beginning of time. If one knows the primordial state of things, it is possible to penetrate their secrets.[54] This is one of the reasons behind theogonical and cosmogonical myths; they serve to justify the present order of things.

As for the capacity to discern the elements that predominate, and in order to furnish an effective treatment (according to the author), of the two elements our body is composed of, fire always has the power *(dunamis)* to move everything, whereas water always has the power *(dunamis)* to nourish everything (I.3.1). In turn, each one dominates and is dominated although neither ever gains complete control (I.3.1–3). Moreover, each of these two elements is composed of two attributes. Fire is composed of hot and dry, and water of cold and wet. But each element also has an attribute of the other; fire has the attribute of wetness and water has the attribute of dryness. In this way, an element is never locked in the same state and many substances become possible (I.4.1).

Since the human body is composed of a mixture of several types of fire and of water, health and sickness must therefore exist in relation to certain mixtures. Thus, the most healthy constitution is a composition of a mixture of the lightest water and the most subtle fire whatever our age or the season of the year. This is obviously not the case for the other mixtures and consequently precautions with respect to age and season must be taken into account. The author of *Regimen* I understands this by discerning elements that predominate in order to furnish a effective treatment *(Regimen* I.32.6).

The author of *Ancient Medicine,* on the other hand, is radically opposed to the use of the philosopher's method for medical ends. This text not only provides important information with regard to the method and content of *peri phuseōs* writings, but it clarifies the other position.

At the beginning of the treatise, *Ancient Medicine,* the author states that medicine, unlike disciplines that study celestial and terrestrial phenomena *(peri tōn meteōron ē tōn hupo gēn),* is not based on postulates or hypotheses *(hupothemenoi)*[55] since it has a real departure point *(archē)* and method *(hodos).* The departure point are the discoveries *(ta heurēmena)* made over the centuries and the method is that of observation.[56] As such, medicine is an art *(technē)* whose primary preoccupation is the treatment of diseases and whose discoveries are the results of real investigations (ch. 2).

What are these *hupothemenoi?* The hypotheses in question are unverifiable postulates; what occurs *peri tōn meteōron ē tōn hupo gēn* are nothing more than speculations and without any real value for the author of this treatise. In sum, contrary to his colleague, neither the seasons of the year, nor the changes in the winds, nor the rising and setting of the stars would have influenced the treatment of this physician. This is also the case for the origin and the formation of man, that is, an anthropogony. The aim of this evolutionary description is to explain the causes behind man's continual existence. We are told this approach is that of Empedocles and the other physicists who wrote works of the *peri phuseōs* type and which were so in vogue among his colleagues. However, the hostility of this author necessitates a closer examination of the influence of Empedocles on the methods of certain physicians.[57]

Empedocles was the first to introduce the doctrine of the four elements (fire, water, air, and earth), or the theory according to which none of the four elements has priority over the others. Each element is an *archē* in the philosophical sense of the term. The influence of this doctrine is particularly important to the author of the treatise, *The Nature of Man.* Like most of his contemporaries, he rejected all the physical and physiological theories which were based on a single element for generation. It would be impossible, he argues, if it originated from a single substance (ch.1–3). The physical bodies, the author continues, are constituted of four substances, namely hot, cold, dry, and wet. Like Empedocles, he contends none of the substances have priority over another. Moreover, each of the substances is considered a power (or *dunamis*) and when these powers are in harmony, each thing (in the present case the human body), has its proper form. This reminds one of his predecessor, Alcmaeon of Croton, for whom health is the result of the balance *(isonomia)* and proportionate mixture *(krasis)* of the powers *(duamis)*, which according to a general law, are opposed pair to pair (wet and dry, hot and cold, bitter and sweet), whereas sickness is the supremacy *(monarchia)* of one of the terms of such a couple.[58] Moreover, once the body dies, each of these substances must return to its proper original nature: the hot with the hot, the cold with the cold, the dry with the dry, the wet with the wet (ch.3).

The body can be seen as a composite of the four humours: blood, phlegm, yellow bile, and black bile, the balance or inbalance of which is responsible for health or sickness respectively (ch.4). There is similar correlation between the four primary opposites (hot, cold, wet, and dry), the four humours and the four seasons. Each of the four humours is associated with one of the four seasons and two of the primary opposites, with each group predominating in turn (ch. 7). This can be schematized as follows:

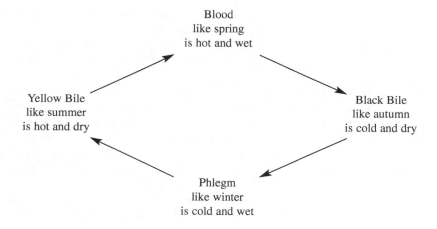

This excessively systematic and speculative theory appears to find support in certain empirical evidence. For example, when it states that "the quantity of phlegm in the body increases in winter because it is the bodily substance most in keeping with the winter, seeing that it is coldest. You can verify its coldness by touching phlegm, bile and blood; you will find that phlegm is the coldest." (*The Nature of Man* 7). Nevertheless, the author of the treatise, *Ancient Medicine,* attacks the theory for its lack of an empirical foundation (just as he castigates the theories of Empedocles). Indeed, his theory, just like that of Empedocles, remains essentially speculative and for this reason the author of *Ancient Medicine* challenges, from the outset, anyone who attempts to treat diseases not from empirical investigations (that is, from reality), but from hypotheses that simply reduce every cause of disease to the four primary opposites: hot, cold, dry, and wet. In chapter 15 he continues, "I am utterly at a loss to know how those who prefer these hypothetical arguments and reduce the science to a simple matter of 'postulates' ever cure anyone on the basis of their assumptions. I do not think that they have ever discovered *(exeurēmenon)* anything that is purely hot or cold, dry or wet, without it sharing some other qualities *(allōi eidei)*."

In fact, if the constitution of man was so simple, he tells us in chapter 20, an edible like cheese, so harmful for one person, must be harmful for all others. But this is evidently not the case. In this regard, he estimates that the first inventors *(hoi prōtoi heurontes)* were much closer to reality both in method and reason: "they never imagined that it was heat or cold, or wetness or dryness, which either harmed a man or was necessary to his health. They attributed disease to some factor *(dunamei)* stronger and more powerful than the human body which the body could not master. It was such factors that they sought to remove." (ch. 14).

For his part, he argues that the human body is much more complex:

> There exists in man saltness, bitterness, sweetness, sharpness, astringency, flabbiness, and countless other qualities *(dunameis)* having every kind of influence, number and strength. When these are properly mixed and compounded with one another, they can neither be observed nor are they harmful. But when one is separated out and stands alone it becomes both apparent and harmful. (ch. 14)

This last passage merits attention for two reasons. First, although the author of the treatise, *Ancient Medicine*, severely criticizes the doctrine of the four elements and their derivatives as a base for medicine because they employ postulates he considers as arbitrary, the fact remains that his own assumptions (albeit more numerous) are no less hypothetical. More important, what we see here is, as Lloyd notes, "a growing interest not just of medical, but of general scientific, method."[59] Second, this passage provides the occasion to open a digression on the term *dunamis,* which assuredly is one of the most important terms in the history of natural philosophy and a key to understanding the word *phusis.*

The term *dunamis,* the most general meaning of which is that of "power" is an action noun derived from the verb *dunamis* the fundamental meanings of which are "to be able, capable." (Chantraine 1968–80, 1.300). The term itself envelops a capacity that is both active and passive. As an active "power" or "force," *dunamis* is the capacity or aptitude to act or to give. As a passive "power" or 'force," *dunamis* is the capacity or aptitude to be acted upon or to receive. Thus, as a body or substance composed of both active and passive properties, it is capable of causing or receiving certain modifications. Since it was the duty of the physician to find the substances capable of modifying our physical states, this explains why the word *dunamis* was so frequently employed by the Hippocratic physicians. The technical or special meaning that the term *dunamis* had for Hippocratic doctors and was so influencial in Greek philosophy is excellently summarized by J. Souilhé following his analysis of the use of the term *dunamis* by the author of the treatise *Ancient Medicine:*

> The term *dunamis* comprises two ideas which are mutually complementary. The substances manifest themselves by their qualities. Things are rendered sensible by these properties, such as the cold, the hot, the bitter, the salt . . . , which enable them to enter into relation with other bodies. These are the *dunameis,* distinct entities which constitute the exteriorization of the substance. But these entities themselves can only be known when in action: action is their *raison d'être,* and action characterises and individualises them. The cold differs from the hot or the bitter or the salt because

it produces a particular determined effect. It can be combined with the other qualities, but will not be confound with them, because its action is not identical to theirs. And this action of qualities is once again their *dunamis*. The term thus designates both their essence and their proper manner of manifesting themselves. (Souilhé 1919, 36)[60]

Later, when Souilhé terminates the group of Hippocratic treatises, he observes that in the treatises where the influence of cosmological ideas is evident:

the term *dunamis* designates the characteristic property of bodies, their exterior and sensible appearance, which permits their determination and specification. Thanks to *dunamis,* the mysterious *phusis,* the substantial *eidos* or primordial element, makes itself known by its action. This explains why it was later possible to pass from the known to the unknown, from appearance to reality, and how easy it was to establish a perfect equation between *phusis* and *dunamis.*[61] To state the nature of a thing or its property becomes the same since the two are inseparable and united by a genuine causal link. (Souilhé 1919, 36)

The terms *phusis* and *dunamis* are sometimes almost synonymous, but there is normally a perceptible distinction as illustrated in the following passage from Menon's *Iatrica:*

Philistion maintains that we are composed of four forms *(ek d'ideōn),* that is to say, of four elements *(ek de stoicheiōn):* fire, air, water, earth. Each of these has its *dunamis* [the quality which characterizes it and makes it known]: fire has the hot, air the cold, water the wet, and earth the dry.

J. Souilhé next demonstrates how the Sophists adopted and transposed this terminology, and finally facilitated its introduction into philosophy. Thus, for Plato, *dunamis* can be defined as the property or the quality, which reveals the nature of a thing. The *dunamis* enables us to give a name to each thing that conforms to its constitution, and to place things in separate groups (Souilhé 1919, 149). Indeed, if the *phusis* designates the substantial foundation of a thing, it is thanks to its *dunamis* that this thing can reveal itself to us. This important relationship will resurface again further on, but now we turn to the third and final series of texts, which should clarify the meaning and scope of the term *phusis* in the expression *historia peri phuseōs.*

The Real Meaning of *Peri Phuseōs*

What follows are five texts, which show that what pre-Socratics understood by the expression *historia peri phuseōs* was a true history of the universe from its origins to the present. This history most certainly includes the origin of mankind. However, I will conjecture with the fifth text that it is probably that the logical starting point was the form of the society in which the philosopher resided. Thus, *historia peri phuseōs* could mean an investigation into the origin and development of the contemporary world (including the society in which the philosopher resided) from beginning to end. Let us examine these texts.

EURIPIDES: FRAGMENT 910 (NAUCK)[62]

The first text is taken from Euripides' famous fragment 910:

> Blessed is he who has devoted his life to scientific research *(tēs historias);* he will neither malign nor harm his fellow citizens, but observing the age-less order of immortal nature, will enquire from what source it was com-posed and in what way *(all'athanatou kathorōn phuseōs kosmon agērōn, † pē te sunesthē chō pēi chō pōs)*. Such men would never take part in shame-ful deeds.[63]

In this fragment, we see that Euripides holds in high regard a certain type of doctrine or physical philosophy (probably that of Anaxagoras),[64] namely, the study or contemplation of "the ageless order of immortal nature, whence and how it was composed (or constituted)." Admittedly, the expression *peri phuseōs* is absent, but the term *historia,* in conjunction with lines five to seven (the italicized Greek) suggests this expression is to be understood. Mean-while, several observations are in order. The expression, *kathorōn kosmon agērōn,* indicates that what is observed is the present *kosmos.* That is to say, the world that surrounds the observer, while that of *pē te sunesthē chō pēi chō pōs* (a corruption of *pēi te sunesthē kai hopēi kai hopōs?*) signifies this *kos-mos* had a beginning and underwent a process of evolution. In this regard, we note that the verb most frequently associated with the nominal *kosmos* is *sunistēmi,* to compose, to put together (Kahn 1960/1993, 223). Moreover, the adjectives employed to describe *kosmos* and *phusis* are the same as those that appear in Homer's works (in the form of formulas) to describe the gods and their attributes. Thus, in *Odyssey* 5.218, Calypso is said to be *athanatos kai agērōs,* as is the famous aegis of Athena in *Iliad* 2.447.[65] These are also terms that Anaximander appears to have applied to his *archē.*[66]

HIPPOCRATIC TREATISE *ON FLESHES* 1.2

The second text is found in the Hippocratic treatise *Peri sarkōn (On Fleshes),* which the author could very well have entitled *Peri archōn.*[67] This text can clarify what may have been understood in the preceding text. The author strongly states that in order to compose a medical treatise, he will use the common opinions *(koinēisi gnōmēisi)* of his predecessors as the starting point. These common opinions are provided in the form of a cosmogony and anthropogony respectively:

> I need only speak of celestial matters *(peri de tōn meterōn)* for as much as it is necessary to show, with respect to mankind and other living things, how they developed and formed *(hopōs ephu kai egeneto),* what is soul; what is health and disease; what is good and evil in man, and for what reason he dies.

Next, he keeps his promise in describing his cosmogony as follows: (1) In the beginning, all things were in a state of confusion *(hote etarachthē panta);* (2) then, the elements from which all things are composed, separated in three stages to form the universe: aether, air, earth; (3) finally, the formation of the parts of the body began, emanating from the putrifactions caused by the heat left in the earth after its initial formation.

This text could not be clearer. It exemplifies without equivocation the common assumption at the time among the *phusiologoi.* According to this assumption, the constitution of all living things is analogous to that of the universe insofar as they originated from the same primordial stuff and are part of the same *kosmos.* There is doxographical evidence for this assumption in *all* of the pre-Socratics beginning with the early Ionians.[68] Moreover, it is obvious the expression *peri tōn meterōn* can be substitued for *peri tēs phuseōs.* I will return to this observation later.

XENOPHON: *MEMORABILIA* 1.1.11–15

The third text is taken from the famous passage in Xenophon's *Memorabilia,* where Socrates, the founder of the teleological method, fails to understand the procedure of the physicists:

> He [Socrates] did not even discourse, as so many others, about the nature of all things *(peri tēs tōn pantōn phuseōs),* or how, what the physicists call the kosmos, came into existence *(hopōs kosmos ephu),* or by which necessary causes the heavenly phenomena occur *(tisin anankais hekasta ggnetai tōn ouraniōn).* Indeed, he showed the folly of those who dealt with such problems. . . . Moreover, in their disturbing research into the nature of all things *(peri tēs tōn pantōn phuseōs),* some hold that there is only one substance, others that there are an infinite number: some that all things are in perpetual motion, others that nothing can ever be moved at any time: some that all life

is birth and decay, others that nothing can ever be born or ever die. Nor were these the only questions he asked about such theorists. Students of human nature, he said, think that they will apply their knowledge in due course for the good of themselves and any others they choose. Do those who pry into heavenly phenomena *(ta theia)* imagine that, once they have discovered the laws by which these are produced *(hais anankais hekasta gignetai),* they will create at their will winds, waters, seasons and such things to their need? Or have they no such expectation, and are they satisfied with knowing the causes of these various phenomena? (trans. Marchant with major revisions)

This text includes several new elements for our thesis. First, not only does the expression *peri phuseōs* appear twice (with explicit allusions, more-over, to the Milesians, Diogenes of Apollonia, Anaxagoras, Democritus, Heraclitus, Parmenides, and Empedocles), but the expression is found each time with its natural genitive: *tōn pantōn*. Indeed, there is always *phusis* of something and when it is a question of the pre-Socratic physicists or *phusikoi, hopōs kosmos ephu* refers not only to the origin and evolution of the universe and mankind, but equally to the causes through which phenomena *(ta ourania,* that is, *ta meteōra)* continue to occur. I stress "continue to occur" for if there is indeed something that distinguishes speculative thought from mythical thought, it is the notion that the "natural" causes behind the initial formation of the universe continue to account for the current natural phenomena. Consequently, it is clear celestial and terrestrial phenomena *(ta meteōra kai ta hupo gēn)* are part of the *peri phuseōs* investigation. Indeed, in his *Meteorology* (which deals with what his predecessors called *meteōrologia*), Aristotle does not restrict himself to treating what falls under the term *ta meteōra* strictly speaking (wind, clouds, rain, lighting, thunder, etc.), but he considers springs, rivers, and even earthquakes (338a27). This explains the use of the expression *peri tōn meteōrōn ē tōn hupo gēn* at the beginning of the treatise *Ancient Medicine*. In fact, according to W. Capelle (1912, 414), meteorology did not originate as a distinct research subject, but as an alternative expression for *historia peri phuseōs*. This may explain the expression, *peri tōn meteōrōn,* instead of *peri tēs phuseōs* in the preceding text.

ARISTOTLE: *PARTS OF ANIMALS* 1.1. 640 B 4–22

The fourth text is taken from Aristotle's *Parts of Animals:*

The ancient philosophers who first studied nature *(Hoi oun archaioi kai prōtoi philosophēsantes peri phuseōs),* investigated the material principle and cause *(peri tēs hulikēs archēs)* to understand its nature and properities; how the universe is generated from it *(pōs ek tautēs ginetai to holon)* and under of influence of what motion *(tinos kinountos),* whether, for instance, by strife or love or mind or chance, the substratum of matter *(tēs 'hupokeimenēs hulēs)* being assumed to have necessarily a certain kind of nature—fire, for instance, to have a hot nature, earth, a cold one; the former to be light, the latter heavy. This, indeed, is how they explain the genesis of the universe *(Houtōs gar kai ton kosmon gennōsin).*

To which Aristotle immediately adds: "And they explain the development of plants and animals in a similar way" (1.640b4–12).

This passage provides additional information on the subject of the expression *peri phuseōs.* First, it is now clear that for his predecessors the temporal and spatial starting point was a material cause or principal *(hē hulikē archē)* which also acted as the efficient or moving cause or principle. In *Generation of Animals* 5.778b7–10, Aristotle maintains the same discourse when he says the first physicists *(hoi d'archaioi phusiologoi)* did not clearly distinguish between material and efficient causes. Initially, he is alluding only to the Monists, but further on he explicitly mentions the efficient causes of Empedocles, Anaxagoras and Democritus.[69] The physicists, meanwhile, begin their investigation *peri phuseōs* by studying the material principal itself, that is, the nature and properties *(tis kai poia tis)* of the principle from which the whole developed. Indeed the expression *pōs ek tautēs ginetai to holon* is abundantly clear. *To holon* refers to the result. Therefore, the *historia* alludes to the entire development from beginning to end. Moreover, *to holon* concerns the completed whole; in brief, the universe *(kosmos)* in which nothing is lacking from its whole by nature *(holon phusei).*[70] That is the reason why he adds animals and plants at the end; they are included in the whole because they are part of the same *phusis* as that of the whole.

Finally, *ho kosmos* is not only synonymous with *to holon,* but also with the expression *hē tōn ontōn phusis* in *Metaphysics* 1.984 b 9. The importance of this resides in its location. Aristotle states that if Anaxagoras postulated *nous* as the separate cause of movement, it is precisely because the *onta* in question (the universe and its entire contents) exhibit goodness and beauty (984b11), and order and arrangement (984b17). This led him to investigate the principle of these things *(tōn ontōn)* that are the cause of their beauty *(tou kalōs tēn aitian archēn einai tōn ontōn ethesan,* 984b21–22). From this perspective, the starting point of an investigation of the *peri phuseōs* type is the present order of things.

PLATO: *LAWS* 10.889 A4–E2

The fifth and final text is taken from Book 10 of Plato's *Laws.* What we have here is the theory *(logos)* which the atheistic materialists were reputed to have employed *peri phuseōs*.[71] This text does not only clearly illustrate the entire thesis for which I am arguing, but it also includes the term *technē*—the final link needed to interpret what the pre-Socratics characterized as a *historia peri phuseōs*.

> The facts show—so they claim—that the greatest and finest things in the world are the products of nature and chance *(phusin kai tuchēn),* the creations of art *(technēn)* being comparatively trivial. The works of nature, they say, are grand and primary, and constitute a ready-made source for all the minor works constructed and fashioned by art—*art*efacts *(technika),* as they're generally called. . . . I'll put it more precisely. They maintain that fire, water, earth and air owe their existence to nature and chance *(phusei kai tuchēi),* and in no case to art *(technēi).* As for the bodies *(sōmata)* that come after these *(meta tauta)*—the earth, sun, moon and stars—they have been produced from these entirely inanimate substances *(dia toutōn gegonenai pantelōs ontōn apsuchōn).* These substances moved at random, each impelled by virtue of its own inherent properties *(tēs dunameōs hekasta hekastōn),* which depended on various suitable amalgamations of hot and cold, dry and wet, soft and hard, and all other haphazard combinations that inevitably resulted when the opposites were mixed *(tēi tōn enantiōn krasei).* This is the process to which all the heavens and everything that is in them owe their birth *(tautēi kai kata tauta houtōs gegennēkenai ton te ouranon holon kai panta hoposa kat'ouranon),* and the consequent establishment of the four seasons led to the appearance of all plants and living creatures. The cause of all this, they say, was neither intelligent planning *(ou dia noun),* nor a deity *(oude dia tina theon),* nor art *(oude de technēn),* but—as we have explained—nature and chance *(phusei kai tuchēi).* Art *(technēn),* the brain-child of these living creatures *(ek toutōn),* arose later, the mortal child of mortal beings *(autēn thnētēn ek thnētōn);* it has produced, at a later stage *(hustera),* various amusing trifles that are hardly real at all—mere insubstantial images of the same order as the arts themselves. (I mean for instance the productions of the arts of painting and music, and all their ancillary skills). But if there are in fact some techniques that produce worthwhile results, they are those that cooperate with nature, like medicine and farming and physical training. This school of thought maintains that government, in particular, has very little to do with nature, and it is largely a matter of art; similarly legislation is never a natural process but is based on technique, and its enactments are quite artificial. (trans. Saunders with minor revisions)

According to this theory, nature *(phusis)* is originally nothing other than the primordial matter (the four elements)—in sum, the temporal or chronological *archē*. As for chance *(tuchē),* it is employed, as in Plato's *Sophist* (265c), in the sense of a spontaneous causality *(aitia automatē)* as opposed to an intelligent causality *(aitia dianoētikē).* Indeed, according to this theory, nature generates everything through its own power. Moreover, when it is said that such and such a stage of the evolution of the *kosmos* is due to the combination of nature and chance, this does not mean that these are external causes. Each stage is only a stage in their proper evolution. Finally, this theory *(logos)* is characterized as a *peri phuseōs* account at 891c8–9. Let us briefly examine the contents.

According to this theory, the *kosmos* appears in the following manner: the four elements which are due to nature and chance (in this case, the same thing), impelled by their respective tendencies *(dunameis),* generate the entire universe *(to holon).* Then the seasons originate from the movement of the celestial bodies. The effect of the seasons on the earth (this is still the result of nature and chance), then leads to the appearance of animals and plants. The greatest and finest works of this cosmogony are thus accomplished.

As for art *(technē),* it is not surprising that the theory argues that its creations are both minor and secondary. Since it is impossible to take into consideration creation *ex nihilo,* to create something that was not originally present is either the result of *phusis* (and consequently is itself *phusis*), or is the result of *technē* (see also Aristotle, *Physics* 3.203b6). However, *technē* always proceeds from what is already there, in this case, the works of nature. This explains why the creations of art are said to be minor and secondary. In my view, the term *technē* is central to the comprehension of the expression *historia peri phuseōs.*

The reason is that the word *technē* is synonymous with human progress which, in turn, is indissociable from the concept of a *Kulturentwicklungslehre* or theory of cultural evolution. Indeed, to query the origin of art is to query the origin of society, for it is inconceivable that society could evolve without *technē.* Thus in book 3 of *Laws,* which delineates the origin and history of constitutions, Plato states that he will describe the conditions from which the Athens of his time emerged *(ta nun gegonen hēmin sumpanta,* 678a8). He begins with a description of the first men. They are the survivors of one in a series of natural cataclysm (677a) that periodically destroy all but a remnant of mankind. They are portrayed as being ignorant of *technai* *(apeirous technōn,* 677b6). With the progress of time *(proiontos men tou chronou),* the inhabited world became what it is now *(ta nun kathestēkota,* 678b6–8). The progress of time is thus indissociable from the discovery of diverse *technai.* And as to insist on this point, Plato employs the substantive *epidosis,* progress (676a5, 679b2)[72] and the verbs *heuriskō* and *aneuriskō,* to discover (677c6, c10) and *epinoeō,* invent (677b8).[73]

CONCLUSION

In Homer, *phusis* designates the whole process of growth of a thing from its birth to its maturity. This is compatible with a linguistic analysis of the word *phusis* which shows that the fundamental and etymological meaning of the term is that of "growth," and that, as an action noun ending in -*sis,* it means "the (completed) realization of a becoming"—that is to say, "the nature of a thing as it is realized, with all its properties." This characterization of *phusis* clearly corresponds with the attempt to describe the process through which the present world order comes about which we see expressed in the earliest philosophical cosmogonies. Indeed, the pre-Socratics were interested (at least initially) in a cosmogony in the literal sense of the word: they were not only interested in a description of the universe as it is, but in a history of the universe: an explanation of its origin (*phusis* as absolute *archē*), of the stages of its evolution (*phusis* as process of growth) and finally of its result, that is, the *kosmos* as we know it (*phusis* as the result). What differentiates the term in its pre-Socratic use from its Homeric ancestor is the reference to the gods. Within the context of the early history of philosophy the term *phusis,* with its primary meaning of growth, arose to express not merely the result of a process or the form of a thing but the process, from origin to end, through which all that is came into being and continues to behave as it does. A number of texts strongly suggest that the *phusis* of "all that is" refers not only to what we call cosmology, but also to the origins and development of human beings and their social organizations or politics. In the final analysis, this may very well be the general meaning of the expression *historia peri phuseōs*.

2

Cosmogonic Myth as an Antecedent to *Peri Phuseōs* Writings

WHAT IS A COSMOGONIC MYTH?

What is a "myth"? The word myth is notoriously difficult to define, and no one definition has been universally accepted.[1] According to some ethnologists, a myth is a message a social group considers to have received from its ancestors and transmits orally from generation to generation (Calame-Griaule 1970, 23). But a myth is not simply a message in the form of an orally transmitted story. According to Henri Frankfort (1949, 16), "Myth is a form of poetry which transcends poetry in that it proclaims a truth; a form of reasoning which transcends reasoning in that it wants to bring about the truth it proclaims; a form of action, of ritual behaviour, which does not find its fulfilment in the act but must proclaim and elaborate a poetic form of truth." Myth exists in an intimate relationship with ritual—with the repetition of demonstrative acts perceived as having been performed at the beginning of time by gods or ancestors (Eliade 1965, 22; Burket 1985, 8; Nagy 1990, 10). In reciting and reenacting myths, people relive the time of origins. Indeed, they leave "chronological" time and return to primordial time, that is, the time when the event took place for the first time. In reliving this time, they experience spectacles of divine works and relearn (and even master) the creative lessons of supernatural beings (Eliade 1965, 30).

As Eliade notes (1963, 14), people consider their myths to be true stories that relate *how* something real came into existence. But in addition, because myth "wants to bring about the truth it proclaims," events that occurred *ab origine* are reenacted in ritual. Myth thus provides both an explanation for the present social and natural order and a guarantee that the present order of nature and society will remain as they are. This dual aspect of explanation and guarantee is especially characteristic of cosmogonical myths.

A cosmogonical myth is a traditional explanation about how (and why) the world order originated.[2] To the extent that a myth of origin always recounts a "creation"—how an object came to be—strictly speaking, the cosmogonic myth enjoys particular prestige. Since the origin of the world precedes all other origins—the creation of humanity or society presupposes the existence of the world—the cosmogonic myth is the exemplary model for all species of creation (Eliade 1965, 25; Burkert 1992, 125). This does not mean that an origin myth imitates or copies the cosmogonic model, but simply that any "new" situation completes the initial totality, that is, the world. In other words, each subsequent "creation" always implies an antecedent state that, in the final analysis, is the world (Eliade 1963, 52). This is why the origin myths of events as diverse as death, sickness, or a people briefly recall the essential moments of the world's creation. It is as if the power of myths of origin depended on the rudiments of cosmogony (Eliade 1965, 102–103; Burkert 1992, 125).

What interests me in particular here is the aspect of myth that guarantees the present state of things, the world in which a given social group resides, will remain as it is. This is precisely the aim of the mythico-ritual scenario of the periodic renewal of the world.[3] This ritual appears to have had two distinct origins: the cosmogonic scenario of a New Year, on the one hand, and the consecration of the king, on the other. The cosmogonic scenario originates from the idea that the cosmos is menaced with ruin if it is not recreated annually, and the consecration of the king is associated with the harvest, which assures the continuity of the life of the entire community. In the mystical rebirth of the king as the Cosmocrator, the two ideas merge into a single ritual.[4] Since the king had to renew the entire cosmos, and since the renewal par excellence occurred when one inaugurated a new temporal cycle, the ritual consecration of the king was celebrated at New Year's celebrations. The king was perceived as the son and earthly representative of the divinity. As such, he was responsible for the regularity of the rhythms of nature and for the general well-being of society. The king guaranteed the permanence of the universal order advocated by the divinity in the beginning. As Frankfort notes: "The ancients . . . saw man always as part of society, and society as imbedded in nature and dependent upon cosmic forces" (1949, 12) This explains why cosmic evolution and cosmic order are modeled on, and expressed in terms of, the sociopolitical structure or life of the community.[5]

From this perpective, the society in which ancient humanity resides is both the logical starting point and the aspired aim of the New Year festival. Thus, in order to explain how the present social order came into being, the cosmogonic myth must necessarily begin with the birth of the world (a cosmogony), then recount the birth of mankind (an anthropogony), and finally relate the birth of society (a sociogony or politogony). For ancient peoples, society comes into existence without a real past in the sense that it only reflects the result of a series of events that took place *in illo tempore,* before the "chronological" time of the people who narrate the myth. However, if the exemplary prototype of the society in which humanity lives seems to precede the effective origin of humanity, the terrestrial society must chronologically follow its origin. In other words, humanity is created or comes into existence before it can take its place in society. An excellent example of such a cosmogonic myth is the great creation epic, the *Enuma Elish,* which means *When Above,* after the opening words of the poem. This myth narrates how the sovereign god Marduk established the present order of things.[6]

THE *ENUMA ELISH*

The cosmogonic poem *Enuma Elish* begins with a description of the watery chaos that preceded the formation of the universe. Within this aquatic chaos are the primordial entities Tiamat (female) and Apsu (male), who represent sea water and fresh water, respectively. Their initial mixture symbolizes a state of total inactivity. The hierogamy of Tiamat and Apsu leads to the birth of successive generations of gods and with them the formation of the universe.[7] Tiamat and Apsu give birth to the couple Lahmu-Lahamu, who in turn give birth to the couple Anshar-Kishar. Their names signify "totality above" and "totality below,"[8] that is, Sky and Earth. Anu, the sky god with whom the generations of "young" (read anthropomorphic) gods begin, emerges from this couple, and he, in turn, is the father of Nudimmund or Ea, lord of the earth (I.1–15).

In this world of silence, immobility, and darkness, an opposition occurs between the old established divinities and the younger turbulent divinities (I.21–50). The older gods are unhappy. Apsu plots to annihilate the younger gods but Tiamat is appalled by her husband's wicked plan. Apsu persists, but the omniscient Ea (I.60) discovers the plot and with a spell, a word of power, puts Apsu to sleep, steals his crown, and slays him.[9] Ea himself becomes god of the waters (I.69).

It is after this initial victory that Ea and Damkina give birth to Marduk, the real hero of this myth (I.78–84). Indeed, the victory of Ea is of short duration. The forces of chaos succeed in rousing Tiamat, the spouse of Apsu. She awakens with a desire for vengeance, rallies her forces, and creates a number of deadly monsters. She makes Qingu her new spouse, appoints him as supreme leader of their coalition, gives him the Tablet of Destinies—the symbol of supreme power over the universe—and confronts the terrified youth (I.125–62; II.1–49).

Anshar, the oldest and the father of the gods, successively charges Ea and Anu to convince Tiamat and her forces of evil and chaos to listen to their words or those of the assembly (II.60–82). However, Ea and Anu are too frightened and intimidated to confront Tiamat; their respective authority lacks force (II.50–94). Finally Anshar asks Marduk, who agrees to be the champion of the gods (II.95–124; III.1–51). However, unlike his predecessors, the young, formidable Marduk demands the elder gods, who are assembled in council, put all their power into his hands and henceforth recognize him as king over the whole universe (III.58–138; IV.1–34). Indeed, it is only when he receives the mandate of the assembly of the gods and is invested with special powers that his "word" will actually fix fate (II.132; this is repeated on several occasions) and in conjunction with this be able to defeat Tiamat and her coalition. Meanwhile, the gods want to see a demonstration of Marduk's magical power, to prove he can effectively do what he is invested to do. At their request, Marduk causes a constellation to vanish and then to reappear at his spoken command (IV.20–28). He is then invested with the emblem of kingship (sceptre, throne, and staff-of-office) and armed for the upcoming battle.

The battle ensues and Marduk, armed with the awesome weapons of a storm/sky god, kills Tiamat and thus becomes the uncontested sovereign of the universe (IV.60f). After contemplating Tiamat's corpse, Marduk decides to divide the monstrous body in half, "like a dried fish," and create beautiful things from it (IV.135–37). One half of Tiamat becomes the vault of the sky, the other half the earth. In the sky, Marduk sets up Esharra, a replica or counterpart of the *apsu* in which Ea established his palace.[10] Indeed, it was in the depths of the *apsu* "in the chamber of destinies, the hall of designs," that Marduk himself was created (I.79–82; IV.143–45). He then founds a place in the sky for each god of the great triad: Anu, Ellil (or Enlil), and Ea, and gives each a constellation as a celestial image and dwelling place (V.1–2). Next, he organizes the planetary universe and thus the calender (V.3–24) so that each of the gods to whom a place and a mission is assigned will know their respective duties (IV.138–V.47; VI.40–47).[11] After organizing the sky, Marduk fashions the earth, that is, Mesopotamia and its adjoining lands with all their geographical characteristics (V.48–64).[12] It is only after the physical universe is created that Marduk fetches the Tablet of Destinies from Qingu and entrusts it to Anu (V.55–56). Indeed, Marduk alone has the right to the precious talisman since he alone is the source of supreme power.

Following this, Marduk decides to create humanity (VI.1–f) to attend to the material needs of the gods (VI.7–8, 131; VII.27–30). Since the vanquished gods are still awaiting their punishment, Marduk, on the suggestion of his father Ea, assembles the gods and asks them to denounce the one responsible for the war, that is, the one who incited Tiamat to revolt. Qingu, the new spouse of Tiamat, is recognized as the only one guilty. His veins are severed and mankind is created from his blood (mixed with clay) by Ea (VI.30–35).[13]

Marduk, for his part, completes his work by organizing the gods and assigning them appropriate tasks, either in heaven or on earth (VI.39–45). He also provides each and everyone with their own lot (VI.46). This is somewhat analogous to land distribution, and, as Nemet-Nejat notes "the gods were seen as an autocracy of great landowners" (1998, 180).

The gods are sincerely grateful to Marduk. To express their appreciation, they shovel and mould brick to construct celestial Babylon and its temple (VI.50f). For Marduk, celestial Babylon will be his place of residence, where he will establish both his cult and his kingship (VI.51, 53, 68). However, the city will also be a place where the gods can assemble to rest (VI.52–54), banquet (VI.70–76), and discuss and decide matters of state (VI.79–82). This celestial city is a prototype, the Platonic Form of terrestrial Babylon, and its temple mankind will build. Indeed, since all that exists must have a paradigm, that is, a "cause" in the sky, the text naturally ends with a synthesis of the entire work accomplished by the demiurge. After all, the particular destiny of Babylon is to be the center of the universe (Cassin 1991, 1:234; Eliade 1965, 14f).

The *Enuma Elish* deals with the origin and evolution of the universe. It begins with a description of primordial reality (or chaos) and then passes through the diverse stages of the universe's genesis. First, it describes the birth and evolution of an embryonic world; embryonic in the sense it is a world that exhibits disorder (or lawlessness) despite the fact the "totality above" the sky (Anshar), and the "totality below" the earth (Kishar), are already present. Second, it describes the birth and evolution of the *present* order of things (natural and social), a universe that exhibits law and order. This is the result of a combat between Tiamat and Marduk—or more precisely, between two generations of gods—representing disorder and order, respectively. Following this, we can easily follow the birth of humankind (and its reason for being) and the type and structure of society in which humans will reside—a society that is not only modeled after divine society but is nearly coeval with it.

The *Enuma Elish,* like all cosmogonic myths that relate how the world was delivered from regression and chaos, was reiterated and reactualized each year in the capital city during the New Year festival. In ancient Mesopotamia, the recitation and reenactment took place at the spring equinox, in the month of Nisan (April), when inundations once again threatened to create the primeval watery chaos. The priests of Esagil of the great temple of Babylon recited the poem before the statue of Marduk, where the king was humiliated before regaining his prestige.[14] In addition, a series of rites reactualized the battle which had taken place *in illo tempore* between Marduk (represented by the king) and Tiamat (the Dragon symbolising the primordial ocean). The victory of God and his cosmogonic work assured the regularity of nature's rhythms and the good state of society in its entirety. The ceremony was attended by the social elite (governors, top officials, army officiers, etc.) who renewed their oath of allegiance to the king just as the gods swore an oath to Marduk when he was elected king.[15]

They would have listened with reverence to the sacred epic and its recital and reenactement would have persuaded them how an ideal state should be organized (and why their loyal support should be unequivocal). Moreover, during the New Year's festival a fertility drama took place in which the king took the hand of Marduk to a shrine where the king took part in the so-called Sacred Marriage. The king, who represented the god Dumuzi, had sexual union with the goddess, Inanna, who was represented by the high priestess or the queen. The result of their action was the fertility of all of nature. This rite is considerably older than the battle drama between Marduk and the Dragon. It goes back to when the gods were identified with the forces of nature rather than with anthropomorphic rulers of state and the view of the world as a state. By enacting the role of a force of nature man could identify with these powers and through his own actions cause the powers to act as he saw fit. Thus the king *is* Dumuzi (just as the king *is* Marduk) and his marriage to Inanna *is* the marriage of the creative powers of spring and the recreative life-giving potency which follows.[16]

HESIOD AND WRITING

In Greek literature, the most important document in the realm of cosmogony is Hesiod's *Theogony*.[17] Although it is virtually impossible to fix the dates of Hesiod with confidence, there now appears to be a general consensus that Hesiod's poetic activity falls somewhere between 750 and 650 BCE.[18] There is also a consensus that writing appeared in Greece around 750 BCE,[19] which means Hesiod was active just as or shortly after alphabetic writing made its appearance in Greece.

But who was Hesiod? For Robert Lamberton, Hesiod, like Homer, is "a mask for many anonymous voices all trained well over generations to sound the same, to speak with the same identity, and to pass on the same traditions" (1988, 2–7). Lamberton is an adherent of the oral formulaic school, which holds that Hesiod's poems must have been originally composed *without* the aid of writing. According to members of the oral formulaic school, this follows from Milman Parry's discovery some 60 years ago that archaic Greek hexameter poetry originated in an oral tradition stretching back generations. Although this thesis entails that composition necessitates performance and that no poet's composition and performance is identical with another,[20] the fact remains that "each performance entails [only] a recomposition of the poet's inherited material."[21] This explains why it is difficult to determine when the poems became fixed, since "Hesiod" would not have relied on writing to "compose" them. Indeed, writing was not necessary to transmit the texts (Nagy 1982, 45). On this view, Hesiod himself is a sort of fiction, an anonymous subject. It is therefore not surprising that proponents of this view do not believe that the biographical elements or geographical locations in Hesiod have anything to do with historical reality.

If this were true, my own thesis would be indefensible. I view Hesiod as a historical figure, and I wish to argue that with Hesiod society was becoming more secularized, that he was witness to (and a participant in) an important historical development.

While it is true Hesiod is part of the oral tradition—committing his poetic activity to writing would not exclude this—there is no reason to associate Hesiod with a tradition that essentially consists of recomposing inherited material. Hesiod is not just recreating values but advocating new ones. Indeed, he is very much a product and proponent of the new age of individualism.

In this interpretation, one would thus assume Hesiod's works were recorded in writing in more or less permanent form during his life. Only oral poetry that had won and retained great acclaim was committed to writing and passed down from generation to generation. Hesiod's works are among the rare works to fall into this prestigious category. It is therefore impossible to deny their influence.

According to Herodotus (5.57.1–58.2), the Phoenicians first introduced the alphabet to Boeotia, Hesiod's homeland. Whether or not this is true, the fact remains that Euboea, which is only a short distance from where Hesiod grew up, employed the alphabet for a variety of uses, including literary.[22] Furthermore, if one considers that the alphabet is a mnemonic script, which is learned by rote, and mastery of the script does not entail a great deal of practice, then there is no reason to believe that Hesiod would not have been capable of writing. Indeed, the fact that oral poetry could be learned by rote should have made the alphabet that much easier to learn in ancient Greece.[23] Whether or not Hesiod first composed his poems orally and then committed them to writing or had them dictated,[24] one would expect his poems to reflect a certain level of critical consciousness. *Works and Days* certainly exhibits a more sophisticated level of consciousness, at least from a socio-political position, than the *Theogony*. However, I do agree with proponents of the oral formulaic school who believe Greek poetry (oral or written) does entail performance. And even if Hesiod did commit his poetry to writing, this poetry was meant to be performed. This is an important point for my thesis and explains how Hesiod's innovative, if not revolutionary, position in *Works and Days* could have been so influential.

THE LELANTINE WAR

A crucial historical reference in Hesiod's work, that members of the oral formulaic school pass over in silence, is to the so-called Lelantine War. Because it refers to a historical fact, this reference in *Works and Days* (654–659) not only enables us to establish *terminus post quem* for Hesiod's poetic activity, but it also suggests Hesiod may have composed with the aide of writing. More importantly for the case at hand, Hesiod's audiences and subsequent aims in the two poems are radically different: the *Theogony* represents a defence of a rigid social stratification while *Works and Days* reflects a new appreciation of social mobility.

In *Works and Days* (654–59 or 725–30), Hesiod boasts of achieving poetic victory at the funeral games at Chalcis in Euboea for King Amphidamas. Plutarch (*Moralia* 153e–f) associates Amphidamas and his death with the Lelantine War. According to Thucydides (1.15.3), the war was exceptional because it divided Greece into two rival camps. The great war was fought between Chalcis and Eretria, the two chief aristocratic communities on the island of Euboea, for possession of the Lelantine plain, the rich arable land located between Chalcis and Lefkandi.[25]

Little is known about the length and the outcome of the war. According to Plutarch (*Moralia* 760f), the Chalcidians won a major land battle over the Eretrian calvary with the help of a contingent of Thessalian horsemen led by Cleomachos of Pharsalos (who fell during a battle and was commemorated with a pillar in Chalcis).[26] It was during a sea battle (again according to Plutarch), that Amphidamas, a Chalcidian nobleman, lost his life (*Moralia* 153f). It was at the funeral games at Chalcis in honor of Amphidamas that Hesiod won his prize (*Works and Days* 654–57).

The fact that Euboean interest practically disappears from Al Mina, an important Euboean trading centre, around 700 BCE,[27] the old town of Lefkandi is abandoned or destroyed around 710 BCE[28] and warrior cremations near the West Gate of Eretria date from the period 720–690 BCE (Murray 1993, 79; Coldstream 1977, 200) and a number of other circumstantial references with respect to the two alliances that date to the last quarter of the eighth century strongly suggest that during this period, probably in the latter part, Hesiod travelled to Chalcis.[29] The city must have had enough energy left to hold games!

As Oswyn Murray notes, the Lelantine war marked the end of an era (Murray 1993, 78; see also Jeffery 1976, 67–68). It was a calvary or gentleman's war, the last war fought in the old style between leading proponents of that style. The aristocracy of Chalcis are called Horse-rearers *(hippobotai),* and ancient descriptions of the fighting emphasize the importance of "cavalry," that is, the aristocratic mounted soldiers. Strabo mentions an impressive display of horsepower in his reference to Eretria, and, more importantly, an inscription in the shrine of Artemis recorded an agreement "not to use long distance missiles," the stones and arrows of the lower classes (Murray 1993, 78–79; see Janko 1982, 94–98). The encounter was recalled by Archilochus (frag. 3.4–5): "No bows will be stretched in numbers, nor slings in multitudes, when Ares joins the struggle in the plain; but it will be dour work of swords, for this is the style of the battle that they are masters of, the spear-famed lords of Euboea."[30]

As Coldstream notes, traces of a seventh-century cult above the West Gate of Eretria show that the warriors were accorded heroic status after their deaths and were worshipped as the guardians of their city.[31] Moreover, the warriors were cremated rather than inhumed although there is strong evidence that other classes and individuals were (see Coldstream 1977, 196–97), and for the most part the cremated graves are associated with offensive weapons. Cremation, of course, was a typical Homeric/epic funeral practice. The fact funeral games were held in honor of the noble, Amphidamas, at Chalcis is another typical Homeric/epic practice or influence. And again, the fact those who knew of Nestor's famous cup (smashed in a cremation burial) and composed Homeric hexameters for a banquet on the occasion, also strongly suggests they were aware of and followed Homeric funeral practices. Coldstream (1977, 350) proposes that the circulation of epic poetry (especially the *Iliad*), may have influenced burial and other aristocratic practices. Whatever the case, there is strong evidence the communities of Chalcis and Eretria were ruled by aristocracies that emulated the Homeric model and there is little doubt the kings or nobles would have been the primary arbitrators in any disputes. Indeed, in the new world of the *polis,* the position of the aristocrats was, at least initially, institutionalized, which meant that they were the magistrates for both internal and external disputes (Murray 1993, 78; but see Gagarin 1986). I will return to this point below.

West suggests Hesiod's *Theogony* may have been designed for the games in honor of Amphidamas. Reinforcing this thesis are the facts that: (1) the *Theogony* is addressed to, indeed an eulogy of, the kings/nobles or *basileis*;[32] (2) there is a reference to a recent bereavement (98–103); and (3) there is a reference that praises men-at-war, cavalry, and men taking part in athletic contests (411–52). (I agree with West, although I do not necessarily draw the same conclusions.) Therefore, the *Theogony* is essentially "conservative," since it tends to praise and support the aristocracy—indeed, it gives the aristocracy mythical justification since it anchors the institution in a cosmogonical myth.

THE *BASILEIS* IN HESIOD'S *THEOGONY*

As noted above, there is evidence the funeral practices of the Euboean kings/nobles correspond to those described in Homer and that Hesiod addressed the *Theogony* to this class of individuals.

In *Theogony* 80–103, there is a long digression on the special relationship between the kings *(basileis)* and the Muses, in particular, Calliope or Fair-utterance. In *Theogony* 84–92, Hesiod describes the kings as follows:

> And the ordinary people *(laoi)* all look to him as he arbitrates *(diakrinonta)* settlements *(themistas)* with straight judgments *(itheiēisi dikēisin)*.[33] His word is sure, and expertly he makes a quick end of even a great dispute *(mega neikos)*. This is why there are prudent kings *(basilēes):* when the people are wronged in assembly *(agorēphi)*, they make amends for them with ease, persuading them with gentle words *(malakoisi epeessin)*. When he goes among a gathering, they seek his favor with conciliatory reverence, as if he were a god, and he stands out among the crowd. Such is the sacred gift of the Muses to mankind. (trans. West with minor revisions)[34]

This passage has long reminded scholars of Homer's *Odyssey* 8.165–77, where the accent is put on the divine gift of eloquence that enables the king "to speak flawlessly in public with conciliatory reverence," distinguishing himself from the crowd (see, e.g., Gagarin 1986, 26). What these two passages have in common is that they both declare that the appropriate behavior of kings—epic kings, that is—along with the ability to be accomplished warriors, consists of being accomplished public speakers and arbitrators who are able to mollify quarrelling parties.

In Homer, it was the duty of the *basileis* to mediate feuds and these mediations were clearly profitable. When the parties agreed to abide by the judgment of the mediator, he received a mediation fee. Thus Agamemnon entices Achilles by offering him seven cities populated by wealthy men "who will honor him with gifts like a god and under his *skēptron* execute his profitable ordinances *(liparas teleousi themistas)*" (*Iliad* 9.156f). In other words, Achilles will gain substantial profit from mediation fees (see Murray 1993, 60). In the *Iliad* (18.497–508) there is also the famous description of a scene, on the shield of Achilles, of two litigants arguing their case before assessors, elders, albeit kings, who declare: "in the middle is a gift of two talents of gold for the assessor who makes the straightest judgment *(dikē)*" (see Robb 1994, 76).

In the context of the *Theogony*, it is clear that the parties to a dispute would come before the *basileis*, state their case, and settle their dispute according to *themis* or precedent.[35] However, it seems that his decision *(dikē)*, straight or crooked, would be "legally" binding; the parties were not in a position to reject the decision (as in the Homeric example). The *basileis* act as judges and not simply as mediators; otherwise, Hesiod would not have abided by their crooked decision in favor of his brother Perses in the *Works and Days*. Moreover, there is no indication in *Theogony* that Hesiod is galled by what he calls "gift-devouring" kings in the *Works and Days*. Indeed, in the *Theogony*, as in the *Iliad,* these gifts are not bribes but the right of the mediator or judge—and there is no suggestion they make a difference to the mediator or judge, which is the case in *Works and Days* (as Murray [1993, 60] notes).

It is important to note that what Hesiod advocates is said to be based on the "truth" (*alēthea,* 28); a truth that pertains to the past, present, and future (38). The Muses inspire his song, and he celebrates them in return (*Theogony* 1–34).[36] However, the Muses also inspire kings; the kings owe them their "conciliatory" expertise, whereas the poets owe them their power of charm. In sum, Hesiod draws a parallel (perhaps a bold one) between the poets and the kings (80–103), although the kings have the important added attribute of being the descendants of Zeus (*Theogony* 96). This does not prevent Hesiod from speaking with the authority of the king; both the king and the poet hold the *skēptron* or "sacred staff."[37] In conjunction with this, it is important to note that the way decisions are made (or should be made) in the human realm is perceived as conforming to the general order of the universe, for the official staff *(skēptron)* and decisions/customs *(themistes)* are seen as gifts from Zeus (see *Iliad* 2.205–6; 9.98). Therefore, decisions or judgments *(dikai)* are considered straight or crooked insofar as they conform to sacred customs. The ideal king should be able to sort out what is *themis* from what is not (Nagy 1982, 58).

The Prelude in the *Theogony*

Hesiod's *Theogony* opens with a long prelude (1–115), which explains the meaning and extent of the poem. In the prelude, the bard describes how, while he was grazing his lambs on the slopes of Mount Helicon, the Muses taught him the art of *aoidē,* the art of singing in verse (22), in order to reveal and celebrate the truth (*alēthea,* 28) both past and future (32), about the race of immortal gods (34). It is not by chance the author of the *Theogony* invokes the Muses. They are the daughters of Zeus and of Memory *(Mnēmosunē),* and it is Memory who enables the poet to have direct access to the events he describes because only she possesses "memory," the power to contemplate the past, present, and future all at the same time (38). In asking the Muses to inspire his songs (104–105), Hesiod asks them to confer on him this gift of memory. This gift, the sine qua non of poetic performance, is the gift of vision through which he will be able to recount events that took place in the "past," that is, *in illo tempore,*[38] which led to the establishment of the "present" order of things. If the future is invoked, it is because it prolongs and thus guarantees in a certain sense, the continuity of this order. From this perspective, it seems that what we have here (in conjunction with the analysis of myth discussed above) is genuine mythmaking, since it is "a traditional expression of a given group's concept of truth" (Nagy 1990, 48).

The events in question are those for which the Muses were created to sing and celebrate; to wit: how Zeus, their father, after a series of socio-political power struggles, defeats his enemies and as the new ruler dispenses privileges and obligations among the immortals, thus establishing and guaranteeing the permanence of the present order of things (69–75; 391f; 885). However, before narrating this story, Hesiod must provide the theater in which these battles for sovereignity between the gods occurred (i.e., the physical universe), and introduce the gods who took part. The list of successive generations of gods provides these elements. It is in this sense that the theogonic and cosmogonic overlap in Hesiod's text.

THE COSMOGENESIS

Hesiod tells us that, in the beginning, Chaos was the very first entity/power to come into being *(genet')*, followed by Gaia (Earth), Tartaros (underworld), and Eros (love). In a certain sense these four primordial powers (two of which are masculine, Eros and Tartaros, and two feminine, Chaos and Earth) are coeval. But in another sense they are not. For some reason, Hesiod refrains from giving them any genealogical connections. Let us begin with Chaos.

Chaos refers to a gap or opening up of a space. The word itself is derived from the root *cha-* and it is related to *chaskō* (gape, yawn) (see Chantraine). However two things appear unclear. First, was Chaos an eternal precondition of a differentiated world or a modification of that precondition? The fact that Hesiod employs *genet'* "came-into-being"[39] rather than *ēn* "was" suggests as Kirk notes (KRS 1983, 39), following Cornford, that it was the later. In this case, *before* the gap or chasm actually occurred, there was a mass of undifferentiated stuff.[40] This, of course, would be an answer to the question: came into being out of what? It was only after the gap occurred that the process of differentiation or the cosmogonical process, strictly speaking, began. On the other hand, some scholars argue (or appear to argue) that Chaos itself is the initial stage, that is, there was, initially, a great abyss. Thus Mazon (1928, 10–11) translates line 116 as *"D'abord fut l'Abîme, puis Terre et Amour."* He therefore believes Hesiod does not reply to the question "How does the earth emerge from the abyss?" Lamberton and Lombardo (1993, 13) follow a similar line: "Hesiod's cosmos begins from a 'gaping' or 'abyss' (Gr. *Chaos*) that simply 'was' in the beginning . . . [and] still exists." It is therefore not surprising they argue that Earth and Tartaros must have coexisted with Chaos (13), as if to say there was no cosmogonical process.[41] What appears logical (if not certain) is that Earth, Tartaros, and Eros were somehow fused in the initial mass of undifferentiated stuff and that a gap, that is, Chaos, somehow occurred in this precosmic stuff, which caused these entities/powers to emerge.

The second thing that appears unclear is the location of the initial gap (Chaos). Hesiod strongly suggests that before the gap occurred Earth, Tartaros, and Eros were mingled together. Cornford, followed by Kirk and others, argues that the gap—the duplication of which occurs again with the castration of Uranos—occurred between earth and sky.[42] Tartaros is thus seen as an appendage or subordinate of Earth, and Eros as the rain/semen that exists between Earth and Sky (KRS 1983, 38). As Kirk notes, "the idea that earth and sky were orginally one mass may have been so common that Hesiod could take it for granted, and begin his account of world formation at the first stage of differentiation" (KRS 39). He cites numerous Greek and non-Greek sources in support of this thesis.[43]

On the other hand, West argues that the gap or space occurred between Earth and Tartaros. West's position appears no less popular that Cornford's (see M. Miller Jr. 1983; Lombardo and Lamberton 1993, 13). It has been forceably argued by Miller Jr. (1983, 134), who observes among a number of other interesting points, that Cornford's position entails that Sky was coeval with Earth (as well as Tartaros and Eros) and that there is nothing in Hesiod's text to suggest this—except perhaps the castration scene further on. West, for his part, finds support for his interpretation in the fact that the same space between earth and tartaros is named *chasma* in 740 and *chaeos* in 814. More to the point, Hesiod informs that *between* dark Earth and misty Tartaros there is murky chaos (*chaeos zopheroio,* 814), that is, an immense gap (*chasma meg',* 740). In conjunction with this, Hesiod says it would take a bronze anvil as much time to fall *from* the earth *to* Tartaros as it would take it to fall *from* the sky *to* the earth: to wit, nine days and nights of falling with arrival on the tenth day (720–25).[44] This strongly suggests that the distance *between* the earth and Tartaros is enormous.[45] Moreover, it entails a sort of three story or stage-symmetrical universe with heaven at the *top,* earth at the *center,* and tartaros at the *bottom.*[46] This gap or chasm is described as dark and windy. More important, it is said that Earth, Sea, Sky, and Tartaros all have roots *(pēgai)* and limits *(peirata),* that is, their beginnings and ends, in this chasm (736–739; 807–810).[47] If the initial gap did occur between Earth and Tartaros, this would help explain why Tartaros has no progeny of its own at the opening of the cosmogony.[48]

Strictly speaking, in the cosmogony Chaos parthenogentically generates Erebos (darkness) and black Night. They, in turn, mingle in love (*philotēti migeisa,* 125) and give birth to Aither (bright sky) and Day. Erebos and Night are indicative of a "dark and humid" condition and are descriptive of the gap itself, one would assume, as it opens. The chronological point of departure in cosmogonical myths is most often described as dark and humid.[49] On the other hand, if Aither and Day are generated from Erebos and Night, it is because Night and Day are indissociable, the one implying the other.[50] From the cosmogonic perspective, day logically and temporally follows night since it represents a more developed state (the sun does not play a role at this stage; indeed as West notes (1966, 197), sunlight and daylight are not seen as the same thing). Consequently, Day, or rather its coming to being, is inseparable from a universe that is in the process of formation. Chaos and Earth are thus closely tied even if there is no genealogical connection at this point. Let us look next at Earth.

According to Hesiod, Earth first *(prōton)* generated (or "gave birth to," *egeinato*) starry sky and then the mountains and the sea (126–32). These were all generated by Earth parthenogentically *(ater philotētos ephimerou,* 132), that is, through a sort of spontaneous generation. This lends credence to those who argue that the initial gap was between Earth and Tartaros. Indeed, as noted above, Tartaros (which is masculine) does not generate, as one may expect at this point, any children of its own. (It may also explain why its only pairing is with Earth involving the production of Typhoeus).[51]

Although Eros is coeval with Earth and Tartaros, like Tartaros, he is no longer mentioned. His generative function, which is taken for granted, is the natural counterpart to that of Chaos: whereas Chaos signifies division and separation, Eros signifies combination and integration. From this perspective, Eros would be connected with the generation of Aither and Day since it is only after Erebos and Night mingle in love that they are generated. Since it is difficult not to connect the coming to be of Aither and Day with the formation of the universe, Eros as a primordial power is no less connected with the generation of the universe than Chaos, Gaia, and Tartaros.[52]

Although every feature of the universe is personified in this account of the origin of the "physical universe," the language at this stage is still devoid of mythical imagery.[53] Indeed, there is a striking absence of personified gods. However, it is unclear if what we have here are several different versions of the formation of the physical universe (e.g., Chaos generating Erebos and Night who in turn generate, Aither and Day, and Earth asexually generating Sky, Mountain, and Sea) or a single version. The fact that Sky is described as "starry" *(asteroenth',* 127) may entail that daylight is still absent, and since Erebos and Night are of the same generation as Mountain, Sea, and Sky (the second generation), then Aither and Day may be considered the next generation (the third generation) and thus a continuation of the same cosmogenesis. Whatever the case, it appears the physical universe (which does not appear to be, at this stage, an embryonic universe as we saw in the opening of the *Enuma Elish)* is now a place for the birth or arrival of successive families of anthropomorphic or noncosmic gods and their battles for supremacy.

The Titans are the first anthropomorphic offspring of Earth and Sky. They include: Ocean, Koios, Krios, Hyperion, Iapetos, Theia, Rheia, Themis, Mnemosyne, Phoibe, Tethys, and finally Kronos (133–38). Of course, the characteristics of the Titans are not without ambiguity. For example, Ocean is more often associated with the great river that encircles the Earth and to which all other rivers were connected (337, 362, 789–92). Ocean is also the brother and husband of Tethys, who is equally connected with water. In Homer, the Titans are the ultimate source of all things (*Iliad* 14.201, 246). Themis and Mnemosyne represent Custom and Memory, the sine qua non of any organized community. Theia and Hyperion (the epithet for the sun in Homer, e.g., *Iliad* 8.480) are the parents of Sun, Moon, and Dawn (371). Phoibe, the bright one, may be connected with the moon (136); Iapetos is the father of Prometheus; Koios and Krios are more obscure while Rheia is the wife of the infamous Kronos, the parents of the Olympians.[54] Gaia and Uranos also gave birth to the Cyclopes: Brontes, Steropes, and Arges (Thunder, Lightening, and Bright Flash and thus personalized phenomena) and the three Hundred-Handers (139–153); all of which are representatives of power and strength and play a fundamental role in the succession story.

THE CASTRATION OF URANOS AND THE SECOND COSMOGENESIS

The famous scene, which recounts the castration of Uranos (154–210) is justifiably seen as a second version (or repetition) of the cosmogenesis (see Cornford 1952, 194; KRS 1983, 38; and Vernant 1991, 1:373). Indeed, the scene relates for a second time how and why Earth and Sky were separated. However in this account, anthropomorphism, with its corresponding motivations and feelings, predominates. The story unfolds as follows: Uranos begets eighteen children (the Titans, Cyclopes, and Hundred-Handers enumerated above), but because of his excessive copulation with Gaia (the negative side of Eros), he prevents them from seeing the light of day (*es phaos ouk anieske*, 157) and from receiving their legitimate *moira* (share) of *timai* (honors). Without light, the generation is stalled, and Gaia asks her children to come to her aid. Kronos, the youngest, takes up the challenge and executes the cruel *(doliēn)* and evil trick *(kakēn technēn)* devised by his mother. Kronos hides in ambush and when the opportune moment arrives (Uranos is engaged in sex with Gaia), he castrates his father. This act represents, for the second time, the separation of earth and sky and thus the appearance of light and the effective birth of the Titans (the Cyclopes and Hundred-Handers, unlike the Titans, are not released from Gaia's womb) and the *timai* (honors) and *gera* (privileges) associated with victory.

Kronos and Rhea then give birth to the Olympians, but like his father Uranos, Kronos treats his children with the same contempt. They are given no share of honor (*moira* of *timē*, 392f, 882.) or privileges (*geras*, 393, 396). Rhea, as unwillingly as Gaia, gives birth to the Olympians (Demeter, Hestia,

Hera, Hades, Poseidon, and Zeus) but Kronos, heeding his father's threat that he would be punished for his evil deeds (210), swallows them one after the other to avert being usurped by one of them (462). However, he is outwitted by his youngest son, Zeus (with the help of Gaia and Uranos) and forced to liberate his children (470f). All the actors, with the exception of Typhoeus, are now in place for the final sovereignty battle.

The Battles for Sovereignty

A violent battle, the famous Titanomachy, ensues for ten years (636) between two coalitions led by Kronos and Zeus. The war continues until Zeus, on the advice of Gaia, retrieves the Hundred-Handers from the underworld where they had been relegated first by Uranos and then by Kronos. With their help, the Titans are finally defeated and dispatched to Tartaros (690–735, 814, 820). However, Zeus is then confronted with a new menace: Typhoeus (820–80), the child of Tartaros and Gaia. Typhoeus represents the return of primordial chaos to the organized world (Vernant 1991, 377). Despite his formidable power, he is defeated in a single combat by Zeus and quickly hurled into his proper place: Tartaros. He is the source of impetuous and unpredictable winds (869–880)—perhaps an indication that the forces of disorder cannot ever be completely vanquished.

Just as the castration of Uranos and its consequences completes the cosmogonic phase of the *Theogony,* the defeat of the monster Typhoeus marks the end of the battles for sovereignty. Following his victory, Zeus on the advice of Gaia (884), is unanimously declared king and he then (unlike Uranos and Kronos), distributes honors to all who fought on his side in accordance with his initial oath *(horkon).* A new political and moral order is thus inaugurated.

The Origin of Humanity

One would expect the origin of humanity to follow Zeus' victory and subsequent marriages, but this is not the case. The origin of humanity, or at least its appearance, is found in the Prometheus episode, which occurs midway between the beginning and the end of the *Theogony* (535–616), *before* the succession battles commence.[55] Whatever the reason for this, the fact remains that Hesiod needed to account for the origin of mankind and the actual human condition—something Homer did not feel compelled to do. In Homer, humans are simply present as part of the world furniture (as part of fate or *moira*). To account for the origin of humanity, an anthropogony is, as we shall see, a primary component of pre-Socratic cosmogonies in general.

The myth of Prometheus explains the origin of mankind and the human condition (Vernant 1983, 238–240). It is unclear if Hesiod was aware of other versions of the origin of mankind or why he choose this version over others.[56] What is common to all of Hesiod's own accounts is that the earliest race of mortals initially lived without toil, cares, fatigue, or sickness. They emerged "whole" from the earth and they never grew old; when they died, it was as in a peaceful sleep.[57]

In the *Theogony*, we learn that there was a time when men and the gods lived peacefully together—a golden age. But, during a feast, Prometheus, who was charged with distributing the food portions, defrauded the gods to the advantage of mortals (we are not told why Prometheus represents mortals).[58] To avenge himself, Zeus hides fire from men, that is, the celestial fire men needed to cook their food. However, Prometheus comes to their aid and again deceives Zeus by stealing fire in the stalk of a fennel plant. Indeed, without fire man can no longer feed himself and is thus condemned, it would seem, to annihilation. Zeus ripostes by creating woman *(gunē)*, Pandora, who will be a primary source of human evil—albeit an equally important asset.[59] The separation of men from the gods necessarily implies a new status for the human race. Humans will no longer emerge from the earth like plants; all new birth will be the result of procreation; and humans will now live painfully in time. However, humanity is not without certain resources. The gift of fire will not only enable humans to feed themselves but will also have a civilizing effect; it will enable them to acquire other techniques and to progress in time.[60] Mankind is thus not left "to a level of solitary brutishness" as Clay (1989, 124) argues. Indeed, the marriages contracted by Zeus following his victory appear to confirm this. This may be, at least in the *Theogony*, the type of socio-political order to which humans must progress. However, the main moral of the story seems to be that to deceive Zeus is to contest the world order established by Zeus, and the punishment for doing so will be exemplary.

THE MARRIAGES OF ZEUS

In the *Theogony*, just as the world order is organized by personal and personalized divinities, all the socio-political concepts are gods and goddesses, as are such nonsocial concepts as Death, Sleep, Lies, Distress, and Sarcasm. In fact, many of the most important concepts were generated prior to the Olympians: Themis and Mnemosyne are the children of Uranos and Earth (135);[61] the Fates, Friendship, and Retribution are the asexually generated children of Night (217–24); Metis and Eurynome are the children of Ocean and Tethys (358). It should be no surprise that Zeus actually contracts a series of marriages following his victory with several of these concepts, beginning with Metis (Cunning Intelligence) and followed by Themis (Custom-Law), Eurynome (Good Order), and Mnemosyne (Memory). These marriages are essential to Hesiod's account.

The first marriage to Metis (Cunning Intelligence) entails that the order of succession will stop with Zeus. Metis is destined to give birth to a child stronger than Zeus. But on the advice of Gaia and Uranos, Zeus swallows Metis instead of his son, as Kronos had done, putting an end to the cycle of succession and assuring that no trick will ever surprise him (886–900). The second marriage to Themis incarnates stability, continuity, and regular order, whence the birth of the Hours (Discipline, Justice/Dike, and Peace) and the Moirai or Fates (901–909), which symbolize the portion and limit attributed to each and therefore the boundary that must not be crossed. The third marriage to Eurynome bears the three Graces: Joy, Festivity, and Abundance (907–909). These are the fruits of a just and durable order, that is, any civilization worthy of the name. The fourth marriage is to Demeter (912–914). The progeny of this marriage is Phersephone, who is later raped by Hades. The rape is particularly important since it symbolizes death and rebirth. Since death can only be that of man, rebirth must be the fruit of the first three marriages in the sense that if man dies, the Muses guarantee his survival through memory of what transpired. This explains the fifth marriage to Mnemosyne and the birth of the nine Muses (915–917) whose function is to conserve everything that characterizes the reign and will of Zeus: the sacred conventions and ways of civilized society (see Havelock 1963, 101).

Hesiod's *Theogony*, therefore, explains the origin of the organizational structure and code of values of the gods and by extension, the heroes and nobles of Hesiod's time. This is clear in the prelude to the *Theogony* (100f), where we are told that the aim of the bard is to celebrate the great deeds (*kleea* 100) of men of old (*proterōn anthrōpōn,* 100) and of the inhabitants of Olympus. The human kings to which Hesiod refers (starting at line 80) are the descendants of these, and "when they make judgments with correct decisions (*diakrinonta themistas itheiēisi dikēisin,* 84–85)," these judgments are based on the *nomoi* and *ēthē* (the sacred conventions and ways) of their human and divine ancestors (and thus the will of Zeus). This is one of the primary lessons of the Prometheus episode: to deceive Zeus is to deceive the new socio-political world order, and it will be met with vengeance from the seat of power.[62]

GENERAL INTERPRETATION OF THE *THEOGONY*

There is no doubt Hesiod's theogonic poem is a hymn in honor of Zeus. That was clearly announced in the prelude. But how is one to interpret the text in general? Hesiod's theogonic poem is a sort of rationalization of the history of the present world order. His method consists in presenting both the history of the world and its system of values—unequivocally based on power—under the guise of an immense divine genealogy.

The series of marriages following Zeus' victory make this interpretation all the more plausible. The result of the fourth marriage, the subsequent marriage of Persephone and Hades, means that despite the precariousness of human life, the *nomoi* and the *ēthē* (66) that derive from the first three marriages and that characterize a civilized society, can and must be preserved. They are preserved through a song, which, like Persephone, is a constant reminder of what is essential for the salvation of society. Moreover, if the Muses are born in fifth and last place, it is precisely to conserve (and not to create or recreate) what preceded them. From this perspective, Zeus' wish becomes that of our ancestors. The fact that gods and men were seen as sharing a similar socio-political structure and value system makes this supposition more plausible.

THE ABSENCE OF RITUAL

The most notable difference between the cosmogonic myth presented by Hesiod and that of the *Enuma Elish* resides in the absence of ritual. Indeed, even if Hesiod's *Theogony* offers an explanation of the origin and the evolution of the world and proposes an exemplary socio-political model of existence for mankind within the world order established by Zeus, what is striking about Hesiod's account is that, in it, the periodic renewal of the world, humanity, and society is no longer necessary.

It is often pointed out that the central organizing principle in Hesiod's *Theogony* is a succession myth and this succession myth clearly has a number of eastern parallels.[63] In each instance, the text exalts the power of a god who rules over the entire universe, the order of which is the product of his victory over the forces of disorder. Such is the case with the *Enuma Elish,* which presents a divine character, Marduk, who in many respects resembles the Zeus of Hesiod's *Theogony*. Both texts narrate the birth and battles of a god who is the central character in the text. The principal protagonists, Marduk and Zeus, are chosen as the leaders of their respective coalitions in order to combat and kill a dragon (Tiamat in the first case, Typhoeus in the second) who personifies confusion and disorder. After slaying the monsters, the protagonists are proclaimed as kings of the other gods. Then they proceed to distribute privileges and destinies in the diverse regions of the universe to those who fought at their sides. This is why these creation stories qualifiy as sovereignty myths. But, how can these two texts exhibit such striking analogies and still diverge on something as fundamentally important (at least in appearance) as ritual? It may be due to a historical event of capital importance: the collapse of Mycenaean civilization. Indeed, there is strong evidence the Mycenaean world was somewhat akin to the kingdoms of the Near East to which it was contemporary. Archeological and documentary evidence (derived from the decipherment of the Linear B script) reveal a system of administration and economic organization based on palace and sanctuary. Mycenaean society (and its corresponding pantheon) was, like its Near Eastern counterparts, markedly hierarchical, with kings and nobles at the top, slaves at the bottom, and farmers, craftsmen, and local community rulers in between.[64] At the top of the hierarchical order was the *wanax*, one of the Homeric words for king. *Basileus*, another Homeric (and Hesiodic) word for king is also found, but seems to be used for the chief of any group (Chadwick 1976, 70). Although *wanax*, in most cases, refers to a human ruler, it seems the word was also applied as a divine title (1976, 70–71). Indeed, even if there is no *certain* evidence of a divine kingship, it is rather odd the king would not be perceived as the son and earthly representative (or counterpart) of the divinity.[65] Despite their mortal nature, the Homeric kings certainly saw themselves as having divine parentage. And these kings were responsible, as were their counterparts in the Near Eastern monarchies, for the regularity of nature's rhythms and for the good state of the entire society. Indeed, numerous documents from the royal archives of various Near Eastern centers all attest to the existence of a powerful hierarchical theocratic state with the king-priest perceived as the son of a god at the summit. Moreover, there is strong evidence these texts were intended to be ritualized, that is, chanted and reenacted. Indeed, not only are these texts/poems based on rhythm and cadence, but in every instance we find that the divine hero must combat a primordial dragon or snake on an annual basis.[66] Finally, in every case, there is a correlation between a sovereignity myth and a fertility myth. Thus, both nature and society are subject to the annual renewal ritual.[67]

If the ritual function connected with cosmic renewal is absent in Hesiod, then it is because the Mycenaen civilization that Hesiod unconsciously refers to collapsed abruptly around 1200 BCE.[68] The collapse of this palace-centred, redistributive economic civilization entailed the disappearance of the character of the divine king and the social practices his presence necessitated. It is therefore legitimate to ask whether the disappearance of the cosmic-renewal ritual did not foster the rejection of Justice as it is envisaged by Hesiod in the *Theogony*, that is, life in conformity with the will of Zeus (or of the ancestors). Indeed, on the one hand, ritual enables people to thwart forces of disorder and, on the other hand, to renew the world in which they live. In other words, ritual guarantees that both the natural and social order willed by the demiurge during the creation remains as it is. It is precisely the king, the son and earthly representative of the demiurge, who is responsible for the stability, fecundity, and prosperity of the entire cosmos. This explains his essential function during the renewal ritual.

But there is nothing of the sort in Hesiod's work or in the work of his successors. In fact, the manner in which the cosmogony is represented in Hesiod's *Theogony* strongly suggests that the renewal ritual no longer has a reason for being. A comparison of the roles played by Zeus and by Marduk in their respective cosmogonies clearly demonstrates this. For example, unlike Marduk, Zeus does not intervene in the natural order of things; he is simply at the origin of a new socio-political order.[69] This explains why Hesiod's theogonic text unfolds in a perfectly linear and irreversible way.[70] Unlike Marduk, Zeus does not recreate what is already in place: the physical universe as we know it. Furthermore, contrary to what occurs in the majority of the other cosmogonic texts, the will of Zeus (or that of our ancestors) has no control over what occurs in "human time." Of course, through the intermediary of the Muses, Hesiod is able to return to the "time of the gods" in order to narrate the will of Zeus. Nevertheless, Hesiod does not create (that is, he does not effectively renew) the series of events that took place in the time of the gods (or "mythical time"). Rather, Hesiod is only the guarantor; he is the one who conserves and transmits. But what Hesiod announces can be accepted or dismissed, retained or not retained, by his audience.

Gregory Nagy correctly notes, "the narrative structure of epic, as is the case with myth and mythopoeic thinking in general, frames a value system that sustains and in fact educates a given society" (1982, 43). And while it may be difficult to determine to what degree Hesiod's *Theogony* is his own creation, there is no doubt that it would have been performed (and thus ritualized, so to speak) before an audience. Furthermore, there is no doubt it was addressed to an aristocratic elite and that it was meant to enhance, if anything, their value system: a Homeric and thus a conservative value system at least by the current standards. It is conservative because Hesiod is (or seems to be) advocating a socio-political model in which the so-called *basileis* or kings are the representatives of Zeus here on earth and in which their word is analogous to the word of Zeus, and should be obeyed. Of course it appears that, as long as the kings do not make unfair judgements, Hesiod has no problem with this conservative value system, which, moreover, is said to cover the past, present, and future. However, *Works and Days* presents a very different position.

WORKS AND DAYS AS A SEQUEL TO *THEOGONY*

If oral literature, tradition, and myth are mirrors in which society observes itself and measures its proper stability, then Hesiod's *Works and Days* is a wake-up call.[71] While it contains several traditional myths (including Eastern elements) that convey messages social groups could have considered as having been transmitted by its ancestors,[72] in many respects *Works and Days* advocates a new type of social reform, a new type of general *aretē*. From this perspective, Hesiod is a precursor of Plato.

Works and Days is composed of two parts. The first, employing myths and moral precepts (consciously composed for the occasion), teaches that no one can trick Zeus without suffering the consequences (the myth of Prometheus and of Pandora), and that when injustice is done, humans are the losers (the myth of the races). The second part offers us a solution to the crisis: work the land the way the gods intended, and with hard work comes success and justice.[73] Even if the Prometheus episode teaches us Zeus cannot be fooled, nothing, including Zeus, can prevent the society in which humanity resides from following its own course. What is proper to humans is to live in time, even if time, in the final analysis, is derived from Zeus, that is, Zeus the "master of time," or "weather god." It is up to human beings to determine how they want to live from day to day.[74]

Thus in the myth of the *genē* (races, ages or generations), war, as work, is characterized either by *dikē* or *hubris*. When war is characterized by *dikē*, as in the age of iron, it is the responsibility of humans. For Hesiod the iron age cannot only be characterized by evil, for good is always mixed with evil (179). This point is fundamental, since it indicates that far from being irreversible, the continual degeneration often stressed by commentators is not, strictly speaking, there to begin with. Hesiod appears to be saying that humans can always become conscious of their mistakes and correct the situation.[75]

Works and Days, considered by many commentators as one of the most somber lamentations ever composed, is in fact much more optimistic when one reads between the lines.[76] Indeed a certain number of autobiographical passages gives us a portrait of Hesiod that contrasts sharply with the pessimistic perception.

BIOGRAPHICAL DETAILS

Hesiod's father, he tells us, was originally a merchant of the Eolian coast of Asia Minor. Tired of the travels and even more tired of the poor remuneration provided by his trade, he settled in Acra where he acquired a piece of farmland (*WD* 633–40).[77] When his father died, the plot was divided between Hesiod and his brother Perses. But the two brothers disputed the division and submitted their litigation to a council of the local nobles (the *basileis*). However, Perses made an arrangement with these nobles to get more than his fair share (35–41). Perses was not only a cheat; he was also lazy and he quickly squandered his part of the familial patrimony. Reduced to a state of mendicancy

(396), Perses seeks help from Hesiod. The latter is at first sympathetic to his brother's state and gives or lends him the essentials of life (394). But Perses is insatiable. Hesiod eventually has enough and refuses to give his brother any more (396–97). He tells him that if he spent less time following the "corrupt" process in the agora (perhaps he was still searching for a means to cheat his brother) and worked the earth, true justice (the justice of Zeus), would prevail. This justice would assure him his subsistence and his happiness, and Hesiod is well placed to know it.

Contrary to what is often argued, the poet was not a poor little peasant at the service of rich aristocrats. He was closer to what Chester Starr calls a "semi-aristocrat or middling farmer" (1977, 126).[78] Hesiod was his own master and economically independent. He had his own cattle, mules, slaves, and salaried men for the work—about whom he often complained (597–608; 765–69). He hoped to sell his agricultural surplus abroad (630–32) and to purchase more land (341). In the heat of the summer, he searched for the shadow of a rock and drank the wine of Biblos (589–96).

But Hesiod is not only a successful cultivator. He was also a renowned poet who won the prestigious poetry contest at Chalcis in honor of Amphidamas (650–62) and a two-handled tripod as a prize. He also doubtlessly won the admiration of his compatriots and perhaps lived to see his poems performed. It is thus difficult to affirm Hesiod did not consider himself as one of Zeus' beloved, or that he seriously believed that justice had really left the earth.

CONFLICTING VIEWS OF *ARETĒ* OR SUCCESS

It should be no surprise Hesiod contests the Homeric conception of *aretē* and offers another in its place.[79] No longer the possession of nobles and heros, the *aretē*-norm now belongs to another class of men. The *panaristos,* the complete man, is the successful farmer, and *aretē* now signifies the qualities that enable a person to prosper and avoid famine.[80] Being a person of *aretē,* in Hesiod's new definition, is a matter of learning to act after sober reflection or after seeking and heeding good advice. Although difficult (289–92), attainment of *aretē* is not restricted to those of noble birth. Hesiod could well say, "Listen, Perses, I am the *agathos,* and not that corrupt judge."[81]

HESIOD AND THE *BASILEIS*

In *Works and Days* as in *Theogony,* kings are again at center stage. However, the description offered by Hesiod in the former is radically different from the latter.

The story of the hawk and the nightingale (235–45) makes it clear that kings have considerable, if not absolute, power over their subjects, and have no qualms about using it. Hesiod is of the opinion, as are most of us, that absolute power corrupts.[82] Kings embody *hubris*, or violence, that is, the Homeric principle that might, or pure self-interest, is right, as opposed to justice. Hesiod believes that people without justice will devour themselves like wild animals and there will be a sort of Hobbesian state of nature—not unlike what preceded the reign of Zeus. However, Hesiod is not as easily intimidated as the story of the hawk and nightingale leaves one to believe. He directly challenges the kings of Thespies with an astonishing free speech; the fact that the poem would have been performed extensively throughout the Greek world only enhances this point. In *Works and Days,* kings are unequivocally characterized as "greedy" and their verdicts as "corrupt."[83] On three occasions he describes them as "bribe-eating" (*dōrophagoi,* 39, 221, 264), and characterizes their sentences *(dikai)* as crooked or unjust *(skoliai)* (221, 250, 262). The kings are also contrasted with the *dēmos* or people (261).

In the *Theogony,* accepting gifts in exchange for delivering judgments is the right of a mediator or king, and Hesiod paints a flattering picture of the custom. But in *Works and Days,* Hesiod is clearly vexed by the system of gifts. He doubts the verdict or *dikē* will be straight, and he suggests he has firsthand knowledge of this. Rulers appear to be clearly more interested in the gift than the sentence, and consequently, at least from Hesiod's perspective, announce a settlement that litigants are surely to return. In sum, they are likely to be the only ones profiting from the system. In Hesiod's eyes, this system must be replaced at any cost, for it clearly has a legal force.[84] What is worse, they see their *dikē* as a question of *timē* or honor. Hesiod advocates nothing short of dispensing with kings, for they embody and indeed endorse the destructive *eris* or competition. This is a bold step— all the more bold in that it will be performed over and over. This is clearly revolutionary. In fact, Hesiod appears convinced that the people will pay for the arrogance of the nobles unless *dikē* rather than *timē* becomes the central virtue (see Murray 1993, 61). This is also clear from his paradigm of the two cities: the city of *dikē* and the city of *hubris* (225–247). *Hubris* is responsible for famine, poverty, plague, et cetera (240f). However, Hesiod contends at 217–18 that *dikē* will eventually triumph over *hubris*. *Dikē* will punish greedy men (220–23). The fact that Hesiod employs *dikē* twenty-one times from line 213 to 285 is indicative of its importance. Hesiod sees justice as a method of procedure and tries to objectify the notion. The fact that *dikē* is personified and becomes the protector of society reinforces this conviction.[85] With the elimination of the kings or nobles, what remains—if not a call for a written code of laws?[86]

THE ADVENT OF LAW

Writing became widespread in Greece between 750 and 650 BCE. Although the evidence indicates that writing was first used for inscriptions (in hexameter, for the most part) of a private nature, it is not by chance that the written law occurs shortly after the advent of writing. The laws of both Zaleukos of Locri, and Charondas of Catana, of Sicily, date around 675 BCE, and there is an extant law from Dreros on Crete inscribed in stone that dates from around the same time (650 BCE).[87] The first laws of Gortyn, another city on Crete (in fact, the first to yield a complete code), also date from around 650 BCE.[88] At Locri and Catana in Western Greece, Zaleukos and Charondas were already trying to fix the penalty for each offense and, in doing so, it appears that they were trying to unify a judicial system and save the citizens from the fluctuations of the sentences, that is, the arbitrariness of the judges/nobles.[89] The main purpose of the extant law from Dreros is (or at least appears) to define the limits of authority, in particular those of the *kosmos* (chief magistrate) of the city *(polis)*.[90] The Gortyn code, for its part, clearly implies that the magistrate is bound by the letter of the law.[91] Something similiar to this develops in Hesiod.[92]

According to Caroline Thomas (1977), the people only became aware of inequalities *after* the codification of law. She sees "critical consciousness" as an effect of both codification and the alphabet.[93] But it is clear from Hesiod that a critical consciousness was well in the works prior to the codification of law. Without the discovery and diffusion of writing, the codification of law would have been impossible, and while it is true that Hesiod's activity began after the introduction of writing, there is no indication that codified law already existed in his native *polis*. This would have to have been the case in order to support Thomas' position.[94]

Customs were initially perceived as immutable, like natural laws. Therefore, something occurred that caused the system to fall apart. Evidently it was the rediscovery of the wealth of the Orient, and the desire to emulate it at any cost, which was behind the subversion of traditional values.[95] The avidity associated with this is a prime example of wealth at any cost. This is what Hesiod characterizes as "mean Eris" as opposed to the "competitive or honest Eris," which he associates with the spirit of competition that arises when an idle farmer sees a wealthy farmer hard at work:

> Such Strife *(Eris)* is good *(agathē)* for mortals
> so potter is jealous of potter
> And carpenter of carpenter,
> beggar is envious of beggar
> and singer of singer. (*WD* 24–26)

This is clearly a new spirit of secular competition at work. It is now wealth rather than birth which makes the man. Does this mean the *basileis* abandoned the title of *agathos?* Not at all. And this is what is interesting: there are now two sorts of activities, with little in common, that claim this powerful title of recognition.

Finally, if one considers that *Works and Days* unequivocally argues that the justice system of the *basileis* must be replaced with a more objective (if not codified) notion of justice (and since it must have been performed on a regular basis), it must have had a lasting and subversive effect on subsequent generations. From this perspective, Hesiod is certainly a catalyst for western political paideia. Indeed, he is an advocate and initiator of a revolutionary way of thinking, which influence political ideals and their corresponding cosmological models.

3

Anaximander's *Historia Peri Phuseōs*

PROLOGUE: ANAXIMANDER AS THE FIRST PHILOSOPHER

While some scholars (e.g., McKirahan, Lloyd, Mansfeld) identify the defining characteristics of philosophy with rigorous proof and questions about the nature of inquiry itself,[1] and others with the rejection of *mythopoesis* and the adoption of rational explanations,[2] there is consensus that Western philosophy (and science) began in the Ionian city of Miletus in the sixth century BCE.[3] There is also consensus that the first philosophical writer was Anaximander of Miletus.[4]

Anaximander's book, *Peri phuseōs,* was one of the first known examples of prose and the first philosophical prose treatise.[5] His choice to write in prose rather than verse may have been an attempt to free the language of philosophy (or what was to become philosophy) from the undesirable preconceptions of poetry. Poetry had long been a vehicle of myth, and its rhythms and diction might (in his eyes), have hindered speculative thought. Of course, poetry as a medium for speculative thought did not disappear.[6]

The famous chronographer, Apollodorus of Athens (ca. 180 BCE) states that Anaximander was sixty-four years old in the year 547/6, the second year of the fifty-eighth Olympiade, and died shortly thereafter.[7] This date is consistent with Hippolytus' claim (DK12A11) that Anaximander was born in the year 610/9 (the third year of the forty-second Olympiade). This means that Anaximander was born around 610 BCE. The dates are important to understand the historical and cultural conditions in which philosophy emerged.[8]

In chapter one, we saw that although *phusis* is absent from the first philosophic writings of early Ionians, it is as unanimously accepted today, as it was

63

in antiquity, that the concept of *phusis* was a creation of Ionian science. The word permitted the Ionians to present a new conception of the world in which natural/rational causes/explanations were substituted for mythical ones. Moreover, we saw that the vast majority of commentators, both ancient and modern, concur that the primary goal of written pre-Socratic works was to provide a *historia peri phuseōs,* an investigation into the nature of things. In conjunction with this, pre-Socratics, beginning with the early Ionians, took "all things" *(ta panta)* or "the universe" *(to pan* or *to holon)* as their primary object of study. In the expression *historia peri phuseōs,* it is this comprehensive sense that must be understood by the word *phusis.* Meanwhile, we saw, following a linguistic analysis of the word *phusis,* that the fundamental and etymological meaning of the term is growth, and as an action noun ending in *-sis,* it means the whole process of growth of a thing from beginning to end. Thus, when the word *phusis* is employed in the comprehensive sense, the term refers to an investigation into the origin and growth of the present order of things from beginning to end. In sum, pre-Socratics were interested in a history of the universe: in an explanation of its origin (*phusis* as absolute *archē*), of the stages of its evolution (*phusis* as process of growth), and finally of its result, the *kosmos* as we know it (*phusis* as the result).

However, the present order of things comprises the physical world (i.e., the natural world conceived as a structured whole in which each constituent part has a place) and the socio-political world in which the investigator/author resides. From this perspective, I concur somewhat with W. A. Heidel, for whom the aim of Anaximander's book *Peri phuseōs* was "to sketch the life-history of the cosmos from the moment of its emergence from infinitude to the author's own time."[9] This is precisely what Hesiod attempted in the *Theogony.* He sought to explain how Zeus established the present order of things, natural, and social. This is the aim of cosmogonical myth in general, and Anaximander clearly attempts to accomplish the same end. This is why he begins with a cosmogony and then moves on to an anthropogony and finally to a politogony. However, his approach is radically different; his explanation is not only naturalistic he clearly and distinctly separates all three developments.

Anaximander was no armchair philosopher. He formulated his theory through investigation and discovery; he travelled extensively, notably (it will be argued), to Egypt via Naucratis. Egypt, or more precisely, the Nile Delta, was in certain respects the center of the universe, that is, the center before the shift to Miletus. There is a good deal of circumstantial evidence for this. But the argument must be read as a whole. Some of the evidence here corroborates Martin Bernal's claims with respect to the relation between Greece and Egypt, albeit for very different reasons. It is all part of what one author calls the Egyptian mirage in ancient Greece (Froidefond, 1971).

The information upon which we must base an examination of Anaximander's investigation is, of course, very limited. In fact, we have only one fragment whose authenticity, either in whole or in part, is uncontested (DK12B1; A9).[10] However, a number of doxographies enable us to reconstruct his *historia* (investigation). Although Anaximander's cosmology has been the focus of much attention, his views on the origin *and* development of humanity have received surprisingly little attention. Most attribute this to a lack of evidence. But there is evidence, although not necessarily from Peripatetic sources, that many scholars consider the only valid testimony. While it is true that a certain amount of conjecture must be taken for granted when reconstructing it, his position is no more conjectural, in my view, than the myriad of opinions on how to interpret (and reconstruct) the often conflicting doxographical evidence concerning his cosmological works. For the case at hand, much of the focus will be on a reconstruction of Anaximander's famous map and how it explains, in light of the doxographical and historical evidence, the real aim of his own *historia*.

I will begin my study of Anaximander's *historia* with an analysis of the origin and development of his cosmological model. This necessitates beginning with an analysis of his chronological starting point, *phusis* as *archē*, and why he choose *to apeiron* to qualify this entity.

THE *PHUSIS* AS *ARCHĒ*

Anaximander used the term *to apeiron* to characterize *phusis* as *archē*. The physical universe emerged from this primordial substance. There is a great deal of controversy concerning what Anaximander meant by *to apeiron*. In a famous passage in *Physics,* in which he mentions Anaximander by name, Aristotle provides some important information on the concept. This text clarifies certain aspects of Anaximander's concept of *to apeiron* as well as what the monists understood in general by the term *archē*.[11]

> For everything is either a principle or derived from a principle *(ē archē ē ex archēs)*. But there cannot be a principle of the infinite, for that would be the limit of it. Further, as it is a principle, it is both uncreatable and indestructible *(agenēton kai aphtharton)*. . . . That is why, as we say, there is no principle of *this*, but it is this which is held to be the principle of other things, and to encompass all and to steer all *(periechein hapanta kai panta kubernan)*, as those assert who do not recognize, alongside the infinite, other causes, such as Mind or Friendship. Further they identify it with the Divine *(to theion),* for it is deathless and imperishable *(athanaton kai anōlethron)* as Anaximander says, with the majority of the physicists. (*Physics* 3.203b6–15; trans. Hardie and Gaye)

Aristotle is clearly distinguishing Monists from those who later postulated the need for a separate moving cause. For the Monists, as the word implies, one *archē* was sufficient to fulfill the two roles. They believed that matter was literally alive, whence the expression, "hylozoism," to qualify this doctrine.[12] According to Aristotle, Thales was the first monist, insofar as he saw water as the *archē* of all things (*Metaphysics* 1.983b7ff). In other words, Thales did not only believe that water was essential for the preservation of all animal and plant life, but he also thought that it was the primary constituent (or ultimate principle) of all things. If the universe were impregnated with life, it was so, from Thales' perspective, because it had a *psuchē* (Aristotle, *On the Soul* 1.5.411a7). The word *psuchē* signifies "life" (it is derived from the verb *psuchein*, "to breath, to blow"), and it was universally accepted as the source of all consciousness and of all life.[13]

Since all things are permeated with soul, soul must necessarily be immortal and imperishable, for it is ultimately inherent in the original *phusis*. Animals, plants, the earth, et cetera, are diverse forms of this same substance impregnated with *psuchē*. If Thales thought that "all was full of the gods," it was because an activity of this sort could only be qualified as divine *(to theion)*.

Aristotle, however, states not only that Anaximander's *apeiron* is uncreatable *(agenēton)* and indestructible *(aphtharton)*, but it is also deathless *(athanaton)* and imperishable *(anōlethron)*. The differences are important, for whereas the first two predicates do not indicate that the principle in question is living and even less again divine, the second two predicates strongly suggest this principle is not only alive (or living) but also divine *(to theion)*.[14]

Therefore, it is comprehensible that, if the *apeiron* is both living and divine, it encompasses and steers all things *(periechein hapanta kai panta kubernan)*. The verb *kubernaō*, "to steer, drive, guide, govern, or direct" is found not only in Anaximander but also in the works of Heraclitus, Parmenides, and Diogenes of Apollonia. On each occasion, the verb has a certain political ring.[15] The verb *periechō*, "to encompass," "to pervade," has essentially a spatial significance, although it can also evoke the meaning of "governing" or "dominating" and again has a political reverberation, as in the case of Anaximenes' conception of air, which is also said to encompass the whole world *(holon ton kosmon, DK13B2)*.[16]

This description gives the impression that *apeiron* is both a conscious and intelligent agent, which initiated the process by which the universe was generated and developed according to natural and inviolable law.[17] It is nevertheless possible that Anaximander did not conceive *apeiron* as a conscious and intelligent agent. As we will see, Anaximander does not explain how the *apeiron* initiated the process. He only says that the *apeiron* secreted a seed, or *gonimon* and that it was impregnated with the primary elements of which the universe is composed. But there is clearly a sense in which the *apeiron* does "control" if one considers that the natural processes it initiates have no "power" to change their own nature. It is thus possible Anaximander considered the whole process from beginning to end as a purely natural process, much like Hesiod does in his semi-philosophical description of the origin of the world in *Theogony*, 114–32. From this perspective, there is nothing to suggest that humanity is seen as a conscious creation of *apeiron*, or that *apeiron* is a god that must be venerated. However, it is easy to see how Anaximander could perceive his cosmological model as worthy of some kind of veneration, as we saw in Euripides' famous fragment 910. Alternatively, we can also see how it contains, in Plato's eyes, the seeds of atheism.

A Linguistic Analysis of the Term *To Apeiron*

What must be understood by the term *to apeiron*, and why was it used by Anaximander? Let's begin with a linguistic analysis. The word *apeiron* is the neuter of the negative adjective *apeiros* which, like its Homeric counterparts, *apeirōn, apeiritos,* and *apereisios* (see LSJ), is a compound with a- privative denoting an absence of something. As for its etymology, there are two apparent possibilities. It may be derived from the noun *peirar* or *peras*, "end, limit, boundary," whence *apeiros* in the sense of "boundless, unlimited, indefinite, and infinite" (Chantraine 1968–1980, 1.870–71). It may also be derived from the verbal root *per-*, "forward, through, beyond," as exemplified in *peirō* ("run through"), *peraō* (traverse) and thus "what cannot be traversed from one end to the other" whence *apeiros* in the sense of "enormous, immense."[18] Whatever the etymology adopted, it is clear Anaximander's *apeiron* must at least be considered as temporally infinite. This, moreover, is the first of the five reasons enumerated by Aristotle for necessitating a belief in the reality of the infinite *(apeiron)* (*Physics* 3.203b4–15). It is clear that he attributes this reason to Anaximander and the other "physicists." It is via this attribution that we will begin the examination of the ancient commentators' points of view before turning to the points of view of modern commentators.

In *Physics* 3.203b4–15, Aristotle states that Anaximander and the other physicists are correct to take the *apeiron* (infinite) as a principle or source *(archē),* since a principle or source must by definition be "temporally infinite." This is why Anaximander and the others qualify the *apeiron* as "deathless and imperishable." But Aristotle understood Anaximander's *apeiron* as *archē*, both as "temporally infinite" and "spatially and quantitatively infinite." This is clear from the following passage: "All the physicists see the infinite *(tōi apeirōi)* as an attribute of some other nature *(heteran tina phusin)* that belongs to the so-called elements: water, air or what is intermediate between them" (*Physics* 3.203a16). It is also clear that the expression *heteran tina phusin* refers to the term *apeiron* and essentially means "spatially infinite." For Aristotle, all monists regarded their *archē* or first principle as spatially infinite.

Aristotle gives two reasons why Anaximander would have chosen the term *apeiron* to designate his *archē:*

1. So that the generation and the destruction of things can succeed each other without fail, there must be an unlimited source (*Physics* 3.203b18–20 = third reason for believing in the infinite).
2. Since the elements are by nature opposed (i.e., fire is hot and air is cold), if one of them were infinite, the rest would be destroyed; the *apeiron* must thus be an indeterminate substance from which the elements come into existence (*Physics* 3.204b22–32).

While the first reason justifies the hypothesis of a primary substance that is spatially infinite, the second justifies a primary substance that is "qualitatively indeterminate." However, even in the case of the second hypothesis, the primary substance is spatially infinite. Aetius, for his part, strongly suggests that Theophrastus attributed to Anaximander at least the first hypothesis, but perhaps also the second (*Placita* 1.3.3 = DK12A14). Meanwhile, Simplicius in his interpretation that follows fragment 12B1 clearly attributes to Anaximander a reasoning which suggests Aristotle's second hypothesis: "It is clear that, having observed the change of the four elements into one another, he did not think fit to make any one of these the material substratum, but something else besides these" (*Commentary on Aristotle's Physics* 24.16–17 = DK12A9; B1; trans. Kahn). Yet, in his *Commentary on Aristotle's On the Heavens* 615.15–16 (= DK12A17), Simplicius clearly credits him with the first hypothesis: "He [Anaximander] was the first to posit the *apeiron* as principle, in order to have an abundant supply for the (subsequent) generations."

In the final analysis, the ancient commentators understood Anaximander's use of the term *apeiron* to mean either a primary substance that was spatially infinite and by implication qualitatively indefinite, or a primary substance that was qualitatively indefinite and by implication spatially infinite. But can we attribute spatial infinity to Anaximander's *apeiron?* Aristotle clearly attributes a "spatially infinite matter" to *all* the physicists (*Physics* 3.203b16–17; 208a3–4), but it may be anachronistic to understand Anaximander's *apeiron* as spatially infinite.

Among modern commentators, the most significant disagreement touches on this "spatial" interpretation of *apeiron*. The commentators are divided into two groups. One group shares Aristotle's opinion (and that of the other ancients) that Anaximander's *apeiron* can mean or means spatially infinite. The other group strongly disagrees. The first group employs the same reasoning as Aristotle in arguing that the term *apeiron* means "without limits" and thus "spatially infinite."[19] The second group argues that the "spatial" and "quantitative" notions of infinity were not envisaged before supplementary progress in geometry was realized. It was only when the mathematicians recognized the possibility of an infinite space (in brief, the need for a space within which straight and parallel lines could be produced "indefinitely") that the physicists admitted an unlimited void in nature.[20]

In the latter case, although Anaximander's *apeiron* is not considered as "spatially infinite," it is considered as "spatially immense." Moreover, some scholars, like Diels (1897) and Cornford, attribute to it the form of a sphere. Cornford (1952, 176) finds support for this in the fact that the term *apeiron* is often employed to designate the spherical or circular form: the circumference of a circle or a sphere has neither a beginning nor an end. In this case, there can be no distinction between beginning and end. Thus Empedocles speaks of a "Sphairos that is well rounded and completely without limits" (*pampan apeirōn Sphairos kukloterēs:* DK31B28). Thus when Anaximander/Aristotle contend that the *apeiron* encompasses all things *(periechein hapanta),* this suggests that the *apeiron* has the form of a sphere.[21]

Until now the accent has been placed on the spatial and/or quantitative meaning of the word *apeiron.* But the word *apeiron* can also have a qualitative meaning. It suffices to take *apeiron* in the sense of "what is without interior limits *(perata)* or internal distinctions," that is, an *apeiron migma.* This is plausible if we consider that Anaximander sought a primary substance from which all things emerged (McDiarmid 1953, 198–200). This meaning is entirely in conformity with the second hypothesis mentioned above. Moreover, since Anaximander's cosmogony commences with a separation/secretion of the opposites from the *apeiron,* this suggests that before the cosmogonical process began, there was no *perata* between the contraries: there was only an indefinite or undifferentiated mixture (Aristotle, *Metaphysics* 3.2.1069b19–24; *Physics* 1.4.187a20–23).[22]

Here is a table of the different possibilities:

APEIRON AS A PRIMARY SUBSTANCE

always	primary meaning	by implication
temporally eternal	spatially infinite	qualitatively indefinite
temporally eternal	spatially indefinite (immense)	qualitatively indefinite
temporally eternal	spatially definite (a sphere)	qualitatively indefinite
	or	
temporally eternal	qualitatively indefinite	spatially infinite
temporally eternal	qualitatively indefinite	spatially indefinite (immense)
temporally eternal	qualitatively indefinite	spatially definite (a sphere)

We have seen that Anaximander's *apeiron* can have several meanings and it is likely he employed the term in more than one sense since technical vocabulary was still nascent. Consequently, if we wish to give an answer to the two questions which we asked at the start of our examination (what must be understood by the term *to apeiron?* and why was it used by Anaximander?), it would be prudent to say that the term *apeiron* suggests an enormous mass that is both spatially and qualitatively indefinite and that he choose this word because it was the best he could find to account for the physical phenomena that were too complex to be reduced to a precise element. In sum, the universe emerged from qualitatively and spatially indeterminate *phusis*. But to get a better idea of this primary stuff, it is important to remember that Anaximander considered it not only as uncreatable *(agenēton)* and indestructible *(aphtharton)*—the *sine qua non* for all principles—but equally as deathless *(athanaton)* and imperishable *(anōlethron)*. These later characteristics are considerably important since they explain how this mass could be contemplated as being divine *(to theion),* and by extension, as being a substance capable of directing itself towards its natural end, that is, the universe as it is perceived by an observer.

Cosmos

Let us now turn to how Anaximander envisaged the formation and shape of the cosmos. This means that we are moving from the notion of *phusis* as *archē* to the notion of *phusis* as process and then to the notion of *phusis* as result.

Cosmogony: The Formation of the Universe

According to a certain number of doxographies, the process by which the formation of the universe begins is described as a "separation (or secretion?) of opposites" *(apokrinomenōn tōn enantiōn)* caused by an eternal movement *(dia tēs aidiou kinēseōs).*[23] This immediately raises two important questions. First, into what opposites is it a separation? Second, how did the opposites manage to separate themselves from the *apeiron*.

The answer to the first question appears to be provided by Simplicius. He states that the opposites in question are hot and the cold, dry and the humid, and the rest *(enantiotētes de eisi theron psuchron xēron hugron kai ta alla)* *(Commentary on Aristotle's Physics* 150.24 = DK12A9). However it is unclear if Anaximander postulated a number of different opposites. Pseudo-Plutarch, whose source is clearly Theophrastus, only mentions hot and cold in the famous cosmogonic passage (see below), and Aetius confirms this in the

Placita 2.11.5 (= DK12A17a), where the heavens are formed from a mixture of hot and cold *(ek thermou kai psuchrou migmatos)*. This makes perfectly good sense. Meanwhile, the opposites, whether one or more, must be considered not as qualities or properties that characterize bodies, but as entities or things. This is the case since in Anaximander's time (as noted above) there was no technical vocabulary that enabled the distinction between a substance (e.g., earth) and its attributes (e.g., cold and dry). Before the cosmogonic process commenced, we can or must imagine opposites as perfectly mingled or blended together in an indeterminate condition, "like a mixture of wine and water" (Cornford 1952, 162), or as in "a state of dynamic equilibrium." (Vlastos 1947/1993, 80; KRS 1983, 130 n2).

Now, how did the opposites manage to separate themselves from the *apeiron?* The answer is related to the movement of *apeiron* itself. The doxographies state that the separation was provoked by the eternal movement or vital force of the *apeiron*. That the movement of the *apeiron* is said to be "eternal" *(aiōn)* is not surprising in itself since it was considered divine. And if the *apeiron* is divine, it is because it is "animated," and what is animated is necessarily in movement. The question is: how did the eternal movement of the *apeiron* enable the opposites to separate (or secrete) from the *apeiron?*

Aristotle suggests that the original movement of the *apeiron* was that of a "vortex" (Robin 1921/1963, 63; J. M. Robinson 1971, 111–18). Aristotle's text reads as follows:

> If, then, it is by constraint that the earth now keeps its place, it must have come together at the centre because of the whirling *(dia tēn dinēsin)*. This form of causation supposed they all borrowed from the observations of liquids and of air, in which the larger and heavier bodies always move to the centre of the whirl *(pros to meson tēs dinēs)*. This is why all those who try to generate the heavens say that the earth came together at the centre. *(On the Heavens* 2.295a7–14, trans. J. L. Stocks)

But shortly after, Aristotle actually distinguishes Anaximander from the majority of physicists by the fact that for him, the earth remains at the center of the universe because of its equilibrium, that is, because it is equidistant from all the points on the celestial circumference *(On the Heavens* 2.295b10–15). In other words, the reason is mathematical, although as we will see, there is also a physical component to this. Moreover, there is no doxographical evidence for a vortex before Empedocles. So the question remains: if we are to imagine Anaximander's *apeiron* as in a state of dynamic equilibrium at point zero, what initiated the cosmogonical process? We saw what appears to be a similar situation in Hesiod. In the beginning, there was a mass of undifferentiated stuff and then a gap appeared (that is, a modification of an initial precondition somehow occurred). Anaximander may, of course, simply have not asked the question. But given that *apeiron* is a natural primordial creative force unequivocally characterized as divine (and, indeed, as a controlling force), it is tempting to see this principle of movement *(archē kinēseōs)* and of beings *(tōn ontōn)* as itself a Being. Homer's Ocean, as we saw in chapter one, fits this description as is also the case with the divine principles of Anaximander's younger contemporaries, notably, Anaximenes and Xenophanes.

From this perspective, it may be more appropriate, at least in the context of Anaximander's cosmogony, to understand the verbs *apokrinesthai* and *ekkrinesthai* as well as the nouns *apokrisis* and *ekkrisis* in the biological/ embryological sense of secrete/secretion rather than a mechancial sense of "separate/separation." Thus the opposites may be understood as being "secreted from" the *apeiron*.

The cosmogonic doxography describing how Anaximander conceived the formation of the universe is found in Pseudo-Plutarch's *Miscellanies* and runs as follows:

> He [Anaximander] states that what produces hot and cold (i.e., a germ) was secreted from (or separated/ejected from) the eternal vital force during the generation of this universe *(to ek tou aidiou gonimon thermou te kai psuchrou kata tēn genesin toude tou kosmou apokrithēnai),* and from this [i.e., the germ] a sort of sphere of flame grew round *(periphuēnai)* the air/mist surrounding the earth *(tōi peri tēn gēn aeri),* like bark round a tree *(hōs dendrōi phloion).* When this [i.e., the flame] was broken off *(aporrageisēs)* and shut off *(apokleistheisēs)* in certain rings, the sun, the moon and the stars were formed. *(Miscellanies* 2 = DK12A10)

This text suggests the following cosmogonic development:

1. The *apeiron* or the "eternal vital force" somehow produces and secretes a germ *(gonimon)* that is capable of engendering the two primary opposites or elements in the cosmogonic process.
2. The fact that the *gonimon* contained (or is pregnant with) the hot and the cold confirms a certain number of other doxographies according to which the first stage in the formation of the cosmos is related to a secretion or separation of opposites.
3. The terminology strongly suggests that Anaximander conceived the universe as growing like a living organism from a seed. (Baldry 1932; Lloyd 1970, 309f; Conche 1991, 142)

Following these observations, it is important to say that the term *to gonimon,* which literally signifies, "that which is capable of engendering," whence "seed, or germ," may very well be Anaximandrean in origin, although it is fairly rare before the Peripateticians (see KRS 131).[24] The word clearly has a biological meaning, although there has been some discussion as to whether the image is basically botanical or embryological. H.C. Baldry (1932, 27), for his part, has shown that the terms *apokrinesthai, aporrēgnusthai,* and *phloios* are in some way all related to embryology. Aristotle employs the expression *sperma gonimon* to qualify a fertile seed as opposed to an infertile one (*History of Animals* 523a25), and Theophrastus uses *gonimon* to characterise the life of animals and of plants (*On Fire* 44). The word *phloios,* which we translate as "bark," is derived from *phleō,* a verb that according to Baldry, is always related to the idea of generation and refers to the skin that envelops a living plant or animal organism during its growth (1932, 30).[25] In fact, the term *phloios* is found not only in Aristotle, to designate the membrane which envelops the egg (*History of Animals* 558a28), but also in another doxography attributed to Anaximander where it is applied to the prickly skin which enveloped the first forms of animal life (DK12A30). Moreover, if one considers the period in question, and the fundamental and etymological meanings of the term *phusis,* it would not be at all surprising if Anaximander's cosmogony was described in terms of organic life. We have already seen a number of Hippocratic texts in chapter 1 that establish an analogy not only between the growth *(phusis)* of plants and the growth of embryos but also between the growth *(phusis)* of the human embryo and that of the universe. These texts and others clearly indicate that such an analogy was the norm rather than the exception, and that this norm traverses the *entire* history of the *peri phuseōs* tradition (including Parmenides and the Atomists).[26] In brief, it is not surprising Anaximander considered as rational and natural the fact that the world was derived from a sort of germ, seed, or egg, and yet still repudiated the anthropomorphic image of sexual mating, which was at the base of cosmogonic myths. What counts is that the process is henceforth due to natural causes.

The central idea, then, is that the cosmos grows like a living being from a seed or germ. This germ contains the two primary opposites hot and cold, which, in turn, are inseparable from the opposites of dry and wet. The germ of hot and of cold develops or grows into in a sphere of flames (the hot and the dry) enclosing a cold and wet center (like bark grows round a tree). The action of the hot (and dry) on the cold (and wet) center (now sufficiently condensed to form the earth) causes a third concentric layer composed of air/mist *(aēr)* to develop (presumably through evaporation) between the two other layers. The pressure of this intermediary layer of air/mist finally breaks the coherent unity by causing the ball of flame to burst and, in the process, forms the celestial bodies. The subsequent action of the heat (from the sun) causes the wet and dry on the earth to separate into land and sea.

This description is confirmed by a certain number of other doxographies. Aetius (2.13.7 = DK12A18.28–29) reports that for Anaximander the celestial bodies are wheel-shaped concentrations of air/mist *(pilēmata aeros)* filled with fire *(puros emplea)*. Hippolytus, for his part, employs practically the same terms *(Refutations* 1.6.4 = DK12A11). And, concerning the sea on the surface of the earth, Aetius states that, for Anaximander, the sea is what remains of the primordial humidity *(tēs prōtēs hugrasias)*, after the greater part was dried up by fire (3.16.1 = DK12A 27.19–21). This is also strongly suggested by Aristotle *(Meterology* 353b5–11 = DK12A27.7–10).

According to this analysis of Anaximander's cosmogony, the cause of all natural change is the reciprocal action of the opposites. Once the separation of the mutually hostile opposites commences, the cosmogonic process perpetuates itself (in a cyclical process) through the natural operation of the reciprocal power of the opposites. This will be examined in more detail when we analyze Anaximander's sole surviving fragment further on.

COSMOLOGY: THE STRUCTURE OF THE UNIVERSE

How did Anaximander imagine (or conceive of) the structure of the universe after its initial development? From this perspective, we are moving from the notion of *phusis* as process to that of *phusis* as result.

Given that Anaximander's cosmological model is the first rational model in the Western philosophical/scientific tradition, it deserves a close examination. It is, however, open to a number of interpretations. Let's begin with the position of the earth. According to Aristotle *(On the Heavens* 295b10 = DK12A26), Anaximander held that the earth is at rest *(menein)* at the center *(epi tou mesou)* of the celestial sphere because of its equilibrium *(dia tēn homoiotēta)*, this meaning that it is equidistant from all the points on the circumference *(homoiōs pros ta eschata echon)*. Hippolytus *(Refutation* 1.6.3 = DK12A11), for his part, states that the earth is at rest because it is not dominated by anything *(hupo mēdenos kratoumenēn)*, in that it is equidistant from everything *(dia tēn homoian pantōn apostasin)*.[27]

The most common interpretation of these passages is that Anaximander's reasoning behind the earth's immobility and position is mathematical and a priori (e.g., Cornford 1952, 165; KRS 1983, 134; Kahn 1960/1994, 77; Guthrie 1962, 99; McKirahan 1994, 40; Wright 1995, 39). Involved is the principle of sufficient reason: if there is no reason for an object to move in one direction rather than another, it stays where it is. This is vigorously contested by some scholars, notably John Robinson (1971) and David Furley (1987, 1.23–30). Robinson argues, with what he sees from Aristotle[28] and Simplicius[29] as textual support, that it is the vortex and air that are behind the earth's immobility. Furley argues that certain images (like the tree trunk analogy in Pseudo-Plutarch's *Miscellanies* 2 = DK12A10.36) imply that the overall shape of the cosmos was not important for Anaximander. He argues further that only a spherical earth could be equidistant from all extremes.[30] Consequently, if the earth is at rest, it is because it is flat, evenly balanced, and floating on air—in sum, for purely physical reasons. While there is little doxographical evidence in Anaximander in support of a vortex or the earth resting on air, the cosmogonical development leaves clearly understood that the explanation for the earth's stability is *physical*. The earth remains at rest at the center of the sphere because of its *inertia* occasioned by the cosmogonical development.[31] Indeed, the two primary opposites behind this cosmogonical development, hot (and dry) and cold (and wet), are characterized by mobility and immobility, respectively, and this in turn explains the earth's inertia. Further, at the end of the cosmogonical development the earth finds itself at the center of a *plenum,* for it is surrounded by a sphere composed of three concentric rings (which contain the heavenly bodies) of fire and mist, with air between them. However, if we consider (a) that the earth is at the center of the sphere surrounded by three concentric rings, (b) that the ratio of the dimensions of the earth is analogous to the sizes and distances of the three rings, and (c) that the earth is, therefore, equidistant from all the points on the celestial circumference as well as the three rings, then we may conclude (d) that the reasoning behind the physical structure of Anaximander's world is mathematical or geometrical. In sum, Anaximander's reasoning may have been something like the following: how can I make the physical structure of the universe, which definitely exhibits order, conform to the most perfect geometrical form, namely the circle?

Meanwhile, Pseudo-Plutarch informs us that Anaximander conceived the *shape* of the earth as cylindrical *(kulindroeidē)* and that its *depth* is a third of its *width,* that is, its *diameter* is three times its *height (echein de [sc. tēn gēn] tosouton bathos hoson an eiē triton pros to platos) (Miscellanies* 2 = DK12A10.32–33). Although this interpretation has not gone uncontested (some prefer to translate it as the *height* is three times the *width*), it is held by the vast majority of commentators. Further, it is confirmed, in a certain sense, by both Hippolytus *(Refutation* 1.6.3 = DK12A11) and Aetius (3.10.2 = DK12A25), who inform us that for Anaximander the earth is shaped like a column drum *(kionos lithōi paraplēsion)*. The earth, as we will see, is also the most important element in determining the *sizes* and *distances* of the other heavenly bodies, that is, their sizes and distances are analogous to the *dimensions* of the earth.

Anaximander imagined the heavenly bodies as rings *(kukloi)* of fire somewhat like chariot wheels *(harmateiōi trochōi paraplēsion)* encased in *aēr* or mist except for an aperture *(stomion, ekpnoē)* through which the fire emerges.[32] He postulated three of these rings: one for the sun, one for the moon and one for the fixed stars.[33] As for their positions relative to the earth, Anaximander placed the sun furthest of all, then the moon, and finally the fixed stars.[34] The texts are clear on this point and are not contested by anyone. However, as soon as one turns to the actual sizes and distances of the three rings, one enters the realm of conjecture, because of the lacunae in our testimonia.

According to Hippolytus, the sun ring *(ton kuklon tou hēliou)* is twenty-seven times *(heptakaieikosaplasiona)* the size (diameter) of the earth. Although the moon is mentioned in the text, the number corresponding to its size is missing because of a mutilated text.[35] The number twenty-seven for the size of the sun ring is confirmed by one of Aetius's doxographies (Aetius 2.21.1 = DK12A21.14–15). However, in another doxography (Aetius 2.20.1 = DK12A21.10–13), Aetius informs us that the circle of the sun is twenty-eight times *(oktōkaieikosaplasiona)* the size of the earth *(tēs gēs)*.

Although the number twenty-eight has been ignored by some (e.g., Sambursky 1956/1987, 15–16) and considered as corrupt by others (Kahn 1960/1994, 62; West 1971, 86), it is the source of a great deal of speculation. Indeed, prior to Paul Tannery (1887/1930) speculation was limited to the sun ring, whereas since Tannery, speculation has spilled over to the moon and star rings.[36] The reason for this is because the only ratio to have come down to us for the size of the moon ring is nineteen times *(enneakaidekaplasiona)* that of the earth (Aetius 2.25.1 = DK12A22), and since the moon ring should, like the sun ring, be a multiple of three, this has led a powerful group of scholars (since Tannery) to conclude that the number missing in the text of Hippolytus, for the size of the moon ring must be eighteen. Although there are no recorded figures for the size of the fixed star ring (or rings), since it forms the innermost ring, in conformity with the examples of the sun and the moon, the same chorus (again since Tannery) recommends 9 and 10 as the corresponding ratios. In sum, what we have here are two series of numbers: 9, 18, 27 and 10, 19, 28. But why two series of numbers?

According to Tannery and a host of others,[37] the smaller numbers (9, 18, 27) represent the inner diameters of the rings and the larger numbers (10, 19, 28) the outer diameters of the rings. However, according to Kirk and his group of followers,[38] this involves an error in computation. For if diameters are meant, and if we assume the rings themselves are one earth diameter thick (and the fact that the sun is said to be the same size as the earth seems to substantiate this),[39] then 2 and not 1 should be added to the multiples to give 11, 20, and 29, respectively.[40] Consequently, Kirk holds that the larger series "might represent the diameter of the ring from outer edge to outer edge" and the smaller series "from points halfway between the inner and outer edges of the actual felloe of air" (KRS 1983, 136 n1). According to Kirk's calculations, the distance from the inner edge to inner edge of the rings would be 8, 17, and 26, respectively.

O'Brien (1967), in one of the more detailed and coherent accounts of the problem, holds that there is no reason (contra Kirk) that we should not think of the thickness of the rings as equal to one half of the earth's diameter, that is, the same thickness as the radius of the earth (1967, 424). Consequently, if we compare the radius of the earth with the radius of the rings, that is, like with like, then the numbers will hold.[41]

However, while it is true that O'Brien's construction shows the celestial rings are equidistant, and are therefore consistent with Anaximander's propensity for *equality* (something everyone appears to agree with),[42] it is also the case that Anaximander appears obsessed with units of 3 and not with the units of 4 which follow from O'Brien's analysis.[43] But what is more important, the language (a *kuklos* 27 times the size of the earth) implies that the earth's *radius* is not the unit of measure.[44]

For my part, I concur with those who hold that the series 9, 18, and 27 comes from Anaximander himself. Indeed, it would be odd for Anaximander to use more than one unit to account for the size of the rings, because the earth is said to be the unit that serves for the size of the rings (and the fact that the sun is said to be the same size as the earth appears to confirm this), and since the diameter of the earth is said to be three times its height, that is, a multiple of 3, then the smaller, rather than the larger series (10, 19, 28), appears to be correct.

Here is a plan view of the cosmological model (figure 1) which also takes into account the larger series 10, 19, 28. The *diameter* of the earth is taken as the unit of measure and the *center* of the earth (and not the outer edge e.g., Hahn 2003, 84) is the primary focal point for each possibility. The assumption is, therefore, that Anaximander would have postulated a value of 3 for π—and is historically appropriate.

In Anaximander's model, the *diameter* of the earth is 3 times its *height* and the *circumference* of the earth is 3 times its *diameter*. According to the hypothesis that the series 9, 18, and 27 refer to the sizes and distances of the three rings with respect to the dimensions and position of the earth, this is what follows:

- The circumference of the star ring is 9 times the circumference of the earth (or 1 x 3 x 3);[45] the diameter (or size) of the star ring from center to center is 9 times the diameter of the earth (or 1 x 3 x 3); the distance from the center of the earth to the center of the star ring is 9 times the radius of the earth (or 1 x 3 x 3).
- The circumference of the moon ring is 18 times the circumference of the earth (or 2 x 3 x 3); the diameter of the moon ring is 18 times the diameter of the earth (or 2 x 3 x 3); the distance from the center of the star ring to the center of the moon ring is 9 times the radius of the earth (or 1 x 3 x 3) and from the center of the earth to the center of the moon ring 18 times the radius of the earth (or 2 x 3 x 3).

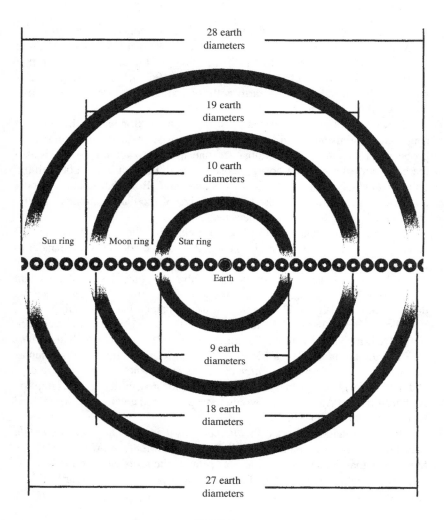

FIGURE 1
Plan View of Cosmological Model

- The circumference of the sun ring is 27 times the circumference of the earth (or 3 x 3 x 3); the diameter of the sun ring is 27 times the diameter of the earth (or 3 x 3 x 3); the distance from the center of the moon ring to the center of the sun ring is 9 times the radius of the earth (or 1 x 3 x 3) and from the center of the earth to the center of the sun ring 27 times the radius of the earth (or 3 x 3 x 3).

In sum, just as the measurements of the earth stand in a relation of 1:3:9 to each other (height:width:circumference), the sizes and distances of the 3 rings stand in a relation of 1:2:3, both to each other and to the dimensions of the earth.

What can one deduce from all this? Simply that Anaximander conceived his universe or cosmological model according to a mathematical or geometrical plan, which reflects a propensity for both geometrical equality and symmetry following the series 3.

THE SOURCES OF THE COSMOLOGICAL MODEL

This hypothesis, first formulated by Tannery in the late nineteenth century, has, in spite of its conjectural nature, been adopted, in one form or another, by the vast majority of commentators.[46] They are, however, far from agreeing about the origin and significance of the numbers and consequently about the origin of the cosmological model. There are, in the main,[47] four hypotheses:

1. the numbers are the result of a sacred or mythical inspiration;
2. the numbers are the result of an astronomical inspiration;
3. the numbers (at least the 3 to 1 ratio) are the result of an architectural or technical inspiration; and
4. the numbers are a result of a political inspiration.

Given the importance of Anaximander's cosmological model for the history of Western/Greek philosophy and science, these four hypotheses merit a closer examination.

The Mythical Hypothesis

The first hypothesis, in one form or other, is that of Tannery, Diels, Heath, Burnet, Robin, Cornford, Sambursky, Rescher, Guthrie, Burkert, West, and Furley.[48] Diels, however, seems to have been its initiator. He and others compare the mythical and religious importance of the number 3 (and 9), and its simple multiples, in the ancient conceptions of many countries, including Greece. Diels concludes that Anaximander's numbers tell us nothing more than what Indians say when they relate that the three steps of Vishnu stretch from the earth to the sky. However, the simple fact (as Kahn [1960/1993, 96] points out), that the numbers refer not to the steps of a god but to the diameters of perfect geometric circles established from a common center, suggests their criteria come from another order. This also holds for West's (1971, 87–93) contention that almost every aspect of Anaximander's cosmological model has Oriental elements: images of the chariot wheels (Babylonian); order of the heavenly bodies (Persian); and dimensions of the cosmos (Egyptian), et cetera.[49] In fact, even if one were to concede that aspects of Anaximander's cosmological model may not be devoid of external influences, the fact remains that it is Anaximander's fertile imagination that transformed these elements into a highly rational model which appears far more advanced than those of his predecessors, including the Orientals.[50]

The Astronomical Hypothesis

The second hypotheses, held notably by Burch (1949/1950, 154), Baccou (1951, 77), Kahn (1960/1994, 96–97), Conche (1991, 208), and Couprie (1995; 2001, 23–48), is that the progression of numbers could very well be the result of observational astronomy (however rough) either on the part of Anaximander himself (Baccou, Burch, Conche, and Couprie) or on data that Anaximander could have used from his Babylonian predecessors (Kahn 97).

However, according to the knowledge available for this particular period, it is more than doubtful that Anaximander had the necessary competence to assert even the approximate sizes and distances of the heavenly bodies among themselves. And it is almost as doubtful that the information, to which Kahn alludes in his book, reached Greece before the second half of the fifth century, for the simple reason that the Babylonians themselves did not have this information.[51] Moreover, if these conclusions are correct, the sizes, distances, and the order of the heavenly bodies could not possibly be based on any sort of astronomical observation.

The Architectural Hypothesis

The third hypothesis, held by Indra McEwen (1993) and Robert Hahn (1995, 2001),[52] is that the inspiration behind the cosmological model is architectural (and hence, technological), although McEwen is far less specific than Hahn. Indeed, for Hahn the inspiration is precisely that of a column-drum earth.[53] Hahn suggests that around this period Ionian Greek architects borrowed from Egyptian architects not only the technical expertise for erecting megalithic masonry buildings, but also the idea of planning construction in advance in terms of plan and elevated perspectives. He also points out a number of interesting features such as the overall structure of archaic Ionian temples being roughly the same: one unit in height by two units in width by three units in length.[54] Consequently, Anaximander may very well have employed plan and elevated perspectives to envision his cosmos. Indeed, as Hahn correctly points out, since Anaximander's cosmos is geometrical, this makes it amenable to graphic representation and several doxographies do credit him with having used diagrams or models. With this in mind, Hahn makes several interesting suggestions in his attempt to show the possible source of Anaximander's inspiration. He begins by comparing the rendition of the cross section of a tree and that of the image of the sphere of flame and inner rings that occurred during the formation of the universe (1995, 115–16; 2001, 193). With these renditions in mind, Hahn then turns to the column-drum construction to show how the technique of *anathurōsis* (a modern term that architectural historians have assigned to techniques for fitting together large blocks and column-drums by dressing only the edge, rather than the entire surface, where the blocks meet) bears a striking resemblance to a *plan* model rendition of Anaximander's cosmos. In fact, according to Hahn's rendition, not only do we have three concentric circles, but in the center of the drum there is a square hole for a wooden pivot—making it all the more suggestive.[55] Finally, Hahn considers Anaximander's possible *elevated* view of the cosmos and considers several renditions. But the problem with the *elevated* view, he points out, is that if we agree with Furley that only a spherical earth can be equidistant from the extremes, then Aristotle in his report on Anaximander is *wrong*. However, a *plan* view can preserve Aristotle's testimony because it shows a round earth, and a round earth *can* be equidistant from the extremes.

The upshot of this suggestive and brilliant thesis is that the rational structure of Anaximander's cosmological model (indeed, the origins of Greek philosophical rationality in general) cannot be understood independent of its "cultural embeddedness" (Hahn 1995, 123). However, it is rather odd to conclude that Anaximander derived his geometrical vision of the universe, something Hahn appears to agree with (1995, 116–17), from his observation of a column-drum. In the final analysis, this would amount to saying that Egyptians were behind the geometrical vision of the cosmos (1995, 117 n75). It seems equally odd to conclude from the fact that the column drum roughly exhibits three concentric circles, that the universe itself must be imagined as having three rings or kinds of heavenly bodies.

In a more recent work (2001), Hahn argues that prose books attributed to architects of the same period as Anaximander were rational prose accounts of techniques for monumental building that were inspired by their Egyptian counterparts. Hahn makes an excellent case for the relationship between Anaximander (and Thales) and the architects in particular in light of the credible list of accomplishments which the *phusiologoi* and *architectones* are credited with (2001, 55–66). It is the shared community of interests and accomplishments that provide the ground for Hahn's hypothesis of their likely

interaction. Moveover, given that many of Anaximander's "philosophical" successors continued to compose in verse, it is quite plausible that his decision to
write his book in prose rather than in verse was influenced by Ionian architects
who composed their treatises in prose. Now, one can well imagine that rational discourse and geometric design, rather than *mythopoesis,* were employed
when difficulties were encountered during the temple construction process.
Moreover, there is clearly a sense in which the architects were engaged "in
activities that revealed physical principles of nature" (2001, 220). That Anaximander may very well have been influenced/inspired by the architects is quite
convincing. But why can't the same case be made for the Egyptian architects,
from whom the Greek architects drew their inspiration and technical knowledge? (2001, 66–86, 97–162) Did they not employ "rational discourse and geometric design rather than *mythopoesis*" in monumental temple building? More
important, while Hahn makes a most convincing case for the influence of
architecture on Anaximander, it is still difficult to imagine that Anaximander's
reflection on the construction of temple building in general and the column
drum in particular explain both his rationalizing mentality and the production
of his famous cosmic and terrestrial maps. Moreover, it is difficult to see how
this rationalizing effect could have influenced his natural and rational explanations concerning the origin and development of the cosmos and terrestrial life
for which Anaximander is equally famous. Despite this, Hahn makes a good
case for the contribution of technology to the philosophical experience, and he
does make a good case for the connection between Egypt and Greece via architecture. In fact, the influence of Egypt on Anaximander and the origin of philosophy may be considerably more important than previously thought.

The Political Hypothesis

There now remains the fourth hypothesis, according to which Anaximander's
model is the result of a political inspiration. This hypothesis was explicitly
formulated for the first time by Heinrich Gomperz:

> In cosmology the political and artistic pattern seem to dominate. The kosmos
> is like a city; it is surrounded by its walls; the order of nature is based on an
> equilibrium of rights and obligations (day, e.g., has a right to last a certain
> time and night a corresponding time), and should this order ever be violated,
> such violation would have to be avenged. On the other hand, it is assumed
> to be a fact that the shape of the earth is that of a drum three times as broad
> as it is high and that the distances of the stars, of the moon and of the sun
> from the center of the earth are in a ratio 1:2:3—not because any measure-
> ments have been made to this effect but because it is fitting that such should
> be the case. (Gomperz 1943, 167)[56]

If I say that Gomperz was the first to have formulated the fourth hypothesis in an explicit way, it is because, prior to Gomperz, the cosmological model was not seen in terms of a socio-political model. Gomperz seems to be drawing an analogy between Anaximander's cosmological model and his famous cosmological law, according to which the order of nature is based on an equilibrium of rights and obligations. However, Gomperz does not go any further; he is content to make the observation. Jean-Pierre Vernant is the first[57] to explicitly expound this thesis in a convincing way.[58]

Vernant's thesis is that the geometrization of space among the Greeks, and in particular among the Milesians (the best example of which is found in Anaximander), does not come from the fact that they were born geometers, but was rendered possible through a political phenomenon, that is, the birth of the Greek *polis*. In support of his hypothesis, Vernant explores the relation between the human cosmos and the physical cosmos in the old oriental monarchies and between the Greek *polis* and Anaximander's cosmological structure. He convincingly shows there is solidarity between the political and physical spaces in both cases.

What characterizes the old cosmological accounts of the oriental type (i.e., the mythical conception of the world) is that the structure of the terrestrial state reflects the celestial state.[59] The reason is that the universe is perceived as a hierarchy of powers analogous in its structure to a human society. Moreover, in accounts of this type, the whole universe is placed under the domination of a sovereign agent, a sort of monarchy. Once the sovereign agent creates the natural order of things, that is, the physical universe as we know it, he assigns to each of the other powers (or gods) their prerogatives and functions in the newly created world. The result, as Vernant justly remarks, is *not* a universe with a homogeneous space, but a universe in the form of a pyramid, or different levels. Furthermore, since the type of socio-political organization the sovereign agent (or divinity) imposes upon the physical universe (following his victory) is the same as the one over which the divine king presides on earth there is a close solidarity between the physical and political spaces; they both reflect a pyramidal structure. In sum, nature and society are confounded.

But how did the birth of the Greek *polis* produce a representation of space that put the stress on the *center* and the *circle?* According to Vernant, the advent of the *agora* explains the transformation of the urban space that lead to the new geometric view of the world.

If there is anything unique about the Greek cities, it is the specific urban plan where all buildings are arranged around a central square (or public gathering place) called the *agora*.[60] Although it appeared for the first time in the Greek colonies, its essence originates with the old warriors' assembly, which took place in a circle and where each man could speak freely on condition that he entered the circle and placed himself *en mesōi,* that is, at the *center.*[61] After a series of economic and social transformations, this assembly of equals became the *agora* of the city where all the citizens (although initially only the aristocracy) could debate and discuss the affairs of the community. The *agora* is thus the circular, centered space that permitted all citizens to affirm themselves as *isoi* (equals), and *homoioi* (peers), and to enter with one another into a relation of identity, symmetry, and reciprocity. In sum, together they form a united cosmos.

The *agora* is first and foremost a space made for discussion. It is a public space as opposed to the private space of the citizen in his dwelling. It is a political space where one argues and debates as one pleases. It is not surprising that this space became the real center of public life. This is why, according to Vernant (1983, 184–85), the expression *en koinōi* (to make public, to put in common) has a synonym, *en mesōi,* whose spatial value is evident. What is debated publicly, *en koinōi,* is always what comes *en mesōi,* to the center.

The *agora* is thus the symbol of a spatial structure radically different from the one which characterizes the oriental monarchies. The power (*kratos, archē,* and *dunasteia*) is no longer situated at the top of the ladder. The power is disposed *es meson,* in the center, in the middle of the human group.[62] And to show that the *agora* was to act as the political center, a communal hearth, the *Hestia koinē,* was erected in the *agora* for the entire community (Vernant 1983, 187–89).[63]

A close examination of the doxographical tradition, which refers to Anaximander, shows there is solidarity between political and physical space. Here are a few examples. According to Anaximander, if the earth remains at rest *(menein)* in the middle *(epi tou mesou)* of the celestial circumference, it is because of the relation of similitude *(homoiotētos)* it entertains with its equals, that is, the points on the celestial sphere *(pros ta eschata)* (Aristotle, *On the Heavens* 2.13 295b10 = DK12A26). Elsewhere, he states that if the earth is situated in the center, *mesēi,* it is because it is not dominated by anything *(hupo mēdenos kratoumenēn),* that is, thanks to the relation of equality it maintains with all the points on the circumference *(dia tēn homoian pantōn apostasin)* (Hippolytus, *Refutation* 1.6.3 = DK12A11). In sum, the terms "centrality," "similarity," and "absence of domination" in Anaximander's cosmology, are clearly linked together as they were in political thought (Vernant 1983, 192) such that, in both cases, what we have is a type of *isonomia,* in the sense that no individual element or portion of the universe would be allowed to dominate another.[64] It is therefore legitimate to say that, just as in the old oriental cosmologies, Anaximander's cosmology exhibits a solidarity between physical and political space. In fact, it seems that Anaximander, like the poet or person who related the cosmogonical myth, kept his eyes fixed on the city (or socio-political structure) when he was imagining the world order. There is, in this respect, an interesting passage in Aristophanes' *The Birds*. Among the characters who come to offer their services to the feathered creatures figures an astronomer by the name of Meton. Meton is also presented as a town planner. Aristophanes introduces him as striding around the town declaring, "I will make my measurements with a set square which I will use so that the circle will be squared and the *agora* will be found at the middle; perfectly straight roads will lead to it, converging toward the center, and as from a star which is itself round, there will be straight rays off in every direction" (*The Birds,* 1002–9). The announcement evokes an admiring chorus from the onlookers. "This man is a true Thales!"

What Meton is doing here is drawing a circle with two perpendicular diameters and a radial crown which represents the *agora* at the center of the city and the streets which converge toward it. In other words, it is the plan of a circular city with radiating streets.[65]

This may be an allusion to a proposal made by Thales to the Assembly of Panionians around 547 BCE, that is, just after Cyrus' victory over Croesus. Thales proposed to create one single *bouleutērion* (i.e., Assembly at Teos), because this island was at the center of Ionia *(meson Iōniēs)* (Herodotus 1.170). The other cities, for their part, would still continue to be inhabited and would have the same situation as if they were *dēmoi,* that is, equals. In sum, Thales' proposal, which translates a geometric vision of the city and puts the stress on the center (i.e., Teos), certainly brings to mind the cosmological model of his fellow citizen and younger contemporary, Anaximander. Of course, this may also be an allusion to Anaximander himself. It is possible that Anaximander, like Meton, could have conceived (or even traced) the plan of an ideal city along the same lines, prior to having projected it on the physical cosmos.[66] Only a few generations after Anaximander, we find Hippodamus of Miletus, who is presented by Aristotle as a town planner, a political theorist, and meteorologist who does not separate physical, political, and urban space.[67] But this is not all. Hippotamus is also presented as an advocate of an ideal city with three distinct (but equal) classes and three distinct (but equal) divisions of territory.[68]

If such is the case, it is fair to ask if, in Anaximander's cosmological model, the numbers which translate the dimensions and distances of the heavenly bodies do not correspond in some way or other to the three social groups of which numerous *poleis,* including Miletus, were composed in Anaximander's day: the aristocracy, the (new) middle class, and the peasantry (or poor).[69] The three social groups, perceived as equals *(isoi),* could each correspond to a celestial ring[70] whose numbers translate the same relation of equality, symmetry, and reciprocity, 9 (1 x 3 x 3): 18 (2 x 3 x 3): 27 (3 x 3 x 3) or 1:2:3, in relation to the earth as the three social groups in relation to the *agora.*[71]

The following points can be emphasized in favor of this hypothesis. The influence of the evolution of the *polis* and, therefore, politics, on Anaximander's cosmology is far stronger and indeed defensible, than any of the other three hypotheses discussed above. Agathemerus informs us that Anaximander was the first to depict the inhabited earth on a chart (DK12A6) and there is strong evidence that the inhabited earth was not only depicted as round, but that the earthly mass itself was divided into three parts of equal size with Delphi, Miletus, or the Nile Delta in the middle (see below). Diogenes, for his part, states that Anaximander was the first to construct a model of the universe (DK12A1).[72] According to Aelian, Anaximander himself directed the founding of a Milesian colony in Apollonia, on the Black Sea, which clearly shows the preoccupation of a philosopher with the problems of his time (Aelian 3.17 = DK12A3). Finally, since the archaic cosmological myths end up at their departure point (the perfect social structure), or, if one prefers, the type of society that was to reflect the will of the creator, is it not possible that Anaximander himself looked for the ideal city that would allow the people of his time to live in complete security or flourish in conformity with the laws of nature?[73] Given that Miletus was torn between economic prosperity and civil strife during Anaximander's time, he may have wished to resolve the situation with his own version of *isonomia*.[74]

ISONOMIA AND NATURE

In conformity with this, what type of constitution would Anaximander be advocating as *isonomical* and how would it conform to his view of the nature of things? According to Anaximander's famous fragment, which explains how the present order of things is maintained, the order of nature is based on an equilibrium of rights and obligations, that is, an equilibrium which results when the constituent powers or primary opposites (the basic components or principles of all things) act as equals: "things [natural things] perish into those things from which they have/derive their being [= the opposites], according to necessity; for these things [the primary opposites] pay penalty and retribution to one another for their injustice according to the assessment of time" (*ex ōn de he genesis esti tois ousi, kai tēn phthoran eis tauta ginesthai kata to chreōn. didonai gar auta dikēn kai tisin allēlois tēs adikias kata tēn tou chronou taxin.* Simplicius, *Commentary on Aristotle's Physics* 24.13 = DK12A9; B1).[75]

Now, powers can only be and act as equals if they can hold each other in check, that is, avoid what Alcmeon calls the domination of one or *monarchia*. Otherwise, the history of the world would be a series of constant unchecked encroachments and this would entail not a cosmos but chaos. It is the immanent law of Time *(Chronos)* which assures that the primary opposites act as equals.

In sum, the natural order of things (and indeed natural things in general) is the result of a constant interchange between the primary powers or opposites, the same powers or opposites which were behind the initial formation of the universe: hot and cold; wet and dry. By nature the opposites encroach on one another, but by nature they must also pay a penalty *(dikē)* and retribution *(tisis)* to one another for this encroachment or injustice *(adikia)* with Time as the assessor or magistrate *(taxis)*. The struggle or interchange between the primary opposites is behind all natural phenomena: night and day; the changing of the seasons; meteorological phenomena; the birth and death of living things, et cetera, with Time as the guarantee that a stalemate will result indefinitely.

If such is the case, how does this law of nature correspond to Anaximander's cosmological model? The answer to this appears to be that the geometrical structure of the cosmological model epitomizes the law of measure. But the cosmological model is not only an ideal example of the law of measure. Since the cosmological model is indissociable from the heavenly bodies and since the movements (and interaction) of the heavenly bodies are behind the cycles of change,[76] in the final analysis, it is the cosmological model which is behind the order of nature. From this perspective, the cosmological model is closely connected with the assessment of Time.[77]

Does this mean that the cosmological model and its corresponding law were influenced or derived from Anaximander's observation of the cycles of change? Or were they influenced or derived from Anaximander's observation of the socio–political conditions of his time?

COSMOLOGY AND SOCIAL ORDER

At different periods of history strong rulers have imposed codes of law that put an end not only to social and political turmoil (at least on a temporary basis) but also to the perception that the forces of nature (e.g., capricious gods) were responsible for the upheaval,[78] as if humans were not yet perceived as autonomous agents. But when a socio-political order crumbles, so does the corresponding cosmological model and the cosmogony on which it depends.

If such is the case, does this mean Anaximander's cosmological model and corresponding law are reproductions of the socio-political conditions of his time? The concept of *isonomia* on the political level, that is, a social balance, entails not only that the parties which make up the society see themselves as equals, albeit hostile equals, but also that they appeal to the impartial principles of law or reason—for otherwise the parties would not be equal.[79] In other words, the three social groups are equal only insofar as they appeal to the impartial principle of "written" law; otherwise, there would be strife. But how can three seemingly hostile groups be made to conform to the law? Only, I believe, if there were a rotation in office among the three social groups (or powers) with the impartial principle of law represented by the *agora*—the official residence of both *hestia* and *nomos*—determining, in advance, the duration of time in office. An abuse of power on the part of one would, well understood, cause the two others to join forces and overwhelm it—whence a sort of conscious equilibrium represented by a center (the *agora*) surrounded by three equal social groups in the form of concentric circles—a model which epitomizes the law it was meant to incarnate.[80] Of course, this would also entail an equitable distribution of duties and honors. The ultimate aim is to create a sort of *krasis,* and to do so one has to avoid encroachments, not to encourage them. It may have been an *isonomia* of this nature that Anaximander had in mind.[81]

But if such is the case, what does it mean to be a man of the middle, as I assume Anaximander, like Phocylides, was?[82] To be a man of the center may have meant simply to appeal to the impartial principle of law, for law is indissociable from moderation, the just measure: *to metron.*[83] Otherwise, the extremes could never be anything more than extremes. From this perspective, citizens could now identify, without fear, with their own social group although there would be no constraints to remain in the same social group, that is, individual elements within a group could be interchangeable. The groups, for their part, would be for all intents and purposes equal, albeit different. In the final analysis, what we have is a sort of reciprocal relation between the microcosm of the city and the macrocosm of the universe.[84] But if it is true that Anaximander's primary preoccupation was with politics, then ultimately, as the language of the fragment implies, the political model came first,[85] although in reality the two models are confounded. Of course, this state is yet to be realized and it is precisely this that would make Anaximander, in many respects, not only the originator of rational accounts of the *peri phuseōs* type—which explains why, with Anaximander, there is for the first time a secular, linear, and progressive conception of history—but also of utopian societies. Indeed, Anaximander was the first to believe that if there is a "golden age," this age is not forever lost in some distant past as it was in mythical accounts (although Hesiod implicitly announces this) but is perfectly achievable in the future, on condition that man realizes that social order like natural order must be based on an equilibrium of rights and obligations, that mutually hostile opposites (as Heraclitus was to observe) are nonetheless equals.[86]

THE ORIGIN OF ANIMALS AND HUMANITY

What was Anaximander's position on the origin of humanity? The explanation that Anaximander gives us of the origin of humanity and of the other living beings (not mentioned by the poets and/or in mythical accounts) is, as in the case of his cosmology, the first naturalistic explanation in this domain. As one might expect, his explanation is entirely consistent with his cosmological system. Indeed, the same natural processes are at work (DK12A27). Living beings emerge from a sort of primeval moisture or slime *(ex hugrou)* which is activated by the heat of the sun after the initial formation of the universe.[87] Life thus results from the action of the hot and the dry on the cold and the wet. Now although Anaximander clearly believed in a "spontaneous generation," he did not believe, as did the poets, that humanity and other animal species emerged "whole" from the earth.[88] Indeed, there is a astonishing consistency to his account. According to Aetius (DK12A30), Anaximander argued that the first animals *(ta prōta zōia)* that arose from primeval humidity *(en hugrōi)* were enclosed (or surrounded, *periechomena*) in a thorny bark *(phloiois akan-thōdesi)*,[89] but that after they grew older and matured, they emerged *(apobainein)* on dry land, shed their thorny coverings, and in a short time after *(ep'oligon chronon)* began a modified form of existence *(metabiōnai)*, that is, adapted to their new environment.[90] Although it is clear that all living creatures arose from the primeval humidity,[91] Aetius is clearly referring to potential land animals in his doxography (12A30). It is therefore unclear if Anaximander thought that all living creatures were originally covered in "thorny bark" *(phloiois akanthōdesi)* or only the first potential land animals. Nor is it clear why Anaximander thought that the first land animals were initially covered this way. The first thing that comes to mind is that it afforded them some sort of protection. But protection from what? Conche (1991, 222) conjectures protection from some sort of marine animal such as carnivorous fish. However, if Anaximander believed that all marine animals once had thorny encasements, even the carnivorous fish would have been protected in a similar way. Indeed, Conche's conjecture presupposes that various species of animals already coexisted in the primeval marine environment (we may assume that Anaximander believed that the first creatures were nourished by the primeval slime). Yet it is unclear (although commentators tend to take it for granted) whether Anaximander thought that the various potential land animal species already had different forms when they inhabited the marine environment. What seems certain from the doxographical evidence is that as some of these thorny creatures matured, they somehow migrated to dry land. And once on dry land, the thorny skin was shed at some point and shortly after this their mode of living was modified accordingly. Of course, it was only after the heat of the sun had evaporated enough of the moisture for dry land to appear that the marine animals could in fact migrate to it (which means that they were not immobile). In sum, the evidence suggests (contra Barnes) that Anaximander recognized a connection between his hypothesis of a drying earth and his zoogonical theories.[92] It was clearly the climatic conditions that were behind the numerous changes or modifications in animals, even though the animals themselves had to adapt, that is, transform, to adapt to their new environment (a point Plato was happy to endorse in *Laws* 6.782a–c). There is thus no doubt that the doxographical evidence suggests that Anaximander defended a doctrine of the transformation of species rather than the immutability of species, although there is nothing to suggest that he also argued (or even suggested) that the transformation was (or would be) ongoing in a manner even reminiscent of Empedocles, let alone Lamarck or Darwin.

What about the human species? The doxographies suggest that according to Anaximander humans did not undergo a transformation completely similar to that of other animal species. Pseudo-Plutarch (DK12A10.37–40) states that Anaximander believed that in the beginning the human species *(anthrōpos)* must have been born from living things (or creatures) of another species *(ex alloeidōn zōiōn)* because humans are the only animals to be in need of prolonged nursing after birth; otherwise they would not have survived. Hippolytus is more precise. He says (DK12A11.16–17) that for Anaximander humans *(anthrōpon)* were originally similar to *(paraplēsion)* another creature, namely a fish *(ichthui).* Censorius confirms this and explains the reasoning behind it. He says that the Milesian believed that humans were initially formed inside fish or creatures resembling fish *(pisces seu piscibus simillima animalia).* When the human embryos reached puberty (and were thus capable of reproduction), the fish-like animals broke open and men and women *(viros mulieresque)* emerged who were capable of nourishing themselves (DK12A30.34–37). Plutarch (DK12A30) corroborates at least part of Censorius' doxography. He also states that according to Anaximander humans were first born in fish and nourished like dogfish sharks *(en ichthusin eggenesthai to prōton anthrōpous apophainetai kai traphentas hōsper hoi galeoi),* and it was only after they were capable of looking after themselves that they came out *(ekbēnai)* and took to the land *(gēs labesthai).*

Some remarks are in order here. According to the doxographical evidence, Anaximander believed that the human species evolved in a distinctive way, compared to the other animal species. Three doxographies mention that Anaximander thought that the human species evolved in a way different from other animal species (Plutarch, Censorius, Pseudo-Plutarch), and three doxographies mention a relation with fish in this context (Hippolytus, Censorius, Pseudo-Plutarch). The general reasoning behind the former is that human infants need their parents to care for them for a long period of time, whereas other newborn animals can quickly look after themselves.[93] This is Pseudo-Plutarch's understanding, and it is confirmed in a sense by both Censorius and Plutarch. Pseudo-Plutarch does not mention fish, but only that humans originated *(genesthai)* from creatures of a different kind *(ex alloeidōn zōiōn),* although he clearly has aquatic animals in mind since *all* land animals have an aquatic origin. Hippolytus confirms a relation between humans and fish, although he only says that the human species was originally similar to *(para-plēsion)* fish.[94] But what does this mean? If we did not have any other doxo-graphical evidence, we would simply say that humans had a marine existence before transforming into land animals. However, Censorius is much more explicit. He says that Anaximander thought that humans were first formed in fish or fish-like creatures. Censorius accounts for the way Anaximander per-ceived this. Originally the primordial sea (or the primeval slime) must have secreted (after being acted on by the heat of the sun) different kinds of embry-onic life forms, albeit not necessarily at the same time.[95] Some of these embryos evolved into fish or fish-like creatures; others evolved into land ani-mals. Human embryos, on Censorius' account, were at some point somehow swallowed by fish or fish-like creatures, but were able to survive like para-sites. The human embryos were able, in time, to mature inside these creatures. When they did reach maturity, the fish-like creature erupted and men *and* women emerged who were already able to fend for themselves and, one would presume, to procreate. Since we can assume from Censorius' account that human beings immediately took to dry land after emerging from the fish-like creatures, it follows either that evolution was rapid or that human embryos were secreted by the sea at a later stage. Plutarch appears to confirm Censo-rius' account when he states that Anaximander (unlike the Syrians, who attrib-uted a common parentage to fish and humans) declares not only that humans and fish are from the same element, as the Syrians do, but also that humans were first born in fish *(en ichthusin eggenesthai to prōton anthrōpous).* Indeed, he also concurs with Censorius that humans were also nourished in fish. What Plutarch adds is the type of fish in which this occurred: the smooth dogfish *(galeoi),* which is, like all sharks, a placental animal that gives birth to live young.[96]

This fish, according to Plutarch *(On the Cleverness of Animals* 982a; and *On Affection for Offspring* 494c) has a number of fascinating qualities, includ-ing viviparous reproduction, nursing of the young within their own bodies and extruding the young and taking them back again.[97] It is because humans were cared for inside of sharks that they were (eventually) able to look after them-selves and, then *(tēnikauta),* come forth *(ekbēnai)* and take to dry land *(gēs labesthai).* Of course, Plutarch does not state that the dogfish ruptures, as Censorius notes, after humans reach their maturity inside. The important point to retain with regard to the testimonia of Censorius and Plutarch is that Anax-imander was genuinely concerned with accounting for the origin of humans based on the fact that, unlike other land animals, they would be unable to sur-vive as a species without some initial help from mother nature. Plutarch and Censorius may be just conjecturing on the source of their own information.[98] However, based on the testimonia it seems safe to say that Anaximander argued that in the beginning members of the human species were born from a different animal species that was capable of nourishing them until such time as they could support themselves.[99]

We do not know, according to Anaximander, at what moment, or under what influence, the embryo becomes male or female, or when humans begin to procreate. Yet one thing is certain, namely that man no longer has the temporal and logical priority over woman that he possessed in the mythical accounts of the Greeks. Moreover, since human beings have a real beginning in time, the origin of humanity and society are no longer represented as coeval; that is, human beings will no longer be seen as coming into existence within the context of a fully functioning society. As we saw, representing society as coming into being without a real past was the norm in mythical accounts, including Hesiod's. Anaximander's anthropogony is the first rational/naturalistic account of the origin of humanity of which we are aware. Let's now turn to the final stage of his *historia*.

THE ORIGIN AND DEVELOPMENT OF SOCIETY

The most important obstacle we encounter in coming to terms with Anaximander's view on the origin and evolution of society is, of course, a lack of testimonia. Nonetheless, there is some non-Peripatician doxographical evidence which is not contested by commentators. These attest to Anaximander as a mapmaker and geographer and are based on the authority of Eratosthenes, the famous Alexandrian geographer and librarian (ca. 275–194 BCE).

The first doxography is transmitted by Agathemeros, a historian and geographer from the third century CE. According to Agathemeros, "Anaximander the Milesian, a disciple of Thales, first had the audacity to draw (or inscribe) the inhabited earth on a tablet *(prōtos etolmēse tēn oikoumenēn en pinaki grapsai);* after him, Hecataeus the Milesian, a great traveler, made the map more precise such that it became an object *(to pragma)* of wonder."[100] The second is from the first century BCE geographer Strabo: "Eratosthenes says that the first two [geographers] after Homer were Anaximander, the acquaintance and fellow citizen of Thales, and Hecataeus the Milesian. Anaximander was the first to publish a geographical tablet (or map) of the earth *(ton men oun ekdounai prōton geōgraphikon pinaka),* while Hecataeus left a treatise *(gramma)*[101] which is believed to be his from the rest of his writings *(ek tēs allēs autou grapsēs)*."[102]

There are a number of important observations to make with respect to these doxographies. First, Anaximander is portrayed as a geographer who was the first to draw or inscribe *(grapsai)* and thus publish *(ekdounai)* a map of the inhabited world *(he oikoumenē gē)*. The verb *grapsein* can, of course, mean both "to write" and "to draw," and, given the period, Anaximander is clearly experimenting with (and thus exploiting) the new medium of *graphein*. By drawing a map of the *oikoumenē*, Anaximander is in fact publishing it (as he did with his book, in prose); he is making it public for all to see, like the publication of a law code. However, there is much more to this than making visible and thus imaginable the form of the earth, that is, of doing what his poetic predecessor, Hesiod, did not or could not do.[103] There is also a practical side to this.

According to Herodotus (5.49), when Aristagoras, the tyrant of Miletus, went to Sparta in 499 BCE to request the Spartan's help in the Ionian revolt against the Persians, he brought with him for the interview "a map of the world engraved on bronze *(chalkeon)*, showing all the seas and rivers." The map appeared to be quite detailed since Herodotus tells us that Aristagoras pointed out in some detail the locations of the various countries of Asia (5.50). Even though Aristagoras failed to convince the Spartan king Cleomenes (ca. 520–490), the practical side of the map is clear. But where did the map originate? Since Herodotus informs us that the Milesian "historian" Hecataeus was also active in the revolt, despite his initial opposition (5.36, 126), it is highly probable that the map of the world that Aristagoras brought with him to Sparta was one inscribed by Anaximander's younger contemporary, Hecataeus. And since Hecataeus' map is clearly modeled on Anaximander's (a point which is uncontested), Anaximander may very well have already constructed his map for practical purposes and, moreover, the map may very well have been more detailed than is often supposed. In conjunction with this, there are two other non-Peripatetic sources which relate that Anaximander himself traveled to Sparta; indeed, that he was highly regarded there. Cicero states that Anaximander was responsible for saving a considerable number of lives in Sparta by warning them of an impending earthquake and by convincing them to spend the night in the open.[104] Favorinus of Arles, for his part, affirms that Anaximander was the first to construct a seasonal sundial in Sparta to mark the solstices and equinoxes.[105] It is clear from these two doxographies that Anaximander was not only a traveler but that he had an exceptionally good reputation in Sparta. It may have been Anaximander's reputation that convinced Aristagoras to seek the Spartans' assistance in the Ionian revolt. In fact, if Anaximander was himself sent by Croesus as one of the ambassadors to Sparta when he sought an alliance with Sparta against the Medes (Herodotus 1.69), then it is possible that Anaximander already brought a map along to make his point, and this may also have prompted Aristagoras to try it again.[106] The famous Laconian cup attributed to the painter of the Spartan king Arcesilas and dated around 550 BCE, the period that coincides with Anaximander's visit to Sparta, would appear to reinforce this conjecture. The cup shows the heavens, supported by Prometheus, surrounding the earth. The earth has the form of a column with the inhabited earth occupying the top. While Atlas is supporting the dome of the earth in the West, Prometheus is represented as bound to a column in the East. Although the second column is clearly taken from Hesiod's *Theogony* (522), the rest of the cup decoration, as a number of recent scholars have pointed out, appears to have been influenced by the theories and teachings of Anaximander.[107] Of course, Anaximander hardly transported his map of the inhabited world on a stone column, but the Spartan artist's rendition would suggest a correlation between the two.

However, are we to envision the famous map of the *oikoumenē* as round? What exactly was on the map? Is there a correlation between the construction of the map and the contention that Anaximander invented or introduced the sundial? And, more important, I think, what is the purpose of the map? But let us begin with the shape of the map.

According to Herodotus, up until his time mapmakers in general depicted the earth *(gē)* as perfectly circular with Ocean running like a river round it and with Europe and Asia of equal size (4.36; although at 4.41 and 2.16 he suggests that Asia, Europe, and Libya were perceived as having the same size). The "father of history" thus gives the impression that the dominant picture in his time was that of a circular earth surrounded by the river Oceanus. However, Herodotus believes that this picture is clearly based on legend and that "there is nothing to prove this" (4.8). The dominant picture is, of course, Homeric,[108] and this may be what prompts Herodotus to ridicule his predecessors: "the absurdity of all the mapmakers" (4.36). Aristotle seems to be making a similar point when he equally ridicules contemporary mapmakers for depicting the inhabited earth *(tēn oikoumenēn)* as round. He also argues that if it were not for the sea (and he bases this on observation), one could travel completely round the earth *(Meteorology* 2.362b12). Of course, Aristotle is imagining not a disk-shaped earth surrounded by the sea (or Ocean) but a spherical earth—albeit with a land/sea ratio of 5 to 3 *(Meteorology* 2.362b20–25). On the other hand, Strabo seems to endorse the Homeric picture when he argues that observation and experience clearly suggest that the inhabited earth *(hē oikoumenē)* is an island and that the sea surrounding it is called 'Oceanus' (1.1.3–9). Agathemerus (third century CE) seems to add more precision to the picture of the map when he says that the ancients drew the inhabited earth *(tēn oikoumenēn)* as circular *(stroggulēn),* with Greece in the center and Delphi at its center as the world's navel *(Geography* 1.1.2 = DK68B15).

These references (but more importantly, Herodotus') appear to suggest that the most significant characteristic of early maps in general, and of Anaximander's in particular, is that they were circular. And there is virtual unanimity among contemporary scholars on this point. However, a few remarks are in order. First, just what is Herodotus ridiculing here? The accent seems to be on the notion of the legendary encircling river and on depicting Europe and Asia of equal size. Herodotus is shocked by the "radical rationalism" of the authors of these maps.[109] Given Anaximander's propensity for perfect symmetery—the most perfect example of which is his cosmological model—it is fair to say that the great Milesian *phusikos* was the inspiration behind the early maps to which Herodotus refers in this famous passage. Of course, we may wonder why the great rationalist would have argued that the legendary river Oceanus encircled the earth. Clearly, Anaximander did not believe in a legendary river just as he did not believe that thunder and lightning were prerogatives of Zeus.[110] As in the case of Strabo, observation, experience, and legend would probably have led him to the conclusion that the earth was surrounded by water. In fact, the earth, for Anaximander, was initially covered with water—a point, in this context, that scholars have ignored.[111]

Some scholars appear convinced that Delphi must be represented as the center of Anaximander's map since it was considered as the earth's navel *(omphalos gēs)*.[112] I find it unconvincing that the great *phusiologos* would succumb to popular belief any more than Herodotus or Xenophanes. Certainly he would have been aware that other civilizations (notably Egypt and Babylon) claimed as much. More importantly, in Anaximander's time the *omphalos gēs* was probably the oracle of Apollo at Didyma near Miletus rather than the oracle of Apollo at Delphi.[113] Agathemerus may have been thinking of maps from a later period (e.g., the same maps to which Aristotle refers) or more hellenocentric versions of similar maps. In sum, I would suggest a more practical (and inspirational) point for the center of the map: Miletus itself—although a good case may also be made for the Nile Delta, as we will see below. Indeed, according to Herodotus (1.170), when Thales, following the defeat of the Ionians, suggested that the Ionians should set up a common center of government at Teos (see below), Teos was chosen for "practical reasons" and not for "religious reasons."

Furthermore, in the famous passage at 4.36, Herodotus states that it was the *gē* or earth in general that his predecessors depicted as round, not the *oikoumenē* or inhabited earth.[114] This comment may explain why Herodotus adds that Europe and Asia, that is the *oikoumenē* strictly speaking, are depicted as being of equal size on the same maps—albeit much wider than taller. Given Anaximander's penchant for perfect symmetry, as noted above, it seems quite plausible that Herodotus is indeed referring to Anaximander's map (or maps modeled on it). It is even more tempting, however, to take as a reference to Anaximander Herodotus' remark at 2.16 that the Ionians argue that the earth consists of three parts: Asia, Europe and Libya. Given Anaximander's fondness for the number three (the most perfect example of which is again his cosmological model), it would appear to be his representation. Are we to imagine that the three were depicted as being of equal size? At 4.41, Herodotus says that the three differ greatly in size. But since Herodotus is clearly speaking for himself in this passage, there is nothing to indicate that the reference at 2.16 is not to three continents of equal size. Whatever the case, there is no reason to see the reference to two and three continents respectively as mutually exclusive. The reference to two continents of equal size may be a reference to a map with a more precise frame, a frame based on the use of the sundial and indicating the equator and the tropics. I will return to this point shortly. Meanwhile, the division of the three continents in Anaximander's time would have been by rivers: the Nile in the south dividing Libya and Asia, and either the Phasis or Tanais (= Don) in the north dividing Europe and Asia.[115] Since Anaximander believed that the earth was encircled by the Ocean, the exterior Ocean would have been seen as the source of the two rivers, canals, so to speak, carrying water to the more centralized Mediterranean and Euxine or Black seas. But the Nile and Egypt clearly have a special status for both Herodotus and his Ionian predecessors which merits a closer examination.

At 2.15, Herodotus states that the Ionians maintain that Egypt proper is confined to the Nile Delta. Indeed, while the Nile is the boundary between Asia and Libya, the Delta is seen as a separate piece of land (2.16). In the passage which precedes this, Herodotus claims that the Egyptians believe that they are the oldest race on earth (2.15; see also 2.1) and that they came into being at the same time as the Delta (2.15).[116] The rich alluvial soil of the Delta enables the Egyptians to get their harvests with less labor than any other people (2.14; see also Diodorus 1.34). Before giving his own opinion on the subject, Herodotus notes that he is surprised that Ionians claim that the earth consists of three parts, Europe, Asia, and Libya, when they should clearly count the Egyptian Delta as a separate and fourth tract of land (2.16). Herodotus' own opinion (2.17) is unimportant here; what is important is what the Ionians claim according to him (2.16). And what the Ionians clearly claim is that Egypt is both the logical and chronological departure point/center for humanity (2.15). Now there was an "almost" universal opinion among the ancients that Egypt was the oldest civilization and the cradle of civilization.[117] But with whom did this opinion/theory originate and why?

There is little if any indication in Homer of the fabulous past of Egypt.[118] Although it is rich in promises, Homer's Egypt is not easily accessible.[119] So when did Egypt become accessible? The Greeks began to inhabit Egypt during the reign of Psammetichus I (664–10).[120] Their residence in Egypt began after Psammetichus awarded a number of Greek mercenaries strips of land. But it intensified in the late seventh century with the foundation of the *emporion* or trading post of Naucratis, which is situated about fifty miles inland on the Canopic branch of the Nile and thus only ten miles or so from the royal capital of Sais (the capital of the XXVI Dynasty, 664–525) and seventy-five miles or so from the great pyramids of Giza (see Herodotus 2.178–79). It has been argued that Naucratis was initially founded by the Milesians (Conche 1991, 29 n9). At the very least, it had a Milesian quarter, as Herodotus clearly notes (2.178–79). Such a quarter is suggested by a large independent sanctuary which dates to the early years of the town (Boardman 1999, 130; Gorman 2001, 56–58). Although Naucratis acquired the status of a fully fledged polis, it was ultimately under the control of the pharaoh. The importance of Naucratis in Egyptian history from the time of Psammetichus cannot be exaggerated. It was in fact the chief port of Egypt until the foundation of Alexandria; and it was not much less important than Alexandria in its own age, thanks in particular to the Philhellenic pharaoh Amasis (570–26).[121] Moreover, since the Saite dynasty relied heavily on mercenaries,[122] it was only with the Persian conquest of Egypt by Cambyses in 525 that the presence of Greek (and Carian) mercenaries ceased to overshadow the country (see Herodotus 3.11). Indeed, the Persian invasion had an adverse effect on Naucratis itself. At one point Darius suppressed the priviledged commercial relations with the city, and the archeological evidence seems to confirm this.[123] As one recent scholar put it, the "heyday" of Naucratis must have been *before* the Persian invasion of 525.[124] Meanwhile it is quite possible that commerical (and touristic) relations with other areas of Egypt began to develop after the foundation of Naucratis. The Greek influence would have made it considerably easier for other Greeks to travel (not to mention that the mercenaries themselves came from the four corners of Greece) and thus for stories of a fabulous civilization to spread rapidly. It is certainly not by chance, as Hurwit notes, that the colossal stone temples of Artemis at Ephesus and the third Heraion of Samos with their grandiose multiplication of columns date to the second quarter of the 6th century: at a time when Rhoikos, the famous architect of the Samian temple, was visiting Naucratis.[125]

Whether or not the Egyptians initiated claims that they were the oldest race on earth and that they came into being at the same time as the Delta, the fact remains that the Greeks quickly believed this to be the case. Why? Clearly, the sacred colossal stone monuments, veritable museums of the past if there ever were, with their indestructible archives (including a list of dynasties), certainly conveyed the idea that humanity was much older than previously believed, and at least considerably older than the genealogies of the oral tradition claimed. Indeed, exposure to the Egyptian past may very well have incited a whole new breed of individuals, including Anaximander, to rethink the origin and development of humanity and civilization. In fact, Herodotus conjectured that given the alluvial origin of the Nile Delta, it would have taken from 10,000 to 20,000 years to reach its present formation (2.11). This was ample evidence for Herodotus that the Egyptians were indeed as old as they claimed (see 2.142–45). In conjunction with this, the regularity of the

Nile floods—analogous to the regularity of the movements of the heavenly
bodies themselves—and the subsequent annual renewal of the rich alluvial
soil would certainly explain how Egypt escaped the great cataclysms of the
past, real or imagined. Indeed, if the story of the flood of Deucalion were
true—and most Greeks including the likes of Thucycides (1.3), Plato
(*Timaeus* 22e–23d), and Aristotle (*Meteorology* 352a30) thought it was—then
the story would have to be either reconsidered, or the event considerably older
than originally thought.[126] Alternatively Egypt, that is, the Nile valley and
Delta, escaped the cataclysm that supposedly destroyed humanity.[127] There
were other ways or reasons, that is, more rational ways or reasons of con-
ceiving of, or postulating, a flood or something analogous. Herodotus (2.12,
13) concluded that the earth was once covered by the sea from the observation of sea shells on the hills of the Nile Delta and from the fact that salt
exudes from the soil. Whether or not he thought that this was a cyclical occurrence is unclear. What is clear is that according to Herodotus geography/geol-
ogy and history are closely connected.

Herodotus informs us (2.143) that Hecataeus of Miletus (560–490 BCE)
conjectured that Egypt had existed for at least 11,000 years after the start of
the records he was shown by the Egyptian priests in Thebes. Since Arrian
informs us that Hecataeus, in his *History of Egypt,* believed that the Delta was
formed by the continual deposit of silt, he probably assumed that the Nile culture was even older and originated in the Delta.[128] In sum, as in the case of
Herodotus, for Hecataeus geography/geology and history are closely connected. Given that this connection is similar to that made by Herodotus and
given that Hecataeus is the source or inspiration behind Herodotus' own
encounter with the Egyptian priest, it is reasonable to assume that Hecataeus
is also the source (or inspiration) behind's Herodotus' geological observations
about the Nile.

The early Ionian *phusikoi* were also interested in geology and in cyclical
occurrences. Xenophanes argued that humanity (and life in general) emerged
from a sort of slime, that is, a combination of earth and water (DK21B29, 33),
and that it was periodically destroyed (DK21A33). He based his theory on the
observation of various kinds of fossils (fish, plants, shells) in different locations including Syracuse, Paros, and Malta (DK21A33). This was clear evidence that the sea once covered what is now dry land. Did Xenophanes and
Hecataeus and by implication Herodotus have a common source, namely
Anaximander of Miletus?[129]

Diogenes Laertius (on the testimony of Theophrastus) informs us that
Xenophanes was an auditor of Anaximander (*Lives* 9.21 = DK21A1) and
gives his *floruit* (probably on the authority of Apollodorus) as the Sixtieth
Olympiade (540–37), which suggests that he was born around 575 BCE. In his
autobiographical verses of fragment 8, Xenophanes informs us that he was

alive and writing at ninety-two. There is a good deal of consensus that Xenophanes lived from 575–475 BCE.[130] Given the consensus on Anaximander's
dates (610–540 BCE), if we assume that Xenophanes left his home town of
Colophon after Cyrus the Mede's conquest of Lydia and thus the reign of
Croesus in 546 (Colophon fell to Harpagus shortly after), then he would have
been around thirty at the time and Anaximander around sixty-five.[131] Considering the short distance between Colophon and Miletus, the facility of travel
by sea, and the reputation of Miletus as an intellectual center, Xenophanes
could have heard about Anaximander's investigations and decided to attend
his private and/or public lectures (or even initially have read his famous
book), view his famous maps, et cetera, somewhere between, say, 556 and
546 BCE. Since Anaximander appears to have been a well-traveled man, this
may have incited Xenophanes to do as much. This is where he may have heard
of "cultural relativism" for the first time as well as the relation between geology, geography, and history. We do not know where Xenophanes first traveled
after leaving Colophon for Western Greece. He was certainly interested in the
origins and development of civilization and the arts that foster it, and his
approach seems to be both rational and secular. Although none of the references to fossils and sea shells appear to be in Egypt (two are proper to the area
of Sicily and the third to Paros in the Aegean sea—unless the reference is to
Pharos in Egypt), his reference to the Ethiopians as portraying their gods as
flat-nosed and black (DK21B16) suggests, if not a visit, at least some famil-
iarity with the culture.[132] Indeed, when Hecataeus states at the opening of his
Genealogies that what the Greeks believe is silly (of course, his criticism of
anthropomorphism of the poets at DK21B11 is also in order here), he may
very well be referring to Xenophanes' contention concerning how the various
peoples portray their respective gods. Since Egypt and thus Naucratis did not
fall to the Persians until 525, given the reputation of Naucratis as a cosmopolitan intellectual center until 525, then if Xenophanes did visit Egypt, it
would probably have been before 525 (one exile at the hands of the Medes
being enough!).[133]

Heidel puts the birth of Hecataeus at around 560 BCE.[134] This strikes me
as entirely plausible if one considers that Hecataeus was probably an elder
statesman during the Ionian revolt of 499, which he initially opposed. Now if
Anaximander did live until at least 540 BCE (and there is nothing to indicate
the contrary), Hecataeus may also very well have been a young pupil/auditor
of Anaximander (see Hurwit 1985, 321). Although he is generally supposed
to have visited Egypt during the reign of Darius (521–486 BCE), who was very
favorably disposed toward the Egyptians and their sancturaries after the lawlessness of his predecessor Cambyses (see Diodorus 1.95.5), Hecataeus may
also have visited Egypt prior to this.[135] Whatever the case, that Hecataeus was
a source and inspiration for Herodotus is uncontested by scholars. However,

if Xenophanes and Hecataeus drew their inspiration from Anaximander, then clearly the great Milesian *phusikos* was also keenly interested in "chronology and geography," although these were not, in my view, his main interest, as Heidel contends.[136] Was Egypt the source of his own observations? Given the importance of Naucratis as a cosmopolitan intellectual center with a Milesian quarter and given that Anaximander (610–540 BCE) had a reputation as both a traveler and a geographer, it would appear strange if he had not visited the great country (few doubt that his friend Thales did). Moreover, Naucratis probably reached its zenith prior to the Persian invasion of 525 and thus during Anaximander's lifetime. Was it a visit to Egypt that initiated his book on nature?[137] Was Egypt the catalyst?

Scholars tend to associate Anaximander solely, or almost solely, with cosmological speculation. But Strabo is quite emphatic that Anaximander the philosopher (and his fellow citizen Hecataeus) were very much concerned with the science of geography (1.1) and he goes on to say that this was also the opinion of Eratosthenes (1.11). As we already saw, there is substantial evidence that geography/geology and history are clearly and closely related. Moreover, geography as Strabo sees it (again on the authority of Eratosthenes and reaching back to Anaximander) is equally connected with both politics and cosmology in a practical and theoretical context (1.1, 11). Now the Suidas informs us that Anaximander wrote a treatise entitled *Tour of the Earth (Gēs periodos)*, and Athenaeus (11.498a–b) mentions a *Heroology (Hērōologia)*. As Heidel notes (1921, 241), *Tour of the Earth* was one of the first accepted names of a geographical treatise, and Strabo's references to Anaximander's geographical work (and not just a "map") on the authority of Eratosthenes certainly appear to confirm this treatise (1.1, 11). *Heroology,* on the other hand, may have been another title for *Genealogies*. Both were employed by (or attributed to) Hecataeus, as Heidel correctly notes (1921, 262). Titles of course were not yet employed at this time, so these references may have been part of his general work on nature (that is, chapters or sections in the general account), which would include, in addition to cosmogonical and cosmological speculation, an interest in the early history and geography of culture. After all, to explain (or describe) how the present order of things was established (as it is clear from Hesiod's paradigm in the *Theogony*) entails offering an explantion of how the *present* socio-political order originated.

This brings us back more specifically to Egypt. As we saw, one of the primary differences between a mythical approach to the origin of humanity and the rational approach is that the former assumes that humanity did not have a real beginning in time but is the result of a series of events that took place *in illo tempore* (or mythical time) involving supernational entities, whereas the latter (beginning as far as we know with Anaximander) conjectures that humanity is the result of the same natural causes that there were behind the original formation of the universe. Of course, Anaximander was much more specific. He saw the human species as having evolved in stages. It developed in a sort of primeval slime before migrating and adapting to dry land. While it may be true that spontaneous generation was perceived as a fact of nature by the Greeks, the mythical antecedents (humans emerging from the earth like plants) are unrelated to their rational counterparts. However, the question is to what degree was Egypt the inspiration behind his own rational account? Did Anaximander postulate that the human species could have evolved simultaneously in several places on the earth's surface, or did he conjecture that it must have originated in one particular place, to wit, the one that presented the best/ideal conditions? For the case at hand, Anaximander need not have believed that humanity (as other living animals) emerged exactly as the Egyptians contended—through spontaneous generation following certain eniromental conditions.[138] Nonetheless, they certainly made a convincing case for why they were the most ancient of all the races in the world (Herodotus 2.2). Not only were climatic conditions in Egypt conducive to some sort of spontaneous or evolutionary development, but, as both Diodorus (1.10) and Herodotus (2.14) contend, there was also a spontaneous supply of food. In sum, the Egyptians could make an excellent case for their claim to be the most ancient people—indeed the cradle of civilization. The question now becomes, did Anaximander believe that other peoples migrated from Egypt? Given the fact that the Egyptians could demonstrate (or corroborate) their claim to be the most ancient of peoples with a series of wooden statues representing previous generations, as Herodotus, Hecataeus, *and* probably Anaximander observed, there was little reason to deny this formidable claim. More important was the fact that the Egyptians used writing to record chronological events. At 2.145, Herodotus states that the Egyptians are quite certain of their dates going back 15,000 years before Amasis because "they have always kept a careful written record of the passage of time." This explains his contention at 2.100 that the priests read to him from a written record the names of the 330 monarchs. Of course, we know that writing did not exist in Egypt for 15,000 years, but it did exist for a very long time before Herodotus and it was clearly employed for recording chonological events. Indeed, the famous Palermo Stone not only lists names of the rulers from the pharoah Min (with whom the first dynasty begins) but also includes a year by year record of each king, the height reached by the Nile flood in that particular year, and outstanding events that occurred and could be remembered in each year.[139] Moreover, the awe inspiring, monolithic sacred stone monuments reinforced the Greek conviction. Also important is that Ionians began to reflect on the geological evidence in support of the Egyptian claim. Given the amount of silt deposited in the Delta each year and the size of the Delta itself, the earth could not be less than 20,000 thousand years old, as Herodotus (2.13) and his Ionian predecessors claimed, and thus the Egyptians themselves could very well have been round for 341 generations or 11,340 years as they claimed to Hecataeus (Herodotus 2.143), with a statue of a high priest representing each generation.[140] The difference between the two numbers could then account for the period of time it would/may have taken for the human species to adapt to the land environment and discover the necessities of life before discovering the various arts and crafts (I will discuss this in more detail below).

In the face of this, the Hellenic claim or conviction that humanity—or at least the Greeks—originated sixteen generations ago looked, as Hecataeus quickly realized, ridiculous. Hecataeus' critical approach is reflected in the opening of his *Genealogia:* "Hecataeus the Milesian speaks thus: I *write* [my italics] these things as they seem to me; for the stories of the Greeks are many and absurd in my opinion" (*FGH*1, frag. 1). The spirit behind this critical statement is analogous to Xenophanes' critical analysis of the anthropomorphism that permeates the theology of Homer and Hesiod. For his part, Hecataeus wants to rationalize the genealogies of the heros, to recreate a history of the past based on these genealogies and their respective myths. There is no doubt that Hecataeus like the Greeks in general firmly believed that the Homeric poems contained more than a kernel of truth. The problem was separating the truth from the fiction, the rational from the fantastic. The relatively new medium of writing would help both to record the oral tradition and to critically evaluate it. Indeed, Anaximander and Hecataeus were among the first to have written their accounts in prose. Now, as we saw, Hecataeus was already well aware of this because of Anaximander's previous research. He must have *read* Anaximander's prose treatise and *observed* his map and the geographical treatise that accompanied it. Moreover, given the dates, he may have even *heard* him lecture and/or narrate his *logos,* that is, his rational and descriptive account. The question now becomes to what degree are Hecataeus' *Genealogies* and *Tour of the Earth* based on Anaximander's *Tour of the Earth* and *Genealogies/Heroologies?*

The description of the earth and of its inhabitants *(oikoumenē)* is the subject of the science called geography, and, as W. A. Heidel (1921, 257) judiciously remarked, history and geography go hand in hand. This moreover is entirely in keeping with our hypothesis according to which the logical point of departure of a work of the *peri phuseōs* type is none other than the society in which man lives. In fact, it is clearly possible that Anaximander the historian, called the young in the *Souda (ho neōteros historikos),*[141] or simply called the other Anaximander the historian by Diogenes Laertius[142] is none other than Anaximander, the *phusiologos,* of Miletus.[143] This could be the same person that Diels Kranz mentions in fragment C (*Zweifelhaftes* or Doubtful Fragment) as the Anaximander who declared that the alphabet was brought from Egypt to Greece by Danaus before the time of Cadmus.[144] The testimonia in question is taken from Apollodorus' *On the Catalogue of Ships,* and the fact that great chronologist mentions the three Milesians in the following order, Anaximander, Dionysius, and Hecataeus, appears to confirm that it is indeed the "father" of philosophy. The doxography in question clearly indicates that the ancients were divided on how the alphabet originated in Greece: Ephorus (fourth century BCE) argues that the alphabet was invented by the Phoenician Cadmus and introduced to Greece; Herodotus and Aristotle argue that Cadmus was only the transmitter of the Phoenician invention into Greece; Pythodorus and Phillis, for their part, argue that the alphabet predates Cadmus and was imported into Greece by Danaus. Anaximander, Dionysius, and Hecataeus of Miletus all confirm this.[145] A few words are in order here on Danaus and the transmission of the alphabet in the context of ancient Egypt.

There is now consensus that writing appeared in Greece around 750 BCE. The steady stream of inscriptions around or after 750 BCE point to this period for the adoption of the alphabet into Greece.[146] Precisely where the alphabet may have started is still open to debate. According to Herodotus, the Phoenicians who came with Cadmus first introduced the alphabet to Boeotia, Hesiod's homeland (5.57.1–58.2). In fact, he contends that they also settled there. Herodotus is, however, ambiguous on when this occurred. At 2.145, he mentions that the period of Cadmus' grandson, Dionysus, goes back 1,600 years *(hexakosia etea kai chilia)* before his time. This would entail that Cadmus and the Phoenicians introduced the alphabet to Boeotia in the third millenium BCE. However, the approximate period Herodotus notes for the Trojan war in the same passage is close to the current consensus: the 13th century BCE. Meanwhile, Herodotus contends that the Cadmean letters he saw at Thebes in Boeotia were not that different from the Ionian. This would leave us to believe that he was somewhat confused about how and when the transmission of the alphabet occurred.[147] Moreover, while most scholars associate the mythical Cadmus with Phoenicia, there are other traditions that associate Cadmus with Egypt, as in the Egyptianization of the story of Io.[148]

Although Herodotus believed that the Phoenicians introduced writing or *grammata* to Greece, he may have believed that the Phoenicians, in turn, borrowed their writing system from the Egyptians (just as the Greek alphabet, by adding vowels, represented an advance over the Phoenician writing system). At 2.36, he clearly states that the Egyptians believed that their own way of writing from right to left was superior to the Greek manner of writing from left to right and that they have both sacred and common or demotic writing. There is no doubt, of course, that Herodotus believed in the diffusion. Indeed, he believed that a considerable amount of Greek culture, including their religion, was borrowed from the Egyptians (2.49–52). We could legimately assume that this would also be the case for the story of Io; that is, Io is identified with Isis and was thus borrowed from Egypt.

On the other hand, Anaximander (and Hecataeus) argue that it was actually *before* the time of Cadmus that the alphabet was introduced into Greece; and the person who imported *(metakomisai)* it was Danaus (DK12C1.11). There is no doubt here that Danaus is associated with Egypt and its high culture. The fact that Hecataeus affirms that originally Greece was populated by Barbarians led from Phrygia by Pelops and Egypt by Danaus *(FGH* 1, frag. 119) lends credence to the idea that they thought that the alphabet (or *an* alphabet) was introduced many generations before the date we now associate with its introduction. Anaximander may have traced this in his own *Heroology* or *Genealogies.* But on what may Anaximander have based his opinion on an Egyptian origin of the alphabet? Semiticists have no problem calling West Semitic writing "the alphabet" since each alphabetic sign in the repertory stands for a single consonant and thus a phoneme, that is, a class of sounds different enough from others sounds to change the meaning of a word. But if West Semitic writing is an alphabet, can the same be said about ancient Egyptian? According to Alan Gardiner (1961b, 23), the Egyptians very early developed a body of 24 uniconsonantal signs or letters that he also calls an alphabet. In fact, he is convinced that this is the origin of our own alphabet (1961b, 25–26). For the case at hand, it is not important that some linguists and scholars may disagree with Gardiner. The fact is that there is no good reason to believe that Anaximander was not convinced that this was also the case after an Egyptian or someone else brought this to his attention (how could he contest what he could not read). The Egyptians could demonstrate that writing had existed in Egypt before even the Greeks could trace their first ancestors.[149] Moreover, even if Anaximander may not have been aware of the Linear B script, he may very well have been aware of the Cypriote syllabary and thus some form of transition from the introduction of an Egyptian alphabet to his own alphabet. In sum, this does not exclude that Anaximander may still have thought that some individual Greek genius innovated, at a more recent stage, by adding the five vowels to the consonants—thus creating, as Powell (1997, 25) notes, the first technology capable of preserving by mechanical means a facsimilie of the human voice. There is nothing to exclude that he saw Danaus and the Egyptians as the original inventors of the alphabet and yet the Greek alphabet as far superior to its predecessors. The Greeks at this early stage (or at least their intelligentia) were already well aware of the powers of their own alphabet and sought its true inventor. Thus Anaximander's contemporary Stesichorus (ca. 630–555 BCE), in the second book of his *Oresteia,* says that Palamedes invented the alphabet *(heurēkenai ta stoicheia),* that is, the Greek version of the alphabet.[150] Clearly, Anaximander and his generation see themselves as "writers" heavily influenced, it is true, by oral tradition, but writers just the same.[151]

Herodotus as noted above believed that a great deal of Greek culture and civilization originated in Egypt—a point also noted by Plato in the *Phaedrus*

(274c–d). And the famous statement by Hecataeus of Miletus that Greece was originally populated by barbarians brought from Phrygia by Pelops and from Egypt by Danaus means the same thing. This is the same Danaus whom he believed brought the alphabet with him. Now since the opening remark in his *Genealogies* (*FGH* 1, frag. 1) strongly suggests that he denied the gods any influence in civilization, then Danaus is seen as a historical individual. One function of his genealogies may have thus been to retrace the origin of certain cultural icons with the help of information received from Egyptian sources. In fact, if it is true as Herodotus claims that Hecataeus attempted to trace his family back to a god in the sixteenth generation (2.141), and the Egyptian demonstrated to him that this was patently absurd, then it was clearly the Egyptians who were instrumental in developing his critical approach and in giving him a clearer sense of chronology and history.[152] At any rate, Hecataeus' contemporary Xenophanes believed human civilization was the result of human progress and that this progress was based on inquiry involving travel to various places and discovery through new encounters with people, places, and things (DK21B18).[153] The poem (consisting of some 2,000 verses) that he is purported to have composed about the foundation of Colophon, which was settled before the Trojan War,[154] would have been based on a rational approach to genealogical/chronological research (DK21A1). It is difficult to know if Xenophanes was able to resist the fascination with Egyptian culture, but Colophon was initially settled by Thebans (now an ambigious word), and the son of one of its founders, Mopsus, is purported to have migrated to Egypt.[155] Miletus, for its part, was founded by Neleus, a son of the Athenian king Codrus, in the eleventh century. If Herodotus/Hecataeus understand by generation "thirty years," then clearly Hecataeus is tracing his descendants back to this period (that is, sixteen generations). And given that the population of each district would insist on their autochthonous origin, an origin that they would (or could) trace, at best, a few generations before the Trojan war, it was painfully clear that the Egyptian claim to have a much older civilization was demonstrably true.

Given the information we have concerning Anaximander, it seems to me that he was no less interested in the distant past than Hecataeus. Indeed, Anaximander appears to be the inspiration behind Hecataeus' own account. This seems clear from the testimonia that Hecataeus developed Anaximander's map in more detail. Given that history and geography, as we saw, were closely connected (if not indistinguishable) at the time, then the map clearly had a dual function, a function which was amplified and clarified in the treatise which must have accompanied it. Moreover, given that the aim of an *historia peri phuseōs* is to give a rational explanation of the origin and development of the present order of things from beginning to end and that the present world order included the society (or civilization) in which one resided, then the two treatises entitled *Tour of the Earth* and *Genealogies* (or *Heroology*) which the later tradition attribute to Anaximander may have simply been different sections, as noted above, of the more generic treatise *Peri phuseōs*. These two treatises were, I believe, intimately connected with Anaximander's map. So what did they intend to achieve?

ANAXIMANDER'S MAP: THE CANVAS OF THE *OIKOUMENĒ*

We saw above that the Nile and Egypt clearly had a special status for the early Ionians. More important, given that they considered the Nile Delta, as Herodotus notes, as a "separate piece of land" (2.16; or in Diodorus' words: "an island" *(hē nēsos)* 1.34)—indeed as Egypt itself (2.15)—and that it was here that humanity originated, there is a sense in which the Delta may be considered (and thus represented) as the *omphalos gēs* of the first *phusiologoi*. From this perspective, the Delta is the center of Anaximander's map (and the Nile, the north-south meridian). Indeed, from the moment Egyptians could empirically demonstrate theirs was the oldest civilization; that living creatures appeared to generate spontaneously; and that the rich alluvial soil provided food with little labor, et cetera, the claim to autochthony by other peoples including the Greeks, seemed untenable, if not absurd. The question is, how did civilization originate, develop, and spread from Egypt throughout the known world? This is where geography, astronomy, and history become contiguous. The map could show the current *oikoumenē* and the treatise that accompanied it could explain in lecture form as rationally as possible how and why this occurred. The treatise itself would have begun with a cosmological introduction. This would initiate the tenor for the whole rational explanation. From Anaximander's rational perspective, the same causes that were behind the initial formation of the universe are the same causes that are currently active in the universe. These causes also account for meteorological phenomena, including, thunder, lightening, wind, and rain. There is no room here for supernatural causes—at least one point the Egyptians failed to see. After explaining how life emerged in the swamps of the Nile Delta (again with reference to natural causes and geological evidence), he would then conjecture how civilization developed. Given the climatic conditions which existed in the region, including an absence of winter and an abundant and effortless food supply, he may have seen humanity living a golden age type existence.[156] But the Nile was not without its dangers, for numerous wild animals including crocodiles and lions were abundant; so this is difficult to assess. Whatever the case, Anaximander would have postulated the early conditions of humanity before proceeding to the various cultural discoveries (*heurēmata* or *technē*) that were behind a more civilized existence (or humanity's progress). Whether or not he thought humanity acquired various arts through experience or necessity is difficult to know, but what is certain is that he would have given a rational explanation consistent with the rest of his *historia*. Nor would it have been unimaginable that Anaximander reflected on the origins of the socio-political structure in the land of the pharaohs; after all, this was the world from which civilization spread its wings. More importantly, Anaximander would have to account for the origin of the various peoples that made up the *oikoumenē*. If the Nile Delta was indeed the one and only cradle of humanity (and this appears to be the case for at least Anaximander and Hecataeus), then how did the other peoples come to inhabit their present locations? Was it at this stage that genealogies (or the *Genealogies*) entered into the picture? As we saw above, Anaximander argued that an Egyptian cultural and political hero, Danaus, was responsible for introducing the alphabet into Greece. Anaximander may have placed a special importance on the alphabet since he was well aware that his enquiry was founded on the testimonies that the alphabet allowed him to collect.[157] And we can conclude that this was also the case with a number of other *heurēmata* generally attributed to the Egyptians (e.g., stone monument building). Somehow Anaximander acquired enough genealogical information, presumably, but not exclusively, from Egyptian sources, to construct a sort of chronological explanation of the diffusion of Egyptian culture.

The section on the *Tour of the Earth* meanwhile may have begun with the Nile Delta where life and civilization originated and then proceeded either clockwise or counter clockwise about the *orbis terrarum,* the whole of Europe and Asia and Libya, indicating the possible migrations of the various peoples with which he was familiar from travels and various documented accounts. The current location of each people would also have been sketched on the map as well as known routes for migration, trade, and military campaigning.

Of course, the question naturally arises as to how he would account for some peoples being clearly less civilized than others if Egyptian civilization was transmitted with the migrations? The logical answer would be because of the periodic occurrence of natural catastrophies. Indeed, even Thucydides believed in the legendary flood, and there is evidence in Anaximander that he believed that natural disasters were ongoing—albeit on a localized rather than on a cosmic scale. Nor does this mean that there was nothing left to discover or that all past discoveries could be attributed to the Egyptians. Clearly Anaximander, one of the founders of the new enlightenment, was well aware that his own rational approach was novel and exciting; indeed, far superior to the current Egyptian approach. How could such a rationalist concur with Egyptian religious practices without lamenting their deficiencies! As for the fundamental differences between the different languages, Anaximander could observe that given the fact that contemporary Greek dialects varied considerably, it is not surprising that the Greek language appears considerably different from

Egyptian (or Phoenician). But given that certain similarities could be attributed to both (as in the case of religious syncretisms), this would be ample evidence that Greek language and civilization originated in Egypt.

Although we do not have a great deal of information on this aspect of Anaximander's *historia,* when the information is put into a historical perspective, it seems Heidel and Cherniss (contra Guthrie [1962, 75] and the vast majority of classical scholars) were not far off the mark when they contended that the aim of Anaximander's book was "to sketch the life-history of the cosmos from the moment of its emergence from infinitude to the author's own time" (Heidel, 1921, 287) or "to give a description of the inhabited earth, geographical, ethnological and cultural, and the way in which it had come to be what it is" (Cherniss, 1951, 323). Let us remember again that what Hesiod is attempting to do in the *Theogony* is to explain how the present order of things was established.

Meanwhile, an excellent example of this manner of proceeding comes to us from Diodorus of Sicily, an historian from the first century BCE. What is striking is that before undertaking his history of the Greeks (which will include not only a chronological table of events from the Trojan War to his own time, but also events and legends previous to the Trojan war), Diodorus begins with a cosmogony (1.7.1–3), then moves to a zoogony (1.7.4–6), and then finally to a politogony (1.8–9). After briefly expounding these three phases, Diodorus then turns to Egypt (to which he dedicates several books) to start his history strictly speaking because tradition considers it as the cradle of the human species; his descriptions of the ideal conditions of the Nile are analogous to what we saw in Herodotus (1.9f.). It is worth noting that Diodorus believes that numerous peoples had autochthonous origins and that this explains, at least in part, the origin of the diversity of languages (1.8.3–4).[158]

What is certain regarding Diodorus's account is that it is impossible to attempt to attribute its contents to the influence of a particular philosopher. In other words, the whole of the text is necessarily eclectic.[159] However, the text is also clearly of Ionian inspiration and there is little in the text that cannot be traced back to the sixth century BCE and ultimately to Anaximander. That one would think that Anaximander (as many scholars contend) would not have reflected on the origin of language (albeit clearly on the origin of the alphabet), that he would have been incapable of initiating a theory of language as sophisticated as Democritus' is, quite frankly, astounding.

Diodorus, for his part, believes that history is the key to happiness *(eudaimonia)* since it commemorates the great deeds of past men and thus incites us to emulate them, that is, to furnish us with examplars for noble living. He thus contends that history is the prophetess of truth and the mother of philosophy (1.2.1–2). The geographer Strabo also makes the same contention when he states that philosophy and geography are both concerned with the investigation of the art of life or happiness (*eudaimonia*, 1.1). This is the same Strabo who contends on the authority of Eratosthenes that Anaximander was among the first geographers (1.1; 1.11). Strabo meanwhile also begins with a cosmogony before introducing his text on Egypt (17.1.36).[160] Moreover, he states, after mentioning Anaximander's geographical treatise (1.11), that the study of geography entails an encyclopaedic knowledge, and this includes a special knowledge of astronomy and geometry to unite terrestrial and celestial phenomena (1.12–15). This connects with Hipparchus of Nicaea's (ca. 150 BCE) contention that it is impossible for any man to attain sufficient knowledge of geography without the determination of the heavenly bodies and the observation of the eclipses, for otherwise it would be impossible to determine whether Alexandria is north or south of Babylon (Strabo 1.1.12).

These observations bring us to another dimension to Anaximander's map. According to Hahn (2001, 204) and Heidel (1937, 17–20, 57), Anaximander's map of the earth was determined by a three-point coordinate system: the terrestrial mark-points corresponding to the rising and settings of the sun on the solstices and equinoxes.[161] This could be achieved, at this point in time, with the aid of the seasonal sundial. Although Diogenes Laertius attributes the invention of the gnomon to Anaximander (DK12A1), this is highly unlikely. According to Herodotus (2.109), the Greeks derived their knowledge of the sundial, the gnomon, and the twelve divisions of the day from the Babylonians. However, since there is evidence that the Egyptians were already familiar with the technique of sundials, Anaximander may have learned it from them and saw them as the "inventors."[162] On the other hand, Anaximander may simply have been the first to make a scientific use of the instrument, as Heidel (1921, 244) contends. The sundial would attest to an impersonal *kosmos* underlying nature as a whole: it would have confirmed the regularity and uniformity of the seasons, times, solstices and equinoxes. It remains, however, that it is difficult to know exactly what Anaximander was able to accomplish in map construction strictly speaking.[163] If the map that Aristagoras is purported to have taken to Sparta is as detailed as generally thought (it apparently contained the course of the famous Royal Road drawn up by the Great King's road surveyors), then distances were somehow measured (see Herodotus 5.50–55). Such a map would provide Anaximander with an additional note of persuasion both in his lectures and on his travels.

This observation brings us back to the general structure of Anaximander's map. As we saw above, on the authority of Herodotus and on the description of the earth as a columnar drum, the majority of scholars tend to give the map a circular form. They divide the earth into three parts: Europe, Asia, and Libya, by means of rivers (the Nile and Phasis) and the Mediterranean/Euxine Sea (the inner sea), and surround the whole with the Ocean-stream (outer sea). Some see Europe, Asia, and Libya as equal,[164] some not.[165] Some place the center in

Delos,[166] some in Delphi,[167] some in Miletus/Didyma.[168] Some add more details than others.[169] Meanwhile since some insist that there is a difference between a map of the earth and a map of the inhabited earth or *oikoumenē*,[170] some scholars continue to imagine it in the shape of a circle,[171] while others see it as a parallelogram[172] and others again as a parallelogram inscribed in a circle.[173]

Now the inhabited earth, on the authority of Ephorus (ca. 340 BCE), was the temperate region and rectangular in shape. To the north of this was the region of uninhabitable cold and to the south the region of uninhabitable heat (and beyond that the outer seas).[174] The rising and setting of the sun on the solstices and equinoxes provided certain fixed points and thus the boundaries for constructing the map of the inhabited world *(oikoumenē)*. The sunrise and sunset on the winter solstice fixed the southwest and southeast boundaries of the inhabitable south while the summer sunrise and sunset on the summer solstice, fixed the northwest and northeast boundaries of the inhabitable north. The inhabited region had, of course, a center and through it ran the main axis or equator, and midpoint between the equator and the outer boundaries were the fixed points (or lines) that would correspond to the summer and winter equinoxes. Heidel (1937, 11–20, 56–59), Thompson (1948, 97), and others argue that Ephorus' map of the inhabited world (which is based on a three point coordinate system) originates with early Ionian mapmakers and thus with Hecateaus and Anaximander.[175] It is possible that maps began to take on the shape of a parallelogram after it became increasingly evident that the eastern land mass (and thus the distance to the eastern ocean on the east/west axis) was significantly longer than perviously realized. Thus the traditional center no longer made any sense. Given Hecataeus' knowledge of the Indus, this would already cause a major problem if he considered Delphi as the center.

Meanwhile, there is no scientific correlation between the fixed coordinates on the map (with the exception of north, south, east and west) and the geographical positions to which they are supposed to refer. The winter and summer tropics are based on the reports of traders and others who had traveled to the most distant inhabited lands at that time. What would matter more would be a central point with east/west and north/south axes or meridians. The fixed points on the map could be the various rivers, seas, cities, and countries and their corresponding peoples. The distances from the center to lands bordering the ocean in each direction would have to correspond.[176]

This brings us back to Egypt and the Nile Delta. In addition to an east-west axis or equator, Herodotus suggests when discussing early Ionian maps that there was a north-south meridian running from the Nile in the south to the Danube/Ister in the north.[177] Was this also on Anaximander's map? This point is interesting from the perspective of Egypt and its place in Anaximander's *historia*. Herodotus contends, as we saw, not only that the early Ionians (and thus Anaximander) divided the earth into three equal parts: Europe, Asia, and

Libya, but also that the Nile Delta was considered separate. Is it possible that the Nile Delta, the land of the eternal summer, as Herodotus called it (2.26), was considered (at least initially) as the center of the inhabited earth? If this were the case, the distance from the Nile Delta (the center of Anaximander's map, see fig. 2) to the eastern ocean would correspond to the distance from the Nile Delta to the western ocean just beyond the Pillars of Hercules. And the distance from the Nile Delta to where the Nile originated in the southern ocean would have to correspond to the distance from the Nile Delta to the northern ocean.[178] From this perspective, the distance from the Nile Delta to the Pillars of Hercules (and there must have been a reasonable idea of this distance given that the route was often traveled) would have to correspond to the

FIGURE 2
Anaximander's Map of the Inhabited World

distance from the Delta to the southern ocean. These are some of the contraints that follow (or would follow) if the map of the earth (inhabited or not) attributed to Anaximander was indeed drawn as round and encircled by the ocean. Moreover, the size of the seas may also have influenced Anaximander's conception of the relative sizes of the land masses of the three continents. The Nile and the Phasis would be the natural divisions of the continents for Anaximander. Since India and the Indus only appear to enter into the world picture with Hecataeus, the eastern-most point of Anaximander' map would be the outermost point of the Persian empire (although an allowance could be made for more land depending again on the distance surmised from the Delta to the Pillars of Hercules, or to the west coast of Libya). The number of fixed points or indications on Anaximander's map (that is, the various rivers, seas, cities and countries and their corresponding peoples) would depend on the dimensions of the map itself.

As I noted above, different scholars postulate different centers for Anaximander's map (including, Delphi, Delos, and Didyma). If the Nile Delta was indeed the center of Anaximander's map, there would be an interesting analogy with Anaximander's cosmological model, which places an immobile earth at the center of three concentric rings representing the sun, the moon, and the fixed stars. This would suggest that Anaximander may have envisioned Egypt as the cosmological, geographical, and political center of the earth, if not, the universe. This would bode well with our previous analysis. However, Anaximander is well aware that the enlightenment has begun, and whatever the Greek debt to their distant cousins, Miletus rather than the Nile Delta should now be the new center.[179] Here geography, politics, and cosmology will find their new home.

4

The *Historia Peri Phuseōs* from Xenophanes to the Atomists

PROLOGUE

In this chapter, I will attempt to show that most of the pre-Socratics not only wrote works of the *Peri phuseōs* type, but that their respective works followed a scheme somewhat similar to Anaximander's. This does not mean that every pre-Socratic was preoccupied with exactly the same content. For example, heroic genealogies are found in some pre-Socratics but not in others. I will argue, however, that all pre-Socratics attempted to account for the origin and development of the present order of things and their respective accounts were comprised in the scheme of three elements: a cosmogony, a zoogony, and a politogony. Of course, an investigation into the origin and evolution of the present state of things, that is, an *historia peri phuseōs*, obviously implies a reflection on the accounts of the predecessors. This reflection often gave rise to a very different system (or conclusions) such that it may appear we are dealing with a different topic or subject matter. But this is only an appearance. For example, even if Pythagoras is much more preoccupied with the meaning of life and death, all this is inherent to his system. Even if Parmenides seems to have abandoned an inquiry of the *peri phuseōs* type in order to pursue an exhaustive study of what it means for something to exist, this only follows from his penetrating analysis of his Milesian predecessors reflections on *phusis* as principle (*phusis* as *archē*). Thus, after completing his exposé on being/existence, Parmenides turns to a cosmogony and an anthropogony that is based, at least in part, on his previous analysis of being/existence. Furthermore, by attempting to show that all pre-Socratics wrote a work of the *peri phuseōs* type, I concur with Aristotle (*On the Heavens* 279b12), the first to postulate that the universe did not have a beginning in time.

In what follows, I will examine each pre-Socratic individually in the chronological order that most scholars would concur with. It is important to be cognizant of the fact that the idea of *phusis,* and the tripartite schema that presupposes the notion, is invariably in the background. Given the importance of the political context, I begin each pre-Socratic with a brief analysis of their respective historical milieu.

XENOPHANES OF COLOPHON

There is consensus among modern scholars that Xenophanes lived an exceptionally long life from around 575 to 475 BCE (KRS 1983, 164–65; Guthrie 1962, 362–64; and Lesher 1992, 3; and above chap. 3). In fact, by his own account, Xenophanes was alive and writing at the age of ninety-two (DK21B8). Xenophanes was born in Colophon, in Ionia. There is a report that Xenophanes was an auditor of Anaximander. Given the dates, the proximity of Colophon to Miletus, and the fact that Miletus was the intellectual and economic center of Ionia at the time, there is no good reason to doubt this. Moreover, Colophon was a member of the famous Panionian League (Gorman 2001, 124–27). This is the same League that Thales was purported to have addressed around 545 BCE, suggesting that they form a common, centrally located government to counter the Persian threat (Herodotus 1.142–52). Colophon was conquered by Harpagus the Mede in 546 BCE, and Xenophanes states he fled his native city—probably not without a good fight—following its conquest around the age of twenty-five (DK21B22). Miletus, for its part, was able to form a special pact *(xenia)* with Cyrus (as with Croseus and Alyattes before him) and thus avoid destruction. This may have prompted Xenophanes to spend some time there before continuing his errant life. He eventually migrated to Western Greece, where he is connected with several cities including Zancle, Catana (home of the first written lawcodes), and Elea (Diogenes Laertius 9.18 = DK21A1; Guthrie 1962, 363–64) and where he eventually died around 470 BCE.

Socially, Xenophanes was an aristocrat like his Milesian counterparts. And he had similar social and political views. He solemnly condemns the excessively luxurious display of his countrymen before the fall of Colophon (DK21B3) and believes that contributions to good government *(eunomiē)* and the material prosperity of a city are far more important than physical feats (DK21B2). Indeed, Xenophanes argues that his own wisdom *(sophiē)* is superior because it has public value rather than just a personal one (DK21B2.11–14). We have here reflections of a moderate; of a man of the center; a man in pursuit of the common good.

Unlike the Milesians, Xenophanes wrote in verse. It is in this form that he composed his work *Peri phuseōs*. A number of scholars have contested the authenticity of a poem called *Peri phuseōs,*[1] but this is due, at least in part, to Aristotle's rather negative opinion of Xenophanes as a philosopher and physicist.[2] Indeed, Aristotle characterizes him as a sort of *theologos*. However, later ancient sources mention a poem called *Peri phuseōs,* and one of those sources has also given us one of Xenophanes more famous fragments (DK21B18 = Stobaeus, *Physical Opinions* 1.8.2).[3] Xenophanes also composed a poem or group of poems called the *Silloi,* or *Satires*. There has been some attempt to assign the fragments to their respective work (e.g., Deichgräber 1938, 1–31), but this appears to be a pointless exercise. The fragments do attest to the same "spirit of Ionian *historia* or 'inquiry'" (Lesher 1992, 4) as his Milesian contemporaries and predecessors (Barnes 1982, 83–4). It is possible to reconstruct from fragments and doxographical evidence the general lines of the same type of *historia peri phuseōs* that we find in Anaximander. Barnes contends that Xenophanes' poem *On Nature* may have begun with fragment 34 on human knowledge (Barnes 1982, 83–4; Fränkel 1973, 128). This makes good sense if one considers that Xenophanes says he will discuss all things (*peri pantōn* B34.2). Alternatively, it makes a good concluding sentence, for Xenophanes also says that what precedes is *tetelesmenon* or "what has been brought to completion" (B34.3).[4] At any rate, fragments B10 through B16 are no less enticing since their intent is clearly to undermine the traditional view about the gods (as expounded, in particular, by Homer and Hesiod) before replacing this view with something more dignified and scientific, that is, involving critical inquiry and reflection.

It is possible that Xenophanes began his *historia peri phuseōs* with a critical assessment of the traditional view of the gods (B10–16). He attributes this view to Homer and Hesiod and for good reason. As Herodotus notes, it was Homer and Hesiod who gave the Greeks their theogonies and described the gods for them (2.53). Moreover, they also explained how the present order of things (natural and social) was established. Several generations later, Plato could still say that many considered Homer the educator of the Greeks and that we should govern our lives according to his teachings (*Republic* 10.606e; also DK21B10). In *Laws* 10 (886c), Plato explicitly states that "the most ancient accounts [about the gods] first relate how the original generation *(hē prōtē phusis)* of the sky and so forth occurred and then, shortly after, relate how the gods were born *(theogonian)* and how, once born, they behaved toward one another" (886c3–6; see also *Euthyphro* 6b–c on a literal interpretation). Plato is referring here to Hesiod and his mythical account of how the present order of things was established.[5] Consequently, a good way for Xenophanes to begin his *historia* is with a critique of (or direct attack on) the two icons of traditional theology: Homer and Hesiod.

Xenophanes, critique begins with the assertion that Homer and Hesiod attributed many things to the gods that humans consider blameworthy and reproachful, including theft, adultery, and mutual deceit (DK21B11, 12). More important, Homer and Hesiod are associated with the idea that gods are anthropomorphic and characterized as "being born" (*gennasthai theous* DK21B14.1). On the other hand, the poets characterize the gods as *aiei* or "eternal" (*theoi aiei eontes*) (Homer *Iliad* 1.290; Hesiod, *Theogony* 21, 33 etc.; see also Lesher 1992, 87). Xenophanes seems to have argued that there is a contradiction here. This may explain Diogenes Laertius' statement that Xenophanes was the first to declare that "everything that comes to be is perishable" (*pan to gignomenon phtharton esti*, DK21A1). Of course, Xenophanes was not the first to hold this position; it was also argued by Anaximander. But it certainly points to Xenophanes' own reason for abandoning the popular poetic conception of divinity.

The anthropomorphic conception of the gods is amplified by the fact that Homer and Hesiod portray the gods as being totally Hellenic in body, speech, and even clothing (DK21B14.2). Xenophanes is clearly aware of the absurdity of this popular conception with the reminder that Ethiopians and Thracians portray their respective gods (according to Xenophanes' empirical investigation) in a like manner: "snub-nosed and black" in the case of the Ethiopians and "blue-eyed and red-haired" in the case of the Tracians (DK21B16). In fact, he contends, if animals could draw, they would do precisely the same thing (DK21B15).[6]

Once the traditional gods are sufficiently deprived of their anthropomorphic attributes, Xenophanes endeavours to reconstruct a new theology based on attributes that would be acceptable, and based on the new rationalism inspired by Anaximander. The new theology takes a radical new twist with the native Colophonian. He contends there is only one god (*eis theos*, DK21B23.1), or rather only one god who is worthy of the name (contra Lesher 1992, 99), and that this divinity does not resemble mortals in body or thought (DK21B23.2).[7] Of this divine entity Xenophanes states that the "whole" (*oulos*) of it sees (*horai*), knows (*noei*), and hears (*akouei*), (DK21B24).[8] Moreover, "he can shake (*kradainai*)[9] all things (*panta*) effortlessly (*apaneuthe*) by the thought of his mind (*noou phreni*)" (DK21B25) and yet "he always remains in the same place, not moving at all (*kinoumenos ouden*)," for "it is it not fitting for him to travel (*meterchesthai*) to different places at different times" (DK21B26).

It is not surprising that Xenophanes, description of god as the greatest god (*megistos theos*, B23.1), has been the subject of much controversy. There seems little doubt Xenophanes is espousing monotheism despite the seemingly polytheistic expression that the one god is the "greatest among gods and men" (*theoisi kai anthrōpoisi megistos*) (see Barnes 89).[10] The primary question is how does the greatest god relate to the physical universe. Following Aristotle (*Metaphysics* 986b24 = DK21A5), a number of prominent scholars have argued that Xenophanes' god is spherical and identical with the universe (e.g., Guthrie 1962, 376–83; for a list of modern scholars see Lesher 1992, 100). Fränkel (1973, 331), following Clement (introduction to B23), contends Xenophanes' god is actually bodiless *(asōmatos)*. What is clear is that Xenophanes' god is an active principle, a true *archē kineseōs,* that pervades the primordial substance and somehow governs or controls its "physical processes" (B25; see McKirahan 1994, 63). From this perspective, there are both passive and active principles, with the latter having an ontological rather than a temporal superiority. Therefore, the greatest god is analogous to Plato's conception of the divinity in *Laws* 10 and *Timaeus* 34b, where there is no distinction between god and the world, although the divinity is portrayed in similar anthropomorphic terms as synoptically governing the universe. But Xenophanes' "greatest god" is clearly inspired by the Milesian conception of the primordial substance. Indeed, there is no reason to believe Xenophanes was not explicating certain implications that would follow from the Milesian conception of the primordial substance from the perspective of traditional religion. In fact, if Anaximander (or Anaximenes) were confronted with Xenophanes' conception of the greatest god, would their own answers be any different? Indeed, is there any good reason to believe that Xenophanes or his Milesian counterparts did not treat his greatest god as a cosmogonical and cosmological principle (contra Broadie 1999, 212)? As we saw above, Anaximander describes the *apeiron* as a conscious and intelligent agent even if the processes it initiated are purely natural. Moreover, there is a sense in which the *apeiron* continues to control all the natural processes. In fact, the terminology employed by Anaximander is no less provocative than Xenophanes'. And this is also the case with Anaximenes! His primordial substance, *aēr,* is again not only characterized as divine, but is what holds together and controls *(sugkratei)* both the macrocosm and the microcosm via *psuchē* or soul (DK13B2). Moreover, gods *(theoi)* and other divine things *(theia)* are said to be the offspring *(apogonoi)* of air (DK13A7.1 = Hippolytus, *Refutation* 1.7.1).[11] Given Xenophanes' connection with the Milesians, he may very well have been thinking along these lines when he stated that his one god is the "greatest among gods and men" (DK21B23).

This last remark suggests that Xenophanes believed the universe did have a beginning in time. There is no fragment or doxographical report explicitly stating this, but a number of fragments and reports certainly suggest it.[12] Xenophanes states all things *(panta)* that come to be *(ginontai)* and grow *(phuontai)* are earth and water (DK21B29, 33). This is not restricted to living things, but includes meteorological phenomena (DK21B30) and the heavenly bodies themselves (DKA32, 33.3).[13] Moreover, water and earth are identified with the primary opposites wet and dry (DK21A29) and these in turn are associated with the great alternating cycles in which land (dry) encroaches on sea (wet) followed by wet (sea) encroaching on dry (land) (DK21A32,33). Xenophanes reached this conclusion after his observations of fossils (DK21A33 and above chapter 3). He conjectures that while living things are derived from a combination of earth and water (land and sea), fossils and shells found inland and on mountains suggests the sea (and mud or slime) must have once covered what is now dry land (whence the imprints). However, he also conjectured that the land will again sink into the sea and when it does and becomes mud, humanity (and no doubt living things in general) will be destroyed but will again regenerate under similar conditions around the earth's *kosmoi*.

The fact that cyclical processes may have been confined to the earth does not preclude the universe having a beginning in time (contra Guthrie 1962, 389).[14] What is certain is that Xenophanes believed, as Anaximander did, that humans and other living things emerged from primordial humidity or slime (no doubt activated by the heat of the sun: DK21A42 = Aetius). Indeed, the evidence for anthropogony and zoogony are uncontested. But did Xenophanes terminate his *historia* with an anthropogony or did he conclude with a politogony? The majority of scholars contend that Xenophanes developed a theory of the origin of civilization. Let's examine the evidence.

The two most famous and most discussed fragments are B18 and B34. B18 states that "the gods *(theoi)* did not reveal to men all things from the beginning *(ap'archēs)*, but, by searching *(zētountes)*, they discover *(epheuriskousin)* what is better *(ameinon)* in time *(chronōi)*." Many scholars understand this statement as an expression of faith in human progress (e.g., Guthrie 1962, 399; Edelstein 1967, 3–19; Fränkel 1973, 121).[15] I concur with this, but a few observations are in order. It is unclear what Xenophanes means by "gods," especially after undermining the anthropomorphic conception. There is also the question of what Xenophanes means by "from the beginning" *(ap'archēs)*. Humans and other living things were not, strictly speaking, created by the gods or the greatest god. What is clear is that humans have a real beginning in time and that they emerged from primordial humidity. At this "beginning" in time, this point zero, humans did not live as they did later in time. This much is also clear. But it is not clear how much time Xenophanes thought had elapsed before the present period. He was aware (via Egypt) that it was indeed a very long time. Did he believe that humans were provided with any of the necessities of life at the outset? Whence the expression that "the gods *(theoi)* did not reveal to men all things *(panta)* from the beginning *(ap'archēs)*." Did Xenophanes have something of this nature in mind? It is difficult to imagine that Xenophanes would not have reflected on this. He clearly has faith in intelligence *(sophiē,* B1.14), the practical intelligence that develops with experience over time (on the meaning of *sophiē,* see Lesher 1992, 55–56). It is possible he associates the discovery of the various arts with the gods, but the gods may be more closely linked here with cultural heros as in Plato (see *Laws* 3.677d). In conjunction with this, we are told he even went so far as to repudiate divination (DK21A51, 52), which is really quite extraordinary given the period. On the other hand, Xenophanes notes that Lydians were the first *(prōtos)* to coin money (DK21B4) and Thales was the first *(prōtos)* to predict an eclipse of the sun (DK21B19). But these references are clearly recent discoveries. While the reference to fossils is a clear indication he believed the earth (and thus humanity) had a relatively long history; the reference that he wrote poems about the foundation of Colophon and Elea (DK21A1) point to a passion for more recent history—although Colophon itself had a rather long history since it appears to date back to the Mycenean period—(see Boardman 1999, 29). Elea was founded by the Phocaeans about 535 BCE (Boardman 189). In conjunction with this, we see that Hecataeus' rational approach to genealogies (in his prose work *Genealogies*) is also closely associated with foundations. More importantly, we see there is a close link between geology, geography and history; these three ingredients are all found in Xenophanes.

The other famous fragment, B34, is more difficult to access: ". . . and of course the clear and certain truth no man has seen nor will there be anyone who knows about the gods and what I say about all things. For even if, in the best case, one happened to speak just of what has been brought to pass, still he himself would not know. But opinon *(dokos)* is allotted to all" (trans. Lesher).

Lesher notes "there is as yet no 'received' or 'standard' view of fragment 34," and he summarizes six existing interpretations: Sceptic, Empiricist, Rationalist, Fallibilist, Critical Philosopher, and Natural Empiricist (1992, 160). This fragment may have less to do with a theory of progress than with the epistemological status of this claim or any preceding claims in his investigation into the origin and development of the present order of things.

Xenophanes is rather emphatic that "the clear and certain truth" *(to saphes)* about the gods, or anything else that preceded *(peri pantōn* B34.2), can be no better than likely *(eoikota* B35),[16] albeit more likely than those of his predecessors (and no doubt certain contemporaries like Pythagoras DK21B7) because his investigations are based on empirical evidence and practical intelligence. Thus, while *to saphes* about the gods may be impossible, empirical evidence leads to the conclusion that gods are not anthropomorphic. In sum, empirical observation is probably the most important criterion in reaching an informed/intelligent conclusion/decision.[17] And it is the same practical intelligence *(sophiē,* B1.14) that assists the state of achieving "good government" or *eunomiē* 21B2.19 (see Fränkel in Mourelatos 1974, n118). In the final analysis, it is practical intelligence combined with empirical evidence that will/may lead in time to what is best. Whether or not humans are capable of attaining truth, the fact remains that the *historia* or inquiry into the present order of things is well worth the effort, for it gives us a better understanding of what is best.

PYTHAGORAS AND THE PYTHAGOREANS

Like Xenophanes, Pythagoras of Samos was born around 570 in Ionia (Von Fritz 1950, 92; Guthrie 1962, 173; Kahn 2001, 6). Although Pythagoras apparently wrote nothing, he is considered as the most famous of the pre-Socratic philosophers. Indeed, because of his mathematical genius his ancient admirers considered him the greatest mind in all antiquity. But much of Pythagoras' fame is shrouded in mystery and this is compounded by the fact that it was a Pythagorean tradition to attribute all discoveries to the master.

There is consensus that Pythagoras believed in the immortality of the human soul and its progress through a series of incarnations. More precisely, he believed in a doctrine of metempsychosis, which is the belief that the same soul can successively animate several bodies, including human, animal, or vegetable.[18] To fully appreciate the novelty and subsequent success of this doctrine (at least in western Greece) we must remember that according to traditional Greek religion, immortality was reserved for the gods.

There has been much discussion on the origin of this theory, of which Pythagoras' contemporary Xenophanes is well aware (DK21B7). Herodotus (2.123; 4.95), who is only a generation later than Pythagoras, contends that it was derived from Egypt and, as M. L. West (1971, 62) notes, "Herodotus' testimony is not to be rejected lightly." Other scholars argue that the Egyptians did not have a theory of metempsychosis although they did believe in the afterlife, and that it must have been derived from India, where such a doctrine did exist (e.g., Kahn, 2001, 18–19).[19] But Egyptian religion is rich enough to allow any number of interpretations (the ability to change forms is certainly native). In any event, one can well imagine that numerous sects were thriving in an open city like Naucratis. There was, of course, an intimate relation between the island of Samos and ancient Egypt before Pythagoras' departure for southern Italy (or western Greece). Diogenes Laertius (*Lives* 8.3) states that the tyrant Polycrates of Samos (ca. 538–23) gave Pythagoras a letter of introduction to his ally, Pharoah Amasis. Pythagoras' travels to Egypt (and elsewhere) were already mentioned by Isocrates (436–338 BCE) in his *Busiris* 28 (see also Herodotus above). We don't know precisely why Pythagoras left Samos. On his return from Egypt, he may have wanted to create a brotherhood analogous to the one he initiated in western Greece (see below), but it was seen as a direct challenge to Polycrates' power. Aristoxenus, a pupil of Aristotle, certainly suggests this when he states that on his return from Egypt,

Pythagoras tried to set up a school in Samos (Atheneus 162c = frag. 91 Wehri). On the other hand, given his puritanical reputation, he may have found the hedonism associated with the court of Polycrates intolerable.

It was during the tyranny of Polycrates (ca. 538–23) that the island of Samos was at the height of its power and prosperity. Indeed, before Pythagoras migrated to Croton, two technical marvels of the ancient world were already initiated by Polycrates: the Dipteros II and the Eupalinos tunnel. Could these two technological wonders and the mathematical precision they entailed have been executed without certain technical expertise derived from Egyptian architects? Did the Egyptian priestly class influence the exclusiveness generally associated with the Pythagorean brotherhood? Given that the pyramid represents "the center of creative forces where ordered life of the universe had begun" (Frankfort 1949, 31)—indeed, where a new beginning will emerge for the deceased—may this not have inspired the famous Pythagorean doctrine of the tetractys and the notion of the tetractys (which has the shape of a pyramid) as the source and root of nature?

There is also consensus that Pythagoras advocated a *tropos tou biou* or "way of life" governed by a moral and religious code of conduct. The Pythagorean way of life is closely connected with his doctrine of immortality.[20] It is not surprising that Pythagoreans played a pivotal role in politics. Indeed, it is said that shortly after his arrival in Italy, Pythagoras gave them a constitution. It is unclear what type of constitution he advocated, but Diogenes Laertius (8.3) contends that he and his followers governed the state so well that it merited the name of aristocracy, or "government of the best." Given that Pythagoras appears to be descended from the merchant class (Guthrie 1962, 173) rather than the aristocracy, what we have here is the emergence of an intellectual aristocracy, albeit one based on a way of life, and Pythagoras' passion to reform society. But it seems that passion coupled with secrecy and exclusiveness could be a mixed blessing.

According to Porphyry, Pythagoras left the island of Samos around the age of 40 (ca. 530) to escape the tyranny of Polycrates, which had become intolerable for a free man (DK14A8). He settled in Croton, in western Italy, which was founded around 710 (see Boardman 1999, 197). Shortly before the arrival of Pythagoras, Croton had been defeated and demoralized by Locri, but in 510 BCE Croton was able to defeat and destroy the famous city and former Milesian colony of Sybaris. The military (and economic) success of Croton is attributed in large part to Pythagoras. It is unclear how this occurred, although Porphyry reports that on his arrival in Croton, he made such a formidable impression on the governing body that he was invited to address the young men of Croton, the children, and finally the assembly of women (*Life of Pythagoras* 18 = DK14A8a). We are also told he married a Crotonian and this may have aided his swift rise to power (DK14A13 = Iamblichus,

Pythagorean Life 170).[21] In fact, the general who lead the Crotonians to victory against the Sybarites was, according to Diodorus of Sicily, the Pythagorean Milo (DK14A14; see also Iamblichus *PL* 177).

Pythagoras and his followers enjoyed uninterrupted power and influence over Croton and neighbouring cities for twenty years. The political power of the Pythagoreans was established through a society or community *(hetaireia),* and its formidable and lasting success is well documented (see Kahn 2001, 7–8; on their influence, see Polybius 2.39). It is this influence coupled with the secrecy that encircled the school (or society) that eventually lead to a number of violent anti-Pythagorean outbursts. One of these occurred during Pythagoras' lifetime and led to his own banishment around 510 BCE. It is reported he died as a refugee in Metapontum shortly after.[22]

What about Pythagoras and *peri phuseōs* tradition? Was Pythagoras interested in an *historia* of the *peri phuseōs* type? Some prominent scholars argue that Pythagoras was a religious prophet rather than a natural philosopher (e.g., Burkert 1972; Huffman 1993). Indeed, they contend Pythagoras was concerned with neither Ionian style *historia* nor with the view that the universe was governed by number and proportion (a view prominent in later Pythagoreans). But if this were the case, it would be difficult to explain why his younger contemporary Heraclitus (ca. 540–480) contended that Pythagoras was a polymath who practiced *historia* more than any other (DK22B129). More important, as Kahn notes (2001, 17), Empedocles (ca. 492–32), a true follower of Pythagoras, is clearly both a natural philosopher and a religious prophet (see below). Most important of all is the fact that Pythagoras' doctrine of the metempsychosis is premised on the kinship of nature. This is not new. Pythagoras' Ionian contemporaries believed the universe, as a whole, was a living creature and that there was a correlation between the macrocosm and the microcosm. Indeed, in the case of Anaximander, there was a correlation between man, nature, and society. However, Pythagoras progressed further. His belief in the kinship of nature was based on mathematics. If the universe exhibits structure and order, it is because it is arranged according to numerical ratios. This is what makes the universe a *kosmos:* a word that connotes order, fitness, and beauty, according to Pythagoras, in the final analysis (albeit not limited to this), the study of these structural principles should enable us to develop (and stimulate) order and structure in our own souls, and to become one with the universal soul, the sine qua non of human existence.

It is often stated that what distinguishes Ionians from Italians, in general, and from Pythagoras and the Pythagoreans, in particular, is that the Ionians were entirely concerned with disinterested cosmological speculations while the Italians were in search of a *tropos tou biou* or "way of life"(e.g., Guthrie 1962, 4 and 1950, 34).[23] But we see the reality as more complex. Just as there is good evidence that the *historia* of the Milesians, in general, and of Anaximander, in particular, has a socio-political connection, there is good evidence that for both Pythagoras and the Pythagoricians the way of life they advocated was premised on an *historia* of the *peri phuseōs* type. This was the only way of establishing and demonstrating an intimate connection between man and the universe.

According to Aristotle, when Pythagoreans undertake an investigation into the nature of all things *(peri phuseōs panta)*, they speak of the effective generation of the universe, *gennōsi to ouranon (Metaphysics* 1.989b3–4). The description Aristotle gives of their cosmogony is analogous to that of the foetus. Aristotle contends that for the Pythagoreans the universe started (or may have started) from a seed *(ek spermatos)*[24] and managed to grow by drawing in *(eilketo)* the parts of the infinite to which it was closest.[25] This comparison was confirmed by the second half of the fifth century Pythagorean, Philolaus of Croton, the first Pythagorean who left us written documents and a work entitled *Peri phuseōs*.[26] According to fragments at our disposal, Philolaus chose unlimited and limiting elements (or unlimiteds and limiters) as his *phusis* as *archē* (DK44B1–4).[27] Since these principles are neither similar nor of the same type, a third principle, *harmonia*, or consonance, is required to bring order to (or unite) the whole and thus form a *kosmos* (DK44B1–3, 6; and Huffman 1999, 81). Thus, according to Diogenes Laertius, Philolaus began his *historia peri phuseōs* as follows: "Nature in the world-order *(ha phusis d'en tōi kosmōi)* was fitted together harmoniously *(harmochthē)* from the unlimited things *(apeirōn)* and also from limiting ones *(perainontōn),* both the world-order as a whole and all things within it" (DK44B1).[28] And according to Philolaus' cosmogonical account, the central fire *(hestia)* in the middle of the sphere, equated with the One *(to hen),* was the first thing to be harmonized and generated (DK44B7; see Huffman 1993, 202: 227–30; 1999, 82).[29] The fact that the first thing to be generated was the central fire (or the hot) and that it draws in air (or the cold) shows to what degree Philolaus was following the Ionian cosmogonical tradition (Huffman 1993, 202; 213).[30] The process suggests the imposition of the limiting on the unlimited in analogy with the form-giving male sperm impregnating the female (on the male/female correlation, see Guthrie 1962, 277–78).[31] It seems that *harmonia* somehow initiates the cosmogonical process by causing the limiting element (or elements) to draw in (and thus impregnate) the unlimited element or elements around it (see Huffman 1993, 140).

Once the cosmogonical process is complete, Philolaus' cosmological model consists of ten heavenly bodies; at the center is the fire or hearth. The ten heavenly bodies are the counter earth, the earth, the moon, the sun, the five visible planets, and the fixed stars.[32] Fire occupies the center because it is seen as the most noble element and the center as the most noble place. The counter earth was postulated to arrive at the perfect number 10. Pythagoreans believed

10 was perfect for two major reasons. On the one hand, the first four numbers whose sum was ten (1 + 2 + 3 + 4 = 10)—the famous Pythagorean *tetraktys* (= the sum of the first four numbers)—were behind the numerical relationships or attunement that held the universe together: the octave 1:2, the fifth 2:3, and the fourth 3:4.[33] On the other hand, the first four numbers were considered the source and root of nature insofar as they represented a point, a line, a surface, and a solid respectively (the so-called building blocks of the universe). The perfect number was illustrated by the sacred figure of the *tetraktys:*

As for human beings, there appears to be a close analogy between their origin and composition and that of the universe (DK44A27 and Huffman 1993, 290f). The primary constituent of the body is the hot and this is associated with the sperm *(to sperma).* But once the animal is born, it breaths in, as in the case of the universe, the external air, which is cold (DK44A27).[34]

It is difficult to know for certain if this cosmogony and anthropogony is essentially that of Philolaus of Crotone or whether it originates with Pythagoras himself. What is certain is that there are clear Milesian influences for much of Philolaus' theory, which in turn strongly suggests that Pythagoras' own doctrine was grounded in an *historia* of the *peri phuseōs* type. The geometrical structure of the universe appears to be an Anaximandrean inspiration. Given the dates and the proximity of Samos to Miletus, Pythagoras may have first studied with Anaximander, as Porphyry states in his *Life of Pythagoras* (11–2; see also Iamblichus, *PL* 11–9 and Kahn 2001, 5). The idea that air plays the same role in the universe as it does in humans, as well as the notion that humans and the universe are constructed and function in a similar manner, is explicit in another Milesian and contemporary of Pythagoras, Anaximenes. The notion of the unlimited is typically Milesian, and the numerical ratios are clearly part of Anaximander's cosmological model. The term *harmonia,* with a cosmic interpretation, is also found in Heraclitus (ca. 540–480), another Ionian and contemporary of Pythagoras. More important, an early follower of Pythagoras, Hippasus of Metapontum, is not only a proponent of fire as a first principle (Aristotle, *Metaphysics* 984a7), but is presented as having done work in the area of music and mathematics (see DK18A7; Guthrie 1962, 320–22; Mueller 1997, 292; Kahn 2001, 35). Given that musical consonances are premised on the famous doctrine of the tetractys, which originated with Pythagoras himself (Kahn 2001, 35), there is no reason to assume that most of the *historia peri phuseōs* found in Philolaus did not originate with Pythagoras. Whether Pythagoras' primary interest was mathematical or religious, the fact remains that the way of life he advocated was contingent on an *historia* of the *peri phuseōs* type.

What about the origin of society and politogony in Pythagoras and the Pythagoreans?[35] According to Porphyry, Pythagoras told his disciples that past events repeat themselves in a cyclical process and that nothing is new in an absolute sense (Porphyry, *Life of Pythagoras*, 19 = DK14A8a). This appears to exclude an idea of progress. But what if Pythagoras believed that he lived in the first cycle? In this case, he may have seen his mathematical discoveries as a contribution to progress for the coming cycles. But whatever the case, the fact remains that two of the primary goals of the Pythagoreans were to discover the laws of the universe and to live in conformity with these laws. In the final analysis, it is through research and discovery that man can progress to understand how to live as social animals in conformity with nature.

HERACLITUS OF EPHESUS

Heraclitus was a native of Ephesus, which is a short distance north of Miletus in Asia Minor. There is consensus that he was born around 540 BCE and died around 480 BCE (on the dating, see Guthrie 1962, 408–408; Kahn 1979, 1–3; KRS 1983, 181–183). Heraclitus was a younger contemporary of Pythagoras, Xenophanes, and Hecataeus, all of whom he mentions by name (DK22B40).

As in the case of Miletus (Herodotus 1.47; 5.65; 9.97), legend has it Ephesus was founded by one of the sons of the Athenian king, Codrus (Strabo 14.632; the sons were Neleus and Androclus respectively). Diogenes Laertius (9.6 = DK22A1), following Antisthenes of Rhodes' *Successions* (second century BCE), contends Heraclitus was a member of the royal house of Ephesus and that he renounced the title of king *(basileus)* in favour of his younger brother. Even if this would make him a direct descendent of Androclus (the Androclids or Basilidai of Ephesus like the Neleids of Miletus), the legendary founder of Ephesus (Strabo 14.632), as some suggest (e.g., Guthrie 1962, 409), it would only mean Heraclitus would have been entitled (or would have been entitled had he chosen) to certain privileges of a religious rather than political nature (perhaps like the Branchadai in Miletus; see Burkert 1985, 95). Many commentators draw the conclusion from this that Heraclitus was indifferent to politics (Guthrie 1962, 408–410; Kahn 1979, 3; McKirahan 1994, 148). Indeed, Diogenes Laertius (9.3) relates the anecdote that Heraclitus preferred playing dice with children to playing politics with his fellow citizens. However, the reality appears much more complex (as McKirahan 1994, 148 correctly notes).

Ephesus was confronted with struggles similar to those of Miletus with its Lydian neighbor.[36] However, it also profited from Lydian largess. It was under the sponsorship of the Lydian King Croesus that the great marble temple of Artemis (a structure that earned a spot in the list of Wonders) was built in Ephesus around 550 BCE. It was in this temple that Heraclitus dedicated his book. When Heraclitus was born, around 540 BCE, the Lydian empire under Croesus (560–546) had since crumbled, and Ephesus was now under the watchful eye of the Persians (Cyrus, 559–30; Cambyses, 530–22; and Darius, 521–486). As part of the Persian Empire, Ephesus and the other Ionian cities, was subject to the wishes of the Great King. During this period, Ionian cities were generally ruled by tyrants, who were more or less endorsed by the Persians. But Heraclitus' blistering attack on his fellow citizens for the expulsion of Hermodorus (in DK22B121) suggests both some degree of local independence and some type of popular government.[37] We know very little about Hermodorus and what we do know is probably anecdotal (see Kahn 1979, 178). However, it is tempting to see him as an enlightened tyrant who was interested in the rule of law, for the anecdote presents Hermodorus leaving for Rome to assist in composing their laws (Strabo, *Geography* 14.25 = DK22A3; Kahn 1979, 178). The only other individual Heraclitus mentions with praise (in the fragments we do have) is Bias of Priene (DK22B39). Bias is a statesman and one of the legendary seven sages who advised the Ionians at a meeting of the Panionium following the Persian victory (Herodotus 1.170) to emigrate *en masse* and found a new city in Sardinia. Bias is also well known for his sharp rebuke of common men. Diogenes Laertius (1.87, 88) attributes to him the expression "most men are *kakoi* or vile." This bodes well for the usual mentality projected on Heraclitus, but would somehow be counterintuitive for a legendary sage and if true, should be put in context. Aristotle (*Nicomachean Ethics* 5.1, 1130a1) quotes Bias as stating that "power *(archē)* will reveal the man." This is like the expression *in vino veritas,* and most of us, whatever our political affiliation, would probably concur with Bias. It may have been the constant infighting for political power that helped formulate many of Heraclitus' rather harsh personal remarks toward his fellow citizens (indeed mankind in general). Moreover, Bias is also reputed as saying that "the strongest democracy is the one wherein all fear the law as their master" (Plutarch, *Moralia* 154d, trans. Vlastos). This bodes well with Heraclitus' exaltation of the "one" in opposition to the "many" as we will see below.

The Ephesians and the Milesians were hostile to tyrants (see DK22B121) and were willing to risk everything to overthrow them. Herodotus (5.100) includes Ephesus among the Ionian cities that participated in the famous revolt against the Persians (499–94) although it was spared the fate of Miletus. Ephesus was, in fact, a member of the Panionian League (Herodotus 1.142–48; Gorman 2001, 124–28) and may even have been at its head (Boardman 1999, 32). Although the League essentially had a religious role, as we saw in the case of Bias of Priene whom Heraclitus compliments, it did meet to discuss political issues.

Scholars never ask what Heraclitus was doing while the city was being attacked by the Persians. In his view, "a right minded people must fight for the law as for the city wall" (DK22B 44, see also B114). And he did consider himself "right minded"! Themistius (*On Virtue* 40 = DK22A3b), describing the life of the Ephesians during the siege by the Persians which took place during the Ionian Revolt, states how Heraclitus convinced them to change their immoderate ways during the siege by consuming more frugally. There may be more than a grain of truth to this anecdote (on the same theme, see also Plutarch, *On Talking too Much* 17.511b = DK22A3b). Clement of Alexandria (DK22A3 = *Miscellanies* 1.65; *sōphronein* "sound thinking/self-control" is the most important excellence for Heraclitus = DK22B112) states that he convinced the tyrant Melancomas, a Persan supported Ephesian tyrant, to leave power. Contrary to Hermodorus, Melancomas may have been an unenlightened tyrant who was not among "the best." Heraclitus may have seen "war as father and king of all" (DK22B53; see also DK22 B22), but he doesn't appear to be adverse to peaceful solutions (DK22B43 "one must quench violence quicker than a blazing fire.")

Heraclitus' political stripes are best revealed in the famous fragment that "One person is ten thousand, if he is best *(aristos)*" (DK22B49). The "best" is he who understands and enacts the law and so "it is law also to obey the council of one" (DK22B33).

But if Heraclitus was not a convinced democrat (the prevalent mood in the Ionian world during the famous revolt), he may have had less sympathy for his immoderate fellow aristocrats whom he clearly didn't consider as *aristos*. To be *aristos* entailed practicing and excelling in the greatest excellence and wisdom *(aretē megistē kai sophiē)*, namely "sound (and moderate) thinking" *(sōphronein)*, which Heraclitus understands as speaking and acting according to the truth,[38] but to achieve this entails understanding things according to their nature *(kata phusin)* (DK22B112), and given that "nature *(phusis)* likes to hide" (DK22B123),[39] thus understanding nature is understanding unity in diversity.

Heraclitus was no man's fool! We can well imagine him refusing Darius' invitation to Persia, if there is any truth to Clement's claim, and given the political and cultural context of the period, it could very well be true.[40] The fragments depict a fiercely independent and highly original thinker who had little tolerance for traditional religion and ritual and who had little fear of publicly saying so (e.g., DK22B14–15, 155, 96; contempt for Homer DK22B42).

Heraclitus, already known as the Obscure in antiquity,[41] is probably the most controversial of all the pre-Socratic philosophers. Few scholars have a similar interpretation of Heraclitus; some modern commentators even doubt he wrote a book. The most sceptical of these commentators is G. S. Kirk (1954, 7). Kirk believes the fragments could be part of a collection of maxims composed by a student soon after Heraclitus' death.[42] Barnes (1982, 58; see also Gigon 1935, 58) argues that fragment one clearly points to the beginning or *prooemion* of an authentic book, and this is reinforced by Aristotle's reference (*Rhetoric* 1407b16) to the same passage with which, according to him, Heraclitus' book begins. As I noted above, Diogenes Laertius (9.6) contends that Heraclitus dedicated/deposited his book in the temple of Artemis and most scholars concur with this remark. This suggests Heraclitus wanted to make his book accessible to the public (Burkert 1985, 310) albeit as a book speaking out with both a human and divine voice (Most 1999, 359). In fact, it seems many copies of his book must have been in circulation soon after, since a whole school of Heracliteans appeared in the fifth century (Burkert 1985, 310; Kahn 1979, 3).[43]

While a number of fragments share certain features of oracles and maxims, Heraclitus' book follows the new Ionian tradition of *historia,* or more precisely, an *historia* of the *peri phuseōs* type, that is "a rational and systematic account of *all* things" (Long 1999, 13; Kahn 1979, 96–100). In conjunction with this, Heraclitus advocates a new way of life based on this *historia* (see Long 1999, 14 quoting Hadot; by quoting Euripides frag 910, Long appears to follow my own general thesis). This means there is an important correlation between nature and politics. Diogenes Laertius contends that "nature" was the unifying theme in the book (9.5), but that it was divided into three parts: cosmology *(peri tou pantos),* politics *(politikos),* and theology *(theologikos).* Diogenes (9.15) says the grammarian Diodotus contends that Heraclitus' book was not actually about nature but about politics *(peri politeias).* This is not surprising since Heraclitus clearly wants to ground, as McKirahan (1994, 148) correctly notes, "his views on law and politics in his cosmic theory." This deserves a closer examination in the context of an account of the *peri phuseōs* type.

At the beginning of his book *Peri Phuseōs,* Heraclitus claims that *all* things happen according to the *logos* (or account) that he provides (DK22B1) and, in conjunction with this, he claims that to give a true *logos* entails "distinguishing each thing according to its nature *(phusis)* and explaining how it is." As we saw in chapter 1, to know the *phusis* or "real constitution" of a thing (what makes it behave and appear as it does) entails knowledge of the processes that regulate its nature. These processes are the same processes behind the origin of the present order of things. But the relation between *logos* and *phusis* is far more complex in the case of Heraclitus. The term *logos* is not only employed by Heraclitus to qualify his true account, but he believes that the world exhibits an objective structure that can be revealed through *logos.*

Indeed, *logos* plays a role analogous to Anaximander's *apeiron* insofar as it is not only a material principle or *archē*, but that it controls all things (*logōi tōi ta hola dioikounti* DK22B72, 30, 66). For Heraclitus, if the most important thing in life is to comprehend the *logos,* the primary excellence is right thinking and wisdom (B112), and right thinking consists in the ability "to know how all things are steered through all things" (DK22B41). Did Heraclitus believe that a cosmogonical account was a necessary part of this?

In the physical universe, *logos* manifests in the form of fire. That is why the thunderbolt, like the *logos,* is said to govern all things (DK22B64–66, 16). It is as a function of the relation of fire to the world, which it governs, that one must judge whether or not one can speak of a cosmogony in Heraclitus' writings.

The world of Heraclitus, like that of the Milesians, is composed of a certain number of opposites. Although these opposites form a unity (i.e., the day and the night form a unity despite their opposition: DK22B53, 80), they nevertheless remain in perpetual conflict (DK22B67). For Heraclitus, in order to maintain an equilibrium in the *kosmos,* there must be an incessant battle between the opposites (DK22B67). In sum, since the combat is universal "combat or war *(polemos)* is the father of all things" (DK22B53), justice *(dikē)* is itself a battle (B80) but only insofar as it attempts to harmonize the opposites (DK22B8; see also 51, 54, 22).

There are two ways to interpret the battle between the opposites and still maintain the idea of justice. Using the terminology of Hussey (1972, 49–50), there is the "tension" interpretation and the "oscillation" interpretation. According to the "tension" interpretation, the battle or struggle between the opposites will *always* be in a state of equilibrium; gains in one region will be *simultaneously* offset by gains in another region by the opposite force or power. According to the "oscillation" interpretation, one of the opposites may completely dominate the other, albeit only for a predetermined amount of time after which the other opposite will prevail for a equal amount of time *ad infinitum.*

Now, if one opts for the first interpretation, it follows that Heraclitus' world is eternal. If one opts for the second interpretation, it follows that the world had a beginning in time and will be annihilated by a conflagration *(ekpurosis)* only to be reborn periodically.

Two notable partisans of the first interpretation are Kirk (1954; 307; 1983, 198) and Guthrie (1962, 450). They find support for their position in fragments DK22B30 and DK22B90, and they interpret the other fragments in light of these. Fragment 30 reads: "This *kosmos,* the same for all, none of the gods nor of humans has made, but it was always and is and shall be: an ever-living fire which is kindled in measures and extinguished in measures." Fragment 90 reads "All things are an exchange for fire and fire for all things, as goods for gold and gold for goods."

These fragments invalidate the Stoic attribution of a periodic *ekpurosis* to Heraclitus, if the word *kosmos* is understood to mean the world order as a whole (as Kirk and Guthrie do) and if one could be certain, on the one hand, that the fire that kindles and extinguishes itself does not affect the entire universe and if, on the other hand, that all the goods (the world in its variety) could never be entirely transformed into gold (fire). In conjunction with this, Kirk (1983, 198) and Guthrie (1962, 457) argue that Heraclitus' fire cannot be the primordial substance of all things, in the same sense as water for Thales, the *apeiron* for Anaximander, and air for Anaximenes. This is the case, they contend, because fire itself is an opposite and could never exist "solely in the form of physical fire" (Guthrie 1962, 457–58; and Kirk 1983, 200). Although fire is the continual source of natural processes (Kirk 1983, 212), it nonetheless has its specific region of the world: the sky. In light of this, Kirk contends Heraclitus' fragment B31 means that the world is, was, and will be composed of three masses: earth, water, and fire. This, in turn, suggests that the transformations occasioned by one or the other occurs simultaneously, and the total of each of the masses always remains the same. For example, if a particular quantity of earth dissolves into water (sea), an equivalent quantity of water (sea) condenses into earth elsewhere (Kirk 1983, 199). In essence, these are the arguments in favour of the "tension" interpretation, that is, the arguments in favour of the universe's eternity.[44]

Notable partisans of the second interpretation are Mondolfo (1958, 75–82), Kahn (1979, 224) and Robin (1921/1963, 97).[45] These scholars find support in their position in the ancient tradition itself. Indeed, there are several doxographical sources, all of which are derived from Theophrastus and which strongly conform to the "oscillation" interpretation.

According to Diogenes Laertius (DK22A1.8 = *Lives* 9.8.), "Fire is the basic element. All things are interchangable with fire, and they come to be by rarefaction and condensation. . . . The All is limited, constituting a single world, which is alternatively born from fire and dissolved into fire, and the succession of this endless cycle of alternating periods is fixed by Destiny."

According to Simplicius (DK22A5), "Hippasus of Metapontum and Heraclitus of Ephesus declare that reality is one and in motion and limited. Taking fire as the first principle they explain all things as derived from fire and resolved again into fire through the complementary processes of condensation and rarefaction; for fire, they assert, is the one essential nature that underlies appearances. Whatever occurs, Heraclitus declares, is a transformation of fire; and in what occurs he finds a certain order and definite time determined by necessity" (Simplicus, *Commentary on Aristotle's Physics* 22.23 = Theophrastus, *Physical Opinions* 1.475 = DK22A5).

According to Aetius (DK22A5), Heraclitus and Hippasus say that the first principle of all things is fire, and that all things both come to be from fire and complete their existence by turning into fire again. As the fire gets extinguished, things take shape and arrange themselves into an orderly universe. First by compression the dense earth is formed; then earth, being relaxed by fire, transforms itself into water; which, in turn, by rarefying, becomes air. At another time the universe and all the bodies that compose it are consumed by fire in conflagration (Aetius, 1.3.11 = DK22A5).

These doxographies agree on three essential points.

1. Fire is not only the continual source of natural processes, but it is also the primordial substance *(archē)* from which all things are derived and into which all things will return.[46]
2. All change is due to the processes of condensation and rarefaction of fire.
3. The world and all that it contains will be periodically annihilated by fire and subsequently renewed from this same substance.

In light of this, it is possible to arrive at an entirely different conclusion from the same fragments that Kirk and Guthrie used in their interpretation. According to Kahn (1960, 225), the term *kosmos,* in fragment B30, can mean "the entire organized cycle of elementary and vital transformation." Heraclitus could therefore be interpreted as saying that the *kosmos* is not the product of human or divine art but that it contains its own autonomous wisdom, which directs all things. From this perspective, the opposition is not between an eternal world and a created world, but between a living, immortal being and an inert object to which a plan of organisation would be applied externally. Thus, a fire which periodically lights and extinguishes itself is the symbol of a universal order that alternates between an extreme heat and an extreme cold. Consequently, the tradition which associated Heraclitus with the doctrine of a *Magnus Annus* and whose culminating points are a Great Summer and a Great Winter, is entirely credible.

As for fragment B90, it may be interpreted as stating that a single substance, in this case fire, can be disguised in various forms provided its transformations (which are its life) are equivalent. However, there is nothing to indicate that all the goods must eventually be transformed into gold for the cycle to be repeated. When Heraclitus states in fragment B125a that he wishes that fortune *(ploutos,* i.e., gold) not be denied to the Ephesians, it is precisely their destruction that he has in view.

Other fragments seem to confirm this interpretation. For example, in fragment B65, it is said that "fire is need *(chrēsmosunē)* and satiety *(koros)."* "Need" *(chrēsmosunē)* strongly suggests the necessity that enables the constitution of the world whereas "satiety" *(koros)* strongly suggests the state of plenitude which results after fire consumes everything it had originally exchanged. Fragment B66 appears to confirm this: "Fire in its advance will catch up with all things and judge them" (see also DK22B28b, where justice seems interchangeable with fire in a similar context). Heraclitus' world thus appears condemned to disappear. However, just as there is a regular return of day and night, and the seasons, Heraclitus must have believed that the universal conflagration was followed by a renewal of the universe which would coincide with the beginning and the end of the Great Year.[47]

If this interpretation is correct, there is indeed a cosmogony in Heraclitus' *historia*. In fact, certain fragments and doxographies suggest how his cosmogonic process unfolded. Heraclitus chose fire as the *phusis* as *archē*. In other words, fire is not only the principle of movement (i.e., the continual source of natural processes), but also the fundamental constituent of all things. According to the Ephesian, there is an upward path and a downward path and these are related to the processes of rarefaction and of condensation (Diogenes Laertius 9.8 = DK22A1.8; Aetius = DK22A5). These two paths determine not only cosmological phenomena (since they represent the two fundamental directions of change), but also how the world came into existence.

Heraclitus' cosmogony could have begun with a downward movement of fire, when fire, by condensing, became a liquid such as sea water (on the cosmogonic process in Heraclitus, see Kahn 1979, 139). This liquid, condensing in turn, would change into earth, or, according to DK22B31a (see also B31b), into half earth and half *prēstēr,* a sort of "fiery storm."[48] This suggests that on the upward path, the rarefaction of a part of the earth, under the influence of the fiery storm, gives rise to dark and humid exhalations which, after transforming into clouds, then transforms into celestial bodies. The processes of condensation and rarefaction of fire, as well as the two fundamental paths of change, which are implied, will obviously continue once the cosmogony is completed. This would explain, among other things, meteorological phenomena. It would only be after an extended period of time (i.e., a Great Year), that fire would terminate this world through a conflagration and then initiate a new cosmogony (DK22A13).

If the universe had a beginning in time, the same must apply to animal species including humans. There is one existing fragment that suggests Heraclitus included an anthropogony/zoogony in his *historia*. In this fragment (DK22B36), Heraclitus states that "life comes from water" *(ex hudatos de psuchē)*. Immediately preceding this statement in fragment 36, Heraclitus notes that "water arises out of earth" *(ek gēs de hudōr ginetai).*[49] Water and earth are, of course, the two primary components of terrestrial life in general in pre-Socratic accounts. But given that Heraclitus associates the wise soul *(psuchē)* with the dry element (DK22B118), and the unwise soul with the moist (DK22B117, 77), it appears there may be an evolutionary factor here although the primordial humidity was both hot and wet. In conjunction with this, it is clear that according to Heraclitus, humans are endowed with *logos* or intelligence. The problem, however, is that humans don't always listen to (or are not conscious of) their *logos* and yet a comprehension of the universal *logos* and how it works is the key to the meaning of life.[50]

Did Heraclitus believe in human progress? According to Heraclitus "a man's character is his fate" (*ēthos anthrōpōi daimōn* DK22B119), but one's character is not predetermined. Indeed, although thinking is common to all (B113, 116), humans have the capacity to increase their understanding and thus change their character (B115; see also Hussey 1999, 103–104; McKirahan 1994, 149). In this respect, there is clearly a notion of progress, but in what does this progress consist? In fragment DK22B35, he informs us that lovers of wisdom should be involved in the *historia* or investigation of many things. Clearly this kind of enquiry is not the same as accumulating what Heraclitus sees as useless facts (see DK22B40). But this enquiry entails a great deal of effort. Discovery and progress take time (DK22B22). This is due in part to the fact that *phusis* likes to hide itself (22B123), and yet to attain truth we must discover the *phusis* of each thing (22B1). It seems that for Heraclitus we often come upon the truth or discover it *(exeuriskō)* when we least expect it (22B18). Then again, we have to be fully and consciously engaged in the enquiry to begin with.

The single most important thing to realize is that there is an impersonal, supreme cosmic principle *(logos)* or law *(nomos)* that regulates *all* physical phenomena (or conversely, all physical phenomena are manifestations of the one; seeB10) and which should be the basis or blueprint for *all* human laws, political, and moral (DK22B124; see also B2). Whatever the individual or culture, this is the key. But this is not without complications. While each individual must discover and understand this universal law, some humans are more apt at this than others (see, for example, B1, 2, 114). Meanwhile, humans are still social animals and as such can only function and thrive in a social setting. What social or political setting is most conducive to the realization of this universal law? Heraclitus is quite emphatic that cities must place complete reliance on what is common. There must be one law code for all. Law or *nomos* must be king. No one is, or should be, above the law, including the tyrant. As Plato notes in *Laws,* even rulers must be slaves to laws (*Laws* 4.715d).

In the final analysis, everyone must feel and ideally know that they are participating in what is common, the sine qua non of their very existence. The problem, of course, is establishing a law code that will incarnate the cosmic principle and that will please the opposing forces; for opposing forces, including democrats and aristocrats, *kakoi* and *aristoi,* rich and poor, and which exist by nature, must learn to be moderate, find a common ground and realize that there must be unity in diversity. Indeed, the cosmic struggle shows that, in the long run, "each side will win equally often" (Hussey 1999, 107). Thus, to be wise is to be moderate and to be moderate is to accept the coexistence of justice and strife. This is best reflected in a political constitution in which a rotation in office is respected for a predetermined amount of time (like the seasons or the succession of night and day). But what are we to make of the famous figure of Hermodorus, whom Heraclitus considered the best among the Ephesians (B121)? It appears Hermodorus may have had the perfect qualities (and plan) that would enable Ephesian society to incarnate the cosmic model.[51] Given that no one could be above the law, including the tyrant/king, Hermodorus devised a code of laws that enabled opposing forces in Ephesian society to flourish in harmony and to have unity in diversity.[52]

While these reflections on the notion of progress in Heraclitus may diverge from the more explicit references we see in some authors with regard to a theory of cultural evolution, Nestle (1942, 103) is surely correct to note that, if Heraclitus did not leave us a theory of culture, he certainly made a significant contribution to the study of the development of civilization.

PARMENIDES OF ELEA

Parmenides was born in Elea in the South Italy around 515 BCE and thus within a generation or so of the foundation of the city.[53] Elea was founded/colonized circa 540 BCE by Phocaeans. Phocaea, a northern Ionian city, was a member of the famous Panionian League and the entire population fled by ship to escape the Persians and settle elsewhere including, after a number of misfortunes, Elea (Herodotus 1.162–170; Huxley 1966; Jeffrey 1976, ch 13; Boardman 1999, 215; Dunbabin 1948, 342–46). Parmenides was of first generation Eleatic/Phocaean stock and of rich and distinguished stock according to Diogenes Laertius (9.21 = DK28A1.23). Given the socio-political turmoil during the years following their departure from Phocaea, it is highly unlikely that Parmenides was not adversely affected. Although there is little written on the history of Elea during this period, we do hear about Parmenides' philosophical exploits and his connection with *eunomia*.[54] According to Plato's successor Speusippus, Parmenides "made laws for his fellow citizens" in Elea (Diogenes Laertius 9.23 = DK28A1.23). Plutarch states that Parmenides' laws were so exceptional that magistrates compelled citizens to take an oath each year to remain faithful to these laws (*Against Colotus* 32.1126a = DK28A12; see also Strabo, *Geography* 4.1.252 = DK28A12). This is a clear indication that Parmenides actively participated in the political developments of his time. In fact, some commentators see a close connection between Parmenides' political affiliations and the content of the poem. However, before examining this, something must be said about the poem and the influence of his predecessors and contemporaries.

While there are numerous readings of Parmenides, in the main, there are two interpretations: a "physical" interpretation and an "ontological" interpretation. Some scholars argue that the subject of the poem is *phusis,* or the material universe, while others argue that the subject is *einai* or being (Lafrance 1999, 265–308). The ancient tradition clearly saw Parmenides as a *phusikos* (e.g., Aristotle, *Physics* 1.184b15–25; 186a11–25; see also Plato *Theatetus* 152d–e; *Sophist* 242c–e). Plato associated Parmenides' doctrine of being and unity with the physical universe (see Brisson 1994, 18–27; Lafrance 1999, 277–79), and this is corroborated by Aristotle (*Metaphysics* 1. 986b24).[55] Moreover, Sextus Empiricus (*Against the mathematicians* 7.11–114), from whom we derive a good part of Parmenides' poem, states that he copied the reference from Parmenides' poem *Peri phuseōs* (see also Simplicius, *Commentary on Aristotle's Treatise On the Heavens* 556.25–30 = DK28A14 and below). In the final analysis, Parmenides' poem must be understood in the context of Ionian *historia* of the *peri phuseōs* type (Curd 1998, 6). What Parmenides is proposing is a new approach to Ionian physics. This is quite clear from fragment B7. 3–8: "Do not let habit born from much experience compel you along this way *(hodon)* to judge your sightless eye and sounding ear and tongue, but judge by reason *(krinai de logōi)* the heavily contested refutation spoken by me" (trans. McKirahan).

According to Parmenides, if we judge with reason or *logos* rather than the senses, a whole new world emerges. What Parmenides discovers is the deductive method, and this enables him to deduce from the basic premise that "the universe is/exists" some stunning consequences for the world of nature which his successors were compelled to address. This explains why Parmenides' philosophical activity constitutes a major turning point in the history of pre-Socratic philosophy. What follows shows what changes and what does not change with Parmenides.

In the proem to his poem *Peri phuseōs,*[56] Parmenides contends that his philosophical inspiration—described as a movement from darkness to light (DK28B1.9–10)—is derived from a goddess. She declares that he must (and will) learn all things *(panta)* concerning the "physical universe," both "the unshaken mind of well-rounded truth" *and* "the opinion of the mortals" (DK28B1.29–30; Lafrance 1999, 294).[57] The focus of the first part of the poem, as Theophrastus observed, is the origin of the universe according to truth and reality, whereas the focus of the second is the origin of the universe according to opinion and appearance.[58]

The young man is first offered the choice between two conceivable ways or paths *(hodoi):* the way of true persuasion and the way of total ignorance (DK28B2).[59] The second way, according to which nonbeing or nonexistence is necessary or even possible, is quickly discarded. This is the case since it cannot even be stated without contradiction and it does not necessitate a demonstration.

Come now, I will tell you—and bring away my story safely when you have heard it—the only ways of inquiry there are to think: the one, that it is and that it is not possible for it not to be, is the path of Persuasion (for it attends upon Truth), the other, that it is not and that it is necessary for it not to be, this I point out to you to be a path completely unlearnable, for neither may you know that which is not (for it is not to be accomplished) nor may you declare it. (DK28B2 trans. McKirahan)

In sum, as soon as one affirms something (the universe) *is* (or *exists*), it is not possible to state that this thing *was* or *will be,* and since existence or being excludes "was" and "will be" (DK28B8.5), the universe is[60] (can only be) "unengendered and imperishable" (DK28B8.5–21), "one and indivisible" (B8.22–25), "immutable" (B8.26–31), and "perfect" (B8.34–49). Thus the image of a well-rounded sphere (or ball) is employed at B8.43 to summarize and describe a physical universe, which follows from the discovery of deductive method. It is an analysis based on "reason."[61]

Now, since being and becoming are mutually exclusive, and since being and existence are one, then the world of plurality and change is relegated to the world of false appearances. This is what Parmenides' predecessors did. They imagined that the world order (or *kosmos*) did not always *exist* in its present state. Indeed, they argued that it evolved from a single substance, which became many things *and* in fact continues to change.

Admittedly, if Parmenides had asked Thales, "what is, is (or exists), is it not?," Thales would have acquiesced without hesitation. But, as Guthrie has judiciously remarked, "In refuting their contentions [i.e., the contentions of the Milesians], Parmenides is not so much *proving* that tautology [i.e., what is, is] as showing that earlier thinkers, as well as the ordinary run of mankind, had never formulated it explicitly, and have evaded its implications" (1965, 16; see also Tarán 1965, 279).[62]

At first glance, Parmenides' metaphysics and epistemology appears to leave no room for an *historia* of the *peri phuseōs* type. However, beginning at fragment B8.53, Parmenides nonetheless initiates a cosmogony. Before examining Parmenides cosmogonical account, a natural question arises: why did he bother to narrate such an account, if according to the conclusion reached in the first part of his poem, such an account is contradictory or "untrustworthy" (B1.30)?[63] The answer, it seems, is found in the poem, where the goddess declares he will learn "all things" *(panta).* Not only the truth (or the way of being), but also the opinions of mortals (*brotōn doxas* B1.30 echoing B8.51; 61), that is, the way of appearances or seeming *(ta dokounta).* Indeed, even if it is not possible to speak of truth with respect to the opinions of mortals, a realistic account of their world can be given. This is what Plato does in the *Timaeus* (see Naddaf 1996, 5–18), and this appears to be precisely the objective of the second part of Parmenides' poem (i.e., starting from B8.50), since the goddess tells him the tale that she will tell concerning "all the likely arrangement" *(diakosmon eoikota panta* 8.60) has the aim of assuring him that the wisdom of mortals *(brotōn gnōmō,* 8.61)—in a similar domain—will never get the better of him (8.61).[64]

It is clear from fragments B10 and B11 that Parmenides intended to propose a treatise of the *peri phuseōs* type: "you will know the nature *(phusin)* of the heavens *(aitherian)* and all the constellations within it and the destructive deed of the shining sun's pure torch and whence they came to be *(hoppothen exegenonto)*, and you shall learn the wandering deeds of the round-faced moon and its nature *(phusin),* and you shall also know the surrounding sky *(ouranon),* from which it grew *(enthen ephu)* and how necessity *(Anankē)* led and shackled it to hold the limits of the stars " (DK28B10) ". . . how the earth and the sun and the moon and the aether which is common to all and the Milky Way and furthest Olympus and the hot force of the stars surged forth (or started) to come to be *(gignesthai)*" (DK28B11, trans. McKirahan with minor changes).

It is difficult to get a clear picture of the manner in which Parmenides conceived of the universe's structure given the fragments and doxographies at our disposal. It is nevertheless possible to reconstruct the key features of his cosmogonical account, the primary interest for the case at hand. Parmenides says the natural world came into existence because mortals decided to name two forms *(morphai)* of opposed powers (DK28B8.53–6 and B9) rather than recognizing a singular true reality (DK28B8.54). These two opposites are: the celestial fire, which is gentle and light, and the obscure night which is dense and heavy (DK28B8.56–8). The fact that the first stage of Parmenides' description of the cosmos's evolution begins with the exposition of two forms of opposed powers rather than postulating a unity like his predecessors confirms that the cosmogony in question and the whole of the poem's second part must be attributed to Parmenides. Furthermore, the fact that he postulated a divinity which governs *(kubernai)* all things from the center *(en mesōi,* B12.3) corroborates this position. This divinity is a separate cause of movement (DK28B12; see KRS 1983, 259), a notion absent from the texts of his predecessors with the possible exception of Xenophanes. Parmenides situates his supreme divinity in a precise location: in the center *(en mesōi,* DK28B12.3) of a spherical universe.[65] The expression *en mesōi* has a strong political connotation and there is no reason to doubt that Parmenides is making a political statement when he employs it. The location may also be analogous to the Pythagorean Hestia, or central earth.[66]

Strictly speaking, the cosmogonical process seems to be related to animal procreation in the sense that the divinity which commands all, sent the female to unite with the male, and vice versa (DK28B12; see also A52–54). In these conditions, the two original forms (light and night from which all things are composed), must have united at the beginning of the process. According to Aristotle (*Metaphysics* 1.986b34) Parmenides associated light with the element fire and night with the element earth. These two elements, of course, correspond to the hot and the cold. Theophrastus associates fire with the active element and earth with the passive element (DK28A7–9). This suggests that Parmenides' cosmogony started with the action of the hot on the cold, or the mingling of fire and earth. There is an interesting correlation with his predecessors. Furthermore, according to Aetius (2.7.1 = DK28A37), the air was separated off *(apokirsin)* from the earth after it was vaporized. This was due to the violent condensation or contraction of the earth. It is quite plausible this separation was provoked by the action of the hot on the cold, which caused a third concentric layer to arise between the original two. The fact that the moon is a mixture of air and fire (Aetius 2.7.1 = DK28A37) suggests an explosion broke the mass of fire, which initially encircled the earth. In this case, it appears Parmenides is following Anaximander. That Parmenides' universe is composed of a certain number of circular bands (*stephanai,* DK28B12; A37), some of which are composed of pure fire and others of a mixture of fire and mist (or fire and night), is strongly reminiscent of Anaximander's cosmological model. These similarities in no way deny Parmenides' originality if it is true that he was the first to demonstrate the sphericity of the Earth, its position in the center of the world (Diogenes Lartius 9.21 = DK28A1), and to have identified that the morning star and the evening star are identical (DK28A40a). Doxographical information informs us that Parmenides did not stop with a cosmogony but continued with an anthropogony, that is, an account of the origin of humanity (DK28B16–19). Simplicius states that Parmenides related the generation of things that come into being and pass away down to the parts of animals (*Commentary on Aristotle's On the Heavens* 559.20). This is corroborated by Plutarch, who informs us that Parmenides recounted in some detail the origin of humanity (*Against Colotus* 13.1114b = DK28B10). Diogenes Laertius (9.22 = DK28A1), for his part, provides several details on the anthropogony. He says that according to Parmenides humans were generated from hot and cold and the sun was a major factor in this generation. This means humans were composed of the same two forms or elements with which Parmenides began his cosmogony. Indeed, it suggests humanity originated from the action of the hot (the sun) on the cold (the earth). There are also several fragments that inform us that Parmenides was keenly interested in embryology (DK28B18) and others that he was keenly interested in the origin of thought and sensation (DK28B16). Theophrastus (*On Sensation* 1 and 3 = DK28A46) provides a certain number of details (see also Aristotle, *Metaphysics* 3.1009b21 = DK28B16). Thought and sensation (which Parmenides considers the same) are connected with hot and cold and thus have a physical origin. While certain mixtures *(krasis)* are at the origin of particular thoughts and sensations, the purest element associated with hot (fire) is at the origin of the best thought, which may be related to the goddess leading the young man from darkness to light in the proem (B1.9–11). In conjunction with this, there is the notion in Parmenides, as Theophrastus observes, that everything that exists has some awareness (DK28A46). Parmenides was well aware that there was stability in the physical world since "Necessity" (B10.6), Justice (B1.14), and the Demiurge (B12.3) would have it no other way (this echos the role of *Dikē and Anankē* in B8). But did he believe there was a correlation between the cosmological model and human society? This brings us to the notion of politogony and human progress in Parmenides and I believe direct and indirect evidence for this is found in the doxographical material.

To start with, it is clear Parmenides associated the discovery of the deductive method with historical progress and his conclusion, that sensation and thought (and thus knowledge) have a material origin rather than divine origin, suggests he believed in historical progression. In fact, his engagement in the legislative arena and his reputation as an excellent legislator strongly suggests he believed in social and technological progress. Vlastos (1947/1993, 67 n71), for his part, sees clear allusions in Parmenides' description of the state of the "wanderers" in B6.5 and B8.54 as references to Aeschylus' description of mankind *before* Prometheus' gift of the arts (Aeschylus, *Prometheus* 447–48). But Vlastos goes much further than this and believes that Parmenides makes a political statement in his famous poem. Vlastos cogently argues that Parmenides' conception of Being is grounded in Justice and Equality and describes it as an entity exhibiting all-around equality links him with the democratic tradition (1947/1993, 84). But this is not only the case with the world of Being, it is also the case with the world of Seeming (1947/1993, 68–9). Indeed, not only are the two *morphai* (Night and Light) equal or self-identical, but they are governed by Just Necessity, which explains why we still have *kosmos* in the physical universe and not chaos or disorder (1947/1993, 68). Parmenides' cosmological model should thus be seen as advocating a democratic socio-political value system. The fact that all things are said to be governed "from the center" (*en mesōi*, B12.3) corroborates this position.[67] Furthermore, since the foundation of his native city only briefly preceded him, he must have been sensitive to the emigration of peoples. In conjunction with this, Strabo (DK28A54a) informs us Parmenides was the first to divide the earth into five zones, and Aetius (DK28A54a) contends that Parmenides was the first to define the borders of the inhabited earth. Whether or not this is true, it is clear that Parmenides had a keen interest in geography, which is an integral part of Ionian *historia*. In the final analysis, while Parmenides, like Descartes, may very well be "consciously looking for an unassailable new starting point"

(Hussey 1972, 105), the fact remains he still works within the *peri phuseōs* tradition of his predecessors, a tradition in which politics and ethics are grounded in cosmological models.

EMPEDOCLES OF ACRAGAS

Empedocles was born in Acragas in Sicily around 492 BCE. (For the dating, see Guthrie 1965, 128–132; DK31A1 = Diogenes Laertius 8.74.) This date is probably related to the foundation of the city of Thurii (445/55), which Empedocles is supposed to have visited soon after, if one believes his contemporary Glaucos of Rhegium (Diogenes Laertius 8.51). According to Aristotle, he died at age 60, circa 432 BCE (Diogenes Laertius 8.51).

Acragas was founded around 580 BCE by the wealthy Sicilian city of Gela, which was itself founded by Rhodians and Cretans around 688 BCE (Boardman 1999, 177). At the end of the sixth century, the city began construction of the massive temple of Zeus Olympios and in the mid fifth century Acragas actually eclipsed its mother city of Gela, when Empedocles was in his prime. Tyrants ruled the city during much of its history. At the end of the sixth century it was ruled by the notorious tyrant Phalaris, who was reputed to have roasted opponents in his brazen bull (Boardman 1999, 188). The city actually reached the height of its fame and power under the tyrant Theron (488–72) during Empedocles' boyhood. Herodotus (7.165–67) contends that Theron and his son-in-law Gelon (of Syracuse) defeated the Carthaginians at Himera on the same days as the Greeks defeated the Persians at Salamis. Acragas became a thriving democracy after Theron's son Thrasydaeus was overthrown around 470 (Diodorus 11.23).[68] Although Empedocles came from a wealthy aristocratic family, as his father Meton before him, he championed democracy and even dissolved an oligarchic organization called the Thousand (Diogenes Laertius 8.66 and 64 = DK31A1; Dunbabin 1948, 323). Aristotle (DK29A10) insists that Empedocles was the inventor of the art of rhetoric, and there is no doubt a correlation between his accomplishments in oratory and being a democrat (as KRS 1983, 282 correctly notes). If it is true Empedocles visited the Athenian colony of Thurii shortly after its foundation (Diogenes Laertius 8.51 = DK31A1), he would have encountered other famous contemporaries such as Protagoras, Aeschylus, Herodotus, Hippodamos, and Anaxagoras who were all associated with this colony around this time.

Empedocles' personality was as legendary as those of Pythagoras and Heraclitus. In one instance, he saw himself as a god living among mortals (DK31B112) and in another he recounts memories of his previous lives, including those of a bird, a fish, and a bush (DK31B117). While the legend about him throwing himself into the craters of Etna is highly unlikely

(DK31A1 = Diogenes Laertius 8.76), other legends are not improbable. For instance, Empedocles, invariably considered as wealthy, may very well have saved the city of Selinus from plague by diverting, at his own expense, the course of neighboring rivers to mingle, purifying the waters of the contaminated river (Diogenes Laertius 8.70). Empedocles was about a generation younger than Parmenides. And if one considers Parmenides' reputation, the reputation of Acragas, and the facility of sea travel, the claim that Empedocles was his pupil is not unfounded (Diogenes Laertius 8.56). In any event, the influence of Parmenides on his *historia peri phuseōs* was as important as the influence of the Pythagoreans on his *Katharmoi* or *Purifications*. The fact that Empedocles wrote two poems of such different character has posed many problems for interpreters.[69] The poem entitled *Peri phuseōs,* explains the origin of the present state of things in a rational, scientific manner, while the other, *Katharmoi* or *Purifications,* is religious and mystical in content and intention. Although it is fair to say that the idea of immortality is certainly not absent in the former (Kingsley 1995, 366), the fact remains that the poems are addressed to very different audiences (initiated and uninitiated) and with very different aims (Kingsley 1995, 368). Dodds (1951, 145), for his part, argues that Empedocles represents the typical character of the ancient shaman who maintains the undifferentiated functions of magician and naturalist. More recently, Kingsley (1995, 226–67, 345) argues that both poems are grounded in mystery. However, it is not difficult to see what Nietzsche understood in his *Birth of Tragedy* as a battle between the Apollonian and the Dionysian tendencies in Empedocles. But let's examine his poem *Peri phuseōs.*

When examining Empedocles poem *Peri phuseōs,* the first thing of note is that he clearly wants to accommodate the consequences of Parmenides way of truth. In fact, Empedocles actually castigates his contemporaries and predecessors for failing to recognize the new sine qua non of any *peri phuseōs* account: that nothing can come into existence from what did not previously exist. "Fools—for their meditations are not long-lasting—are those who expect that what previously was not comes to be or that anything dies and is utterly destroyed" (DK31B11 trans. Inwood; see also B12). But how does Empedocles reply to Parmenides' arguments that change is unreal or illusionary?

Empedocles was not intimidated by Parmenides. Knowledge, as he notes in his invocation to the Muse, is not the prerogative of reason, but any means of apprehending it is worth pursuing (DK31B2–3). Moreover, he rehabilitates the notion of change (although Parmenides appears to rehabilitate change in the second part of his poem), but unlike the Milesians, he denies that a single substance underlies all that exists. To resolve the problem, Empedocles introduces his famous doctrine of the four primordial elements: earth, air, fire, and water. These elements are the four roots of all things (*tessara pantōn rhizōmata,* DK31B6). As such, they are not only unengendered and indestructible but all natural change results from their mixture or separation. The novelty of Empedocles' claim is contained in the famous fragment 8: "I will tell you something else: there is no birth *(phusis)* of mortal things, nor is there any end *(teleutē)* in baneful death, there is only mixture *(mixis)* and separation *(diallaxis)* of what is mixed *(migentōn)* and nature *(phusis)* is only the name given to these by humans."

For Empedocles, nothing new ever comes into existence; there are only four unchanging stuffs. In other words, only the four elements can be qualified as *ousia*. What one normally calls a human, a beast, or a plant, and et cetera, are only mixtures of the four elements. To the question: what is a human? Or what is a plant? One should reply: the four elements. Not only are humans and plants derived from these four elements, but when they pass away, they will separate again into these same four elements. So what humans normally understand by *phusis* and *teleutē* are only, from Empedocles perspective, *mixis* and *diallaxis* of the four elements.

To support his theory, Empedocles provides an attractive simile, which compares nature to a painter. As a painter creates an enormous variety of forms and things from combining a few pigments, so nature creates all natural substances from a few elements (DK31B23.1–8). Empedocles concludes: "so let not deception compel your mind to believe that there is from anywhere else a source of mortal things" (trans. McKirahan).

In a similar manner, Empedocles explains how a finite number of roots generate a seemingly unlimited number of different substances such as blood, skin, or bone. These diverse substances are formed through the combination of the four roots in variable whole number ratios; a given substance always corresponds to a certain fixed, defined combination. For example, bone consists of four parts fire, two parts water, and two parts earth (B96). Blood consists of equal portions of the four elements (B98).[70]

The fact that Empedocles postulated four realities instead of one does not resolve the problem of motion. Parmenides insists that what exists could not move. The Ionian insistence on hylozoism means that the cause of movement was not a factor in their cosmogonical accounts. Since the elements themselves had to be as similar as possible to the Parmenidian One, Empedocles appealed to external moving forces. He called these forces Love and Strife and it is only under their influence that the four elements produce change. In the final analysis, there are six ultimate factors or agents in Empedocles' cosmological system: four passive and two active.

Before considering Empedocles' explanation of the origin and evolution of the present order of things, something must be said about a concept that is particularly important in his *peri phuseōs* account: *krasis*. We have already seen the importance of the term in Alcmeon's medical theory, where *krasis* is the proportional mixture of *dunameis* or qualities. The term is employed by

Parmenides in a similar sense; the change that occurs in the body is directly associated with the *krasis* of the two opposite *morphai* or powers *(dunameis)* of which the body is composed: light and dark (DK31B16; for the term *dunamis,* see DK31B9).

In a *krasis,* the various qualities or powers *(dunameis)* of which a thing is composed combine in such a way that their specific modes of action are annihilated. The result is a uniform composition with its *own* qualities and effects. In this sense, *krasis* is synonymous with *harmonia.* In Philolaus, Heraclitus, and Parmenides an ordered universe is the result of a *harmonia* (and thus a *krasis*) among the opposite powers *(dunameis).* This is precisely what we find in Empedocles. Love or Harmony (DK31B23.4; 27.3; 96.4) is a primary consequence of the formation and the conservation of a *krasis.* On the other hand, Strife separates *krasis* into its constituent parts, which then proceed to combat one another. It is this concept of *krasis* that dominates Empedocles *historia.*

Empedocles' cosmic system is a real puzzle. As Hussey notes (1972, 130), this system was already the most discussed and quoted in antiquity. In fact, there is no consensus on where the cosmogony begins (Guthrie, 1965, 168). Does it commence with the rule of Love or the rule of Strife? What is certain is that the two mutually antagonistic moving forces alternate continuously in a never ending cyclical process (DK31B17.6–7; 26.11–12).

When Love completely dominates, all the elements in the *kosmos* unite in the form of a spherical divinity: a perfect *krasis* or Parmenidian One (B26.5; 27–29). Following this, Strife enters Sphere and begins to separate the elements until each is severed from the other. The separation continues until there is no *krasis* whatsoever. The cycle then recommences in an identical manner. Between these two extremes, there are periods when Love and Strife advance and retreat in turn. During these periods, the world is neither in total *krasis* nor separated into four perfectly homogeneous regions. It is during these intermediary stages in the struggle for supremacy between Love and Strife that a variety of compounds and living things are formed and we find the present world order.

According to Aristotle *(Generation and Corruption* 2.334a5; *On the Heavens* 3.301a14), Empedocles thought the world was at the stage when Strife was gradually progressing (and which may reflect the political turmoil at the time). However, since there is a period of alteration between the two motor forces, there is a form of double cosmogony, whence the remark: "double is the birth of mortal things *(thnētōn)* and double is their disappearance" (DK31B17.5). A universe of "mortal things" designates the world of humans or the world in the process of formation. The mortal things are the compounds (B35.7, 16–17) such as animals and plants as opposed to the four elements themselves which are, of course, "immortal" (B35.14).

If it is true that Empedocles thought that the world was currently dominated by Strife, then the starting point for the current cosmogonical process (and thus the first stage of his *historia peri phuseōs*) must have begun with the state of things following Love's complete dominance; to wit: a well-rounded, joyous, and solitary sphere (DK31B27, 27a, 28–29). At that point in time, the sun, earth, and sea did not exist (DK31B27.1–2). Empedocles relates their origin and the way in which they were formed (DK31B38), and he recounts the origin and formation of living beings (DK31B62), in the second part of the investigation.

The cosmogony in the new cycle begins when Strife enters the perfect sphere of Love, causing "all the members of the god to tremble one after the other" (DK31B31). The physical process or original motion that causes the elements in the sphere (which is immobile in its perfectly blended state) to separate is not, at this stage, the famous *dinē* or vortex associated with Empedocles (B35.3–4; Aristotle, *On the Heavens* 2.295a9–13), but the attraction of like to like. This is the movement that causes the four elements to separate. It is also the movement initiated by Strife.[71] During the course of the separation our universe was formed. According to doxographical tradition (Pseudo-Plutarch, *Miscellanies* = DK31A30; Aetius 2.6.3 = DK31A49), air was the first element to be separated from the original *krasis;* it flowed round in a circle. Fire came after air, and having nowhere else to go, it ran under the solid mass of air. This results in the formation of two hemispheres: one made of fire and the other of air with a little fire (DK31A30, 56). Since fire is heavier than air, this causes an imbalance (A30). Subsequently, a *dinē* or vortex is initiated and causes the hemispheres to rotate (A30, 49). The rotation explains the succession of day and night. The earth, for its part, is restricted to the center under the effect of the vortex and water is finally released from the earth under the force of the rotation (DK31A30, 49, 67; and Aristotle, *On the Heavens* 2. 295 a13–24). But although the basic structure of the universe is established the sun and other celestial bodies still do not exist; nor is the earth's surface yet separated into sea and dry land. This will occur afterwards (DK31B38; see KRS 1983, 300). The sun is explained as a reflection of fire encircling the earth (DK31A56).[72] And the other celestial bodies are explained in a more conventional way: they originate from the elements themselves (DK31A30, 49). The sun meanwhile is behind the origin of the sea and thus the earth's surface as we know it (Aristotle, *Meteorology* 2.353b11; 2.357a24 = DK31A25).[73] Once the universe is in place, Empedocles describes the origin of terrestrial life. This unfolds in several stages.

According to Aetius (5.19.5 = DK31A72), the zoogony unfolds in four stages. The first generation of animals and plants that emerged from the earth were not whole but consisted of isolated organs (see B57, 58 and Aristotle, *Generation of Animals* 1.722b17). The second generation consisted of a mishmash of organs combining to form fantasy-like creatures (31B61). The third generation consisted of whole-natured creatures that emerged from the earth without limbs or sexual distinction (31B62). In the fourth and final generation, creatures no longer emerged from the earth but reproduced amongst themselves. The animal species were distinguishable according to the character of their mixture (some had a more natural inclination toward water, others air and so on). There is consensus that the first two generations or stages correspond to the period when Love was advancing whereas the last two generations or stages correspond to the period when Strife was advancing. There is a sense that only the fittest survived, but this only appears to be the case in the first two stages. Yet this is no more than conjecture since we have no direct quotes from Empedocles on the subject. The last two stages present similarities with Anaximander's description, including a similar relation between the earth and the sun in the generation of living things (DK31A70).

Living things consist of a compound of the four elements in certain ratios. Sex for Empedocles is determined by temperature (Aristotle, *Generation of Animals* 764a1). Like most pre-Socratics, Empedocles was preoccupied with rational account of the origin and evolution of human and other species.[74] Moreover, he was clearly engaged in how thought and sensation actually function. Aristotle (*On the Soul* 427a22) states that Empedocles saw thought and sensation as the same. Empedocles perceived these as purely physical processes with blood as the actual organ of thought (B105). Both sensation and thought are connected to the universal principle that "like acts on like," and there is a certain irony in this if one considers that Strife is the moving principle that attracts like to like. But clearly, there must be mixtures that are more conducive to wisdom and understanding, and these, one can assume, are connected to a special *krasis* under the domination of Love.[75] But the process is more complex and confusing, for we are clearly residing in a period where Strife rather than Love is advancing. This is found both in Empedocles' doctrine of immortality and his socio-political views (or development thereof).

Empedocles believes there is no distinction between the animate and the inanimate (B102, 103, 110) and that a defined hierarchy in nature (B146) largely drives the theoretical side of his doctrine of reincarnation.[76] Empedocles believes in an exile or fall from an initial happy state and the possibility of an eventual return to paradise (B115, 128, 130).[77] Given that the original daimon retains its identity through its reincarnations (B117) and that the daimon must go through a series of reincarnations in order to return to paradise, there is clearly a sense of human development or progress (with political leaders among the best forms of human incarnation, B146). However, it is unclear if, following the "fall," humans find themselves in a primitive social environment (as we saw in Anaximander) or a more sophisticated one (as we saw in mythical accounts). Given that Empedocles believes in some sort of human evolution, it is tempting to go with the former. What is certain is that he had a keen interest in the application of technical ability and some of the feats attributed to him are not impossible, for example diverting the course of rivers to cleanse a contaminated area (Diogenes Laertius 8.70), inventing a system of artificial heating (A68 = Seneca, *Natural Questions* 3.24.1–2); and creating a wind guard (Diogenes Laertius 8.60).[78] These examples suggest that Empedocles thought *technē* could help *improve* human existence. What about the realm of politics?

As we saw above, several doxographical reports clearly state that Empedocles was a strong proponent of democracy. At first sight, this is difficult to reconcile with his contention that he was a god among mortals (B112). But he does believe political leaders are among the higher forms of incarnation (B146). Consequently, Empedocles as a political and social leader may be simply advocating democracy as the most valid political system in assuring humanity advances toward the new paradise. There is no doubt that Empedocles lived in extremely turbulent times. Indeed, political turmoil was so prevalent this convinced him that Strife was advancing. Vlastos (1947/1993, 61–64) argues that, given the principle of successive supremacy in Empedocles, "the universe must be characterized by *isonomia,* for it conforms to the democratic principle of the rotation of office."[79] We see something similar in Anaximander with the question: Is the cosmological system behind Empedocles' penchant for democracy or does his penchant for democracy drive his cosmological system? Whether or not Empedocles wrote one major poem or two, his *historia,* while impregnated with mysticism and magic, still covers, from a synoptical perspective, all the relevant themes already identified with Ionian accounts of the *peri phuseōs* type.

ANAXAGORAS OF CLAZOMENAE

There is a good deal of consensus that Anaxagoras was born in Clazomenae (a member of the Ionian League and a city actively involved in the settlement of Naucratis) in northern Ionia around 500 BCE.[80] If the date of his birth is correct, then Anaxagoras was only a shade older than Empedocles (see Guthrie 1965, 266). It is not surprising there is some controversy as to who was the first to produce his work and who was influenced by whom.[81] There is no doubt Empedocles and Anaxagoras both reply to Parmenides, and that there is a clear allusion to Zeno in DK59B4.

It is argued that Anaxagoras started his philosophical career in Athens at age twenty (ca. 480), but if his arrival in Athens was connected with the reputation derived from his book, he must has arrived in Athens somewhat later, since it is unlikely his book was written before 470.[82] Several doxographies, generally uncontested, state Anaxagoras predicted the fall of a meteorite at Aegospotamie in Thrace (which is nonsense). Since it is generally assumed this event influenced his theory of the cosmic whirl and the origin of the heavenly bodies (see DK59B9), and since the event occurred in 467 BCE, then his book must have been completed after this date (e.g., Guthrie 1965, 266). Schofield (1980, 33–35), for his part, lists a number of other convincing reasons for dating the book, and with it Anaxagoras' *floruit*, between 470–60 BCE.

More attention has been paid to Anaxagoras' life than that of any other pre-Socratic, although we still know very few details. And it is worth remembering that Anaxagoras was born around the time of the famous Ionian revolt. Since Clazomenae was actively involved in the revolt and was captured (Herodotus 5.126), his aristocratic family must have been active participants. It is unclear to what degree Clazomenae suffered following the revolt, but the Persian Wars (490–79/467) must have worsened the political atmosphere in Clazomenae and elsewhere in Ionia. Was it this situation that occasioned Anaxagoras to leave Ionia for Athens? Given that Clazomenae was now part of a Persian province, the Great King would actively seek recruits for his armies of invasion (see Herodotus). It has been argued that Anaxagoras came to Athens as a conscript around the age of twenty (Burnet 1930/1945, 254; Guthrie 1965, 322–23). Diogenes Laertius states that along with impiety, Anaxagoras was accused of "collaborating with Persia" (DK59A1 = Diogenes Laertius 8.12). Politics clearly played an important role in his departure from Athens, although it seems his accusers were political opponents of the famous Athenian statesman Pericles (fl. 461–29), a close friend and associate of Anaxagoras. There is also consensus that Anaxagoras spent around thirty years in Athens, although it is unclear if it was in intermittent stages. What appears certain is that, when Anaxagoras was in fact exiled from Athens, he settled in Lampsacus in Northen Ionia, a city under Persian control, where he founded a flourishing school and died around 428 BCE, the year, ironically, of Plato's birth. But it is worth noting that during Anaxagoras' residence in Athens, that Athens became, with the foundation of the Delian League against Persia, the "New" Persia.

Diogenes Laertius states that Anaxagoras was among the authors who wrote only one book (Diogenes Laertius 1.16 = DK59A1; Sider 1981, 11–13), and this book is the *peri phuseōs* common to all the pre-Socratics. Let us examine its main lines.

The first thing to note in an analysis of Anaxagoras' work is that he, as Empedocles, took Parmenides' canons into serious consideration—which is again indicative of the speed of the word in ancient Greece. This is clear from the following fragment: "The Greeks are wrong to accept coming to be and perishing for no thing comes to be, nor does it perish, but they are mixed together from things that are and they are separated apart" (DK59B17, trans. McKirahan).

However, whereas Empedocles insisted on a twofold process of mixture and separation, on two moving forces, and on a perfectly cyclical cosmic process, Anaxagoras postulated a single moving force and a strictly linear cosmogonic process. Moreover, rather than postulating a finite number of substances as Empedocles had done, Anaxagoras argued for an infinite number. He thus avoids a pitfall in Empedocles' theory. According to the latter, if a natural element such as wood or bone were divided a sufficient number of times, it would no longer be that thing, but the component elements of which it was composed. In sum, the wood or bone would now have perished, and this is quite contrary to Parmenides' canon that coming to be and perishing are logically impossible. Thus Anaxagoras postulated an infinite number of primary or basic substances, which Aristotle later called *homoiomerē* or similar parts (*Physics* 187a23 and *On Generation and Corruption* 314a18 = DK59A46). This suggests that for Anaxagoras each natural entity or substance conceals within itself every other natural entity or substance. What predominates in any particular natural entity (e.g., bone), determines the name of that natural entity or substance.[83]

Anaxagoras was no less original in his explanation of the origin of movement.[84] Like Empedocles (and again under the spell of Parmenides), he accepted that the total primitive mixture would have remained in a state of inertia without a principle of movement independent of the primordial substance itself. Anaxagoras called this cause *nous* or Mind/Intelligence (DK59B11–14). Like Empedocles' Love and Strife, *nous* is understood as an abstract principle and as something corporeal. As an abstract principle, *nous* has knowledge of all things (*gnōmēn ge peri pantos*, B12.10). It has the greatest power (*ischuei megiston*, B12.10–11) and thus governs *(kratei)* all living things (B12.11–12). As a corporeal entity, *nous* is the finest and purest that exists (DK59B12.9–10). In fact, it is unmixed with anything else, and this explains not only its complete autonomy (B12.1–3) but its control over matter (for a succinct description, see McKirahan 1994, 221).

According to Diogenes Laertius, Anaxagoras began his book in the following way: "initially, all things were together *(homou panta chrēmata ēn)*, then *nous* made an organised world" (DK59A1; B1; B4b). Anaxagoras contends that although all things were initially confounded, *aēr* and *aither* (or fire) were dominant (DKB1.4, 2). This contradicts Anaxagoras' contention that all things (that is, the seeds or *spermata*, B4) have a portion of everything.[85] This may mean that in the beginning all seeds were contained or concealed in *aēr* and *aither* (DK59B1–2). Furthermore, once the rotational movement (or vortex) started under the impulsion of *nous*, two laws occur: the attraction of like to like, which caused the indistinct mass to take on particular characteristics, and the tendency of the heavy/*aēr* toward the center and light/*aither* toward the periphery. These purely mechanical laws suggest that *nous* was not always in complete control of the cosmogonic process. Plato (*Phaedo* 97b–98c = DK59A47) and Aristotle (*Metaphysics* 1.985 a17–21 = DK59A47) observed that Anaxagoras did not make *nous* the/a final cause. Indeed, they noted that once *nous* initiated movement the cosmogonical process continued for purely mechanical reasons. But despite the reservations of Plato and Aristotle, the text clearly indicates that Anaxagoras did attribute to *nous* an all controlling power.[86]

To return to the cosmogonic process, the seeds in which the hot, dry, light, and bright dominated were transported toward the periphery, whereas those in which the cold, wet, heavy, and dark dominated were transported toward the center of the vortex (DK59B12, 15). The sky was formed by the first group and the earth by the second. The force of the vortex caused the earth to go through several stages (including, air, cloud, water, earth, and stone; see 59B16) before taking its present form. This, of course, is reminiscent of Anaximenes and his theory of condensation. Meanwhile, the speed of the vortex in certain instances is powerful enough to pick up large stones from the earth's surface and project them into space (DK59B16; Hippolytus, *Refutations* 1.8.6 = DK59A42; Aetius, 2, 13, 3 = DK59A71).[87] The speed and the resistence causes these projectiles to ignite, whence Anaxagoras' contention that heavenly bodies have (again like Anaximenes) a terrestrial origin (DK59A21; A42 = Hippolytus, *Refutations* 1.8.2; Plutarch, *Lysander* 12 = DK59A12). This was one of the purported reasons for which he was prosecuted for impiety (see Plato's *Apology* 26d, *Laws* 10.886d–e). Finally, the action of the sun caused the sea to form on the earth's surface.[88] In brief, this is how the first stage of Anaxagoras' *historia* unfolded. In the second stage Anaxagoras conformed to his Ionian predecessors. He argued that "animals *(zōia)* originated from the wet, hot and earthy *(ex hugrou kai thermou kai geōdous)*, but later from each other" (Diogenes Laertius 2.9 = DK59A1). This is consistent with Hippolytus (*Refutations* 1.8.12 = DK59A42), who says animals originated in the wet *(en hugrōi)*. However, the seeds or *spermata* that correspond to the original animals and plants were also concealed in the primordial mixture. This would explain Anaxagoras' contention (at DK59B4) that humans and other animals were separated out of the primordial mixture. This interpretation is strongly suggested by Theophrastus (*History of Plants* 3.1.4 = A117): "Anaxagoras says that the air contains seeds of all things and that these, when carried down with water, generates plants" (trans. Schofield 1980, 125; n44); as Guthrie (1965, 315; 1957, 35) notes, seeds were germinated by heat. Meanwhile, once animals began to reproduce from each other, Anaxagoras argues that the seed for both sexes came solely from the male.

Anaxagoras equated mind *(nous)* and soul *(psuchē)*.[89] However, all living things do not have an equal amount of *nous*. Living things with the lowest portion of *nous* only have the power to move whereas those with the highest portion also have the power to think. This explains the hierarchy in the natural world. Humans, of course, have the highest portion of *nous*, but there also seems to be a correlation between the portion of *nous* and the structure of the living thing. Aristotle notes Anaxagoras contended that humans are the wisest of animals because they have hands (Aristotle, *Parts of Animals* 687a7 = A102). Since there is no evidence that Anaxagoras believed in a theory of evolution, then the human species (the essence of which would have been contained in the primordial *spermata*), like other animal and plant species, must have emerged from the primordial humidity in their present form. In this case, one could, or should conclude, that wisdom or intelligence (i.e., practical, and later, theoretical) wisdom and intelligence developed over a certain period of time. This bodes well with fragment B21b (from Plutarch, *On Chance* 3.98f), where Anaxagoras notes that if certain properties such as speed and force give animals superiority over humans, humans use their experience *(empeiriāi)*, memory *(mnēmēi)*, wisdom /or art *(sophiāi)*, and craft *(technēi)*—all of which are connected with his superior *nous*—to make animals submit to their interests. It is these specific predispositions of the human species that permitted the development of civilization.[90] This does not denigrate the role of the hand, for without the hand arts and crafts (including the domestication of animals) would never have developed. All this suggests that Anaxagoras was keenly interested in the origin and development of civilization.[91] Indeed, B21b at least suggests animals and humans initially shared a similar, bestial way of life and that humans, at least at the outset, were less fortunate then other animals. As his disciple Archelaus (DK60A1, 4), Anaxagoras argued that the notion of justice, as with other human notions, did not only develop gradually, but also variously (see Farrar 1988, 87). But this thesis, as we know from the historians, tragedians, sophists, physicians, and philosophers (e.g., Democritus) was widespread, if not the norm among the intelligentsia.[92]

As Farrar (1988, 41) notes, Anaxagoras was the first to attempt to establish a causal rather than an analogical connection "between cosmic characters and human ones."[93] With Anaxagoras, for the first time an "independent" (and autocratic) cosmic mind *(nous)* initiates motion and imposes order on primordial matter. Since *nous* controls all living things it somehow controls human minds, however it is unclear what this means. Farrar (1988, 42) argues that we have a "cosmic replica": human actions not only follow a pattern but are also controlled from within. However, human minds are, contrary to the cosmic *nous*, obstructed by embodiment; otherwise, they would be omniscient (for the opposite view, see Schofield 1980, 18–19). Farrar also contends that "the participation of mind in *nous* means indifference to the world of action and sensation" and this in turn explains the reports "that according to Anaxagoras it was the possibility of contemplating the cosmos that made life worthwhile" (= DK59A30).

Anaxagoras states that if cosmic *nous* were mixed with other things it would not be able to rule things with the same consistency (DK59B12.4). Since humans are composed of mind and matter they constitute a mixture. Consequently, humans are not omniscient, autonomous, and free from mistakes. Indeed, as Laks (1999, 266) notes "difference, domination and even violence" are omnipresent in every feature of Anaxagoras' theory. Here Laks is discussing Anaxagoras' theory of sense perception.

Now if Anaxagoras' cosmogonic *nous* is omniscient and continues to govern and control all things, animate and inanimate, then the theory of human progress attributed to Anaxagoras must somehow occur according to divine plan, whether mechanically or otherwise. Therefore, the initial confused, brutish state of human life is also part of a divine plan, and the means by which this initial state was regulated (i.e., reason, speech, arts, crafts, and agriculture) must also be seen as part of a divine plan. But is it possible to understand the plan/will (?) of the cosmogonic *nous* as Plato contends in *Timaeus?* More importantly, given that humans are by nature political animals (the cosmogonic *apokrisis* accounts for human origins and their civilizations, B4), is there a political constitution that best represents the synoptical vision or will of the cosmogonic *nous?* In sum, although humans are mixed they nonetheless have the capacity to understand the cosmogonic *nous* and fulfill its initial plan.

There is consensus that Euripides' famous fragment 910 is a reference to Anaxagoras (see also Aristotle, *Eudemian Ethics* 1216a11 = DK59A30). This fragment suggests that the order of nature is the standard of goodness and thus the model to follow. Indeed, its study will discourage humans from harming one another and doing unjust deeds. Since nature is a paradigm that can (or should) be employed in a "political" education (see Capizzi 1990, 38), for Anaxagoras there is a sense in which the cosmos represents a cosmic republic. If this is the case, it can be argued that Anaxagoras advocates a socio-political model that should be modeled after (or conform to) the cosmic model or republic. Can we conjecture what he had in mind?

Given that the cosmogonic *nous* is described as *autokrates* (B12.2), it is tempting to see an allusion to the One Great Persian Monarch.[94] The Clazomenean, as noted above, was not only raised in a Persian province, but also resided and flourished in one after his exile from Athens.

However, Anaxagoras spent most of his intellectual life in Athens, where he probably wrote his famous book. There is a good deal of consensus, as noted above, that the real reason for which Anaxagoras was accused of impiety was purely political. He was a close associate of Pericles, who had a number of political enemies. Some scholars argue that the *archē* of intelligence was a democratic paradigm, either the domination of Pericles in Athenian politics, or the domination of Athens within Greece (see Capizzi 1990, 384). In any event, as Capizzi (1990, 385) has shown, the Athens-paradigm and the Intelligence-paradigm are clearly associated, if not identified, with each other.[95] According to Anaxagoras' cosmological model, every individual mind like every individual citizen is equal, but in order to live in peace and harmony, the citizens must submit to the rule of law, the dispensation of *nous,* the true *archē* in the democratic paradigm and modeled after the cosmic republic.

THE ATOMISTS: LEUCIPPUS AND DEMOCRITUS

Atomism is clearly one of the more famous theories that has survived antiquity. The doctrine is associated with two names: Leucippus and Democritus. While Leucippus is considered the founder of atomism, his successor and collaborator, Democritus, developed the theory to such an extent and with such success that atomism came to be associated with him alone. Indeed, Epicurus (341–271), who adopted and popularized atomism only a century after Democritus, actually denied the existence of Leucippus (Diogenes Laertius 10.13 = DK67A2). But Aristotle (*Metaphysics* 985b4 = DK67A46a; *Generation and Corruption* 324a24 = DK67A48a), our primary source for the theory, is quite emphatic that Leucippus was the founder.

Democritus was from Abdera in Thrace, as was his famous elder contemporary, the sophist Protagoras. He was born about 460 BCE.[96] According to Herodotus (1.68), Abdera was settled in the mid-sixth century by Greeks from the island of Teos, who fled the Persians. Whether Leucippus was also from Abdera is an open question (Abdera, Miletus, and Elea are all given), but what is certain is that atomist theory is strongly Ionian. It is unclear if Leucippus was a generation older than Democritus, but it seems he "proposed the atomic theory in the decade 440–430" (McKirahan 1994, 303).[97] This treatise was entitled the *Great World-System.* It seems that Democritus took Leucippus' theory[98] and applied atomism to every aspect of the world. He was an encyclopaedic author. The Alexandrian catalogue lists over sixty works in order by tetralogies or groups of four (see Diogenes Laertius 9.45–49), covering almost every conceivable field. Both the scope and volume of the work confirms the tradition that he lived to be over 100 years old. As with other pre-Socratics, Democritus came from a wealthy family and he used his inheritance wisely (Diogenes Laertius 6.35–6 = DK68A6; *Suidas* = DK68A7). Democritus was an exceptionally well-traveled individual and there is little doubt his travels influenced certain facets of his philosophical worldview (DK68B299). Given the prominence of war, Democritus was a strict realist and advocated thorough military training for all citizens (DK68B157).[99] In conjunction with this, Democritus was a convinced democrat (e.g., DK68B251, 252).[100] Moreover, there is evidence that Abdera had a democratic constitution during Democritus' lifetime (Lewis, 1990, 151–54; Procopé, 1989/1990, 309, 313–14). In fact, there is some numismatic evidence Democritus actually held office around 414 BCE (Procopé 1989/1990, 309–10) and a number of fragments reflect his reports on the situation in Abdera, in particular, the importance of fostering social cohesion (Procopé 1989/1990, 313–17).

Democritus states that when he came to Athens no one knew him (DK68B116). Although no one doubts that Democritus visited Athens, it is unclear when he arrived or the length of his visit (or visits). Protagoras (ca. 490–21; on the dates see Guthrie 1969, 262; Kerferd 1981, 42) was already well-known and respected in Athens by 444, since he was selected by Pericles (whose supremacy runs from 461–29) to draft the new constitution for Thurii (Heraclides Ponticus frag. 150). Around this time, or shortly thereafter, Leucippus invented atomic theory. Did Democritus visit Athens before the death of Pericles (429 BCE) or during the Peloponnesian War (431–404)? He would only have been around thirty years old at the time. Given that the gods were associated with physical phenomena (DK68B166 and A74) and thus purely conventional, Democritus would have been a prime target for the charge of impiety, as Anaxagoras and Protagoras were for their own unorthodox views.[101] There is no reason to believe that Protagoras the fellow citizen did not know of Democritus before he arrived in Athens (he was also a contemporary of Thucydides, Archelaus, Zeno, Socrates, Hippocrates; see Diogenes Laertius 9.41–42 = DK68A6). There is clearly an epistemological and political debate between Democritus, whose *historia* is synoptical and for whom the cosmic order and the human/political order are fused together, and Protagoras (and Thucydides), for whom cosmic order and human/political order are incompatible (see Farrar 1988, 196–97).[102]

Among the works listed under the rubric *phusika* are *Great World-System* and *Little World-System,* and it is generally agreed that taken together, their aim is to describe the origin and development of the universe, humanity, and society and culture (KRS 1983, 405; Guthrie 1965, 385; C. C. W. Taylor 1999a, 233–34, 1999b, 181; Farrar 1988, 228–230; Vlastos 1945/1993, 340). There is consensus that *Great World-System* should be attributed to Leucippus (e.g., McKirahan 1994, 303; Guthrie 1965, 385; KRS 1983, 405; Taylor 1999a, 157) and *Little World-System* to Democritus. But for the case at hand, we will examine both in the context of atomism.

Atomism, as with the cosmological systems of Empedocles and Anaxagoras, is a reply to Parmenides and Eleatism (although it is clearly more than this).[103] This is clearly attested by Aristotle (in *Generation and Corruption* 324b35–326b6), for whom atomism was a reaction to those who maintained that being must necessarily be one, and motionless. Aristotle notes that while Leucippus wanted to avoid their madness,[104] he nevertheless wanted to satisfy the conditions of their ontology. But he also wanted to safeguard the physical world and made concessions to each group. On the one hand, he admits plurality and movement, generation and corruption. On the other hand, he admits true being has no void and that without the void there was no movement. Since the reality of movement is admitted, the void must constitute a nonbeing as real as being itself. Since plurality is admitted, this must exist in the nonbeing of the void and not in being from which it could not derive. The introduction of the void led to the possibility of plurality and movement.

While atoms themselves had no perceptible qualities (qualities are dependent on atoms forming compounds), they did have different shapes and sizes. Aristotle (*Metaphysics* 985b15–19 = DK67A6; see also *Generation and Corruption* 315b6–15 = DK67A9) notes that atoms differ in shape *(rusmos)*, arrangement *(diathigē)*, and position *(tropē)* (see also Simplicius, *Commentary on Aristotle's Physics* 28.15–26. = DK67A8; 68A38). However, arrangement and position are the sine qua non for the formation of compounds. In the final analysis, only size *(megethos)* and shape *(rhusmos)* are intrinsic to the atom themselves (for a good discussion, see Taylor 1999a, 171–84). The question of knowing how the atoms move in the void did not seriously preoccupy the atomists (Aristotle, *Metaphysics* 985b19). If atoms are in movement now, there was no reason to think this was not always the case. This is one of the fundamental differences between the atomist response and those of Empedocles and Anaxagoras to Eleatism. Having considered the void inadmissible, Empedocles and Anaxagoras had to postulate a separate cause of movement. Without a separate cause, the primordial state of things would have remained as it was. But this was not the only radical difference between their respective replies to Eleatism. For Empedocles and Anaxagoras, primary substances were observable, material entities, whereas for the atomists, for the first time, the primary substances, atoms, were unobservable and thus purely theoretical entities (see Taylor 1999a, 182).

Meanwhile, if atoms moved freely in the void, then there was no reason to believe they would move in one direction rather than another; this must have always been the case. There is a sense in which the so-called original motion could be qualified as random (see KRS 1983, 424). But collisions between atoms are always occurring, and it was secondary motions, which resulted from atoms colliding and rebounding, that Aristotle qualified as unnatural or compelled rather than natural.[105] However, the character of the secondary motions that ensue from the rebounds of colliding bodies/atoms are determined by their previous history (and no doubt the size and form of the colliding bodies as well). The movement of atoms is determinable because their movements follow certain natural laws. This seems to be the sense of Leucippus' sole surviving fragment: "Nothing happens in vain *(matēn)*, but everything happens from a reason *(ek logou)* and by necessity *(hup'anankēs,* 67B2).[106] Since the notion of purposeful intelligence is absent in atomism (the atomistic universe is subject to purely mechanistic laws), the sense here is that nothing happens without a reason *(logos)*. All events are due to the necessary interaction of atoms; they can be explained (Taylor 1999 art., 186–87; McKirahan 1994, 321). This bodes well with Simplicius' contention that, according to Democritus, "chance is the cause of nothing" (*Commentary on Aristotle's Physics* 330.14–17 = DK68A68). Moreover, it is in this sense one should understand Democritus' contention that "in reality, we know nothing, since truth is in the abyss" (B117). In this quote, Democritus suggests that if one had all the facts, any problem could be resolved. More importantly, the desire to know is always present (see 57B118).

The effects of the collision were seen as twofold. First, they could simply rebound off one another as in a billiard game, second, if atoms of similar form (e.g., hooked, concave) collided, they could unite to form composite bodies, notably water, air, and earth. Fire, for its part, was composed only of spherical atoms and these are conceived as "soul" and "mind" atoms.[107]

In the final analysis, the collision of atoms and their subsequent entanglement explains how *kosmos* (or *kosmoi*) originates and develops. Diogenes Laertius (9.30–33 = DK67A1) has the most detailed account of atomistic cosmogonical process. When a large number of atoms or bodies *(sōmata)* of various shapes are separated from the infinite *(ek tēs apeirou)* and move in a great void *(eis mega kenon),* a vortex *(dinēn)* is produced. While the whirling motion causes similar atoms to come together, it also drives the smaller, lighter atoms back into the void. The remaining atoms, which continue to rotate, become entangled and form a spherical shell or membrane *(humēn).* The larger, heavier atoms congregate at the center to form the earth, while the outer shell or membrane becomes thinner. However, the outer membrane is then increased by the influx of atoms from the outside.[108] As it whirls around, some of these atoms interlock and form a structure that is at first wet and muddy, but, as the whirling continues, dries and eventually ignites, forming the stars and the other heavenly bodies.[109]

While the cosmogonical account is due to blind mechanical movements, the formation of the cosmos is described in terms proper to the birth of animals (Guthrie 1965, 408; G. E. R. Lloyd 1966). In conjunction with this, the atomists contend that once the *kosmos* grows to maturity, it becomes, as a plant or animal, old and then dies (Diogenes Laertius 9.33 = DK67A1; Hippolytus, *Refutations* 1.13). Since atoms are innumerable and the void infinite, atomists argue that there must be innumerable coexisting worlds *(kosmoi)* that are constantly coming into being and passing away. Indeed, with the atomists, we have the first uncontested reference to infinite worlds.[110] Again, with the atomists, for the first time there is no reference to a primordial substance or entity that is qualified as divine. Indeed, the mental in general no longer has a descriptive role to play.

In fragment DK68B34, Democritus calls a human being a *mikros kosmos,* that is, a miniature *kosmos* or world order. For Democritus, humans, like the universe or *megas kosmos,* are composed of the same elements (atoms and void) and follow the same laws. Democritus was the first to employ the term *mikros kosmos* in this context but he was not the first to draw an analogy between man and the universe. The idea was common to most pre-Socratics and is a common theme in mythical accounts. The same observation can be made with regard to the origin of life. The doxographical tradition (DK68A139) informs us that Democritus, who is the only atomist named, contended that humans and other animals arose from water and mud. It is clear Democritus would have added a more detailed description. Diels, in fact, attributes and thus appends the famous account by Diodorus Siculus to Democritus (DK68B5). Whether or not this text faithfully translates Democritus' position on the origin of life, the fact remains that most of the information in this text can be traced to his predecessors, including Anaximander. What is clearly novel in the atomistic account is the notion that soul, the source of life, consists of spherical atoms, which are by nature mobile.

Few scholars contest that atomists in general and Democritus in particular did not leave a detailed account of the origin and development of civilization and culture, a fundamental component of an *historia* of the *peri phuseōs* type.[111] In fact, there seems to be a good deal of consensus that such a descriptive account was contained in Democritus' *Little World -System.* The text that is generally cited in conjunction with this is taken from the historian Diodorus Siculus (DK68B5). According to this account, the first men lived like animals. With no social organization each sought his own food and shelter. Attacked by wild beasts, they banded together from expediency *(hupo tou sumpherontes)* and for mutual protection. During this association humans came to know one another and develop speech.[112] While the first utterances were unclear, they eventually made conventions or contracts *(sumbola)* among themselves for every object and created words to communicate. This occurred, we are told, each and every time humans banded together for similar reasons, and this explains why there are so many different languages. Meanwhile, since humans had no technical skills, they initially lived without houses, clothes, fire, and agriculture. In fact, they didn't even have the notion of storing wild fruits and plants and died in winter from cold and hunger. But humans soon learned from experience *(hupo tēs peiras)* to seek shelter in caves and store food. Later, fire and other useful things were discovered and finally the arts and crafts conducive to civilized existence. In general, it was need and necessity *(chreia)* that taught humans, although necessity also has assistants, notably hands, reason, and a quick mind (Diodorus of Sicily 1.7–8). While much of this account can be traced to sixth-century Ionian accounts, there are clearly elements congruent with certain features of Democritus' own account.

In fragment B26, Democritus contends names are not natural but conventional.[113] Although language is conventional, it is nonetheless understood, for both Diodorus and Democritus, as the result of natural necessity. Thus in B258 and B259, Democritus contends that a necessary condition for a well-ordered society *(en panti kosmōi)* is protection from menacing wild beasts. Moreover, as with Diodorus' account, Democritus (B144) argues that the arts were separated out by necessity *(apokrinai tanagkaion)* (see Vlastos 1945, 592; 1993, 340). That is, humans first discovered arts that were indispensable to their survival. Once this was secured (associated with the notion of abundance), arts such as music developed (B144). In B154, Democritus contends we learned to sing from observing birds singing. Whether or not he considers this as a later development, as with music, he recognizes some of the more necessary arts were due to observations of animals: from the spider, the notion of weaving and mending; from the swallow, the art of housebuilding. Regardless of the period of social evolution, and regardless of the arts under consideration, it is not divine intention that explains the proper way of life to mankind, but the inevitable reaction to human needs and circumstances.

The fact that humans learn from experience is a major ingredient in the reshaping of their souls. Before examining this in the context of politics and ethics, which are also accounted for in the atomic physical theory, it is important to examine the relation between sensation and thought. The atomists contended that the only objective realities were atoms and the void. It follows from this that thought and sensation can be reduced to the interaction of atoms; they can be reduced to a physical mechanism, or more precisely, a form of touch. Aetius (4.8.5; 10 = 67A30) states that, for the atomists, sensations and thoughts are alterations of the body, that is, they are due to the impact of images from outside (see Guthrie 1965, 451).[114]

This deserves closer examination. Like other pre-Socratics, atomists maintained that the soul *(psuchē)* distinguished living things from inanimate things. The soul, like fire, consisted of spherical atoms (there is a natural correlation between heat and life). The spherical shape proper to these atoms enabled them both to permeate the entire body and to draw the whole body into motion since mobility is proper to their nature (Aristotle, *On the Soul* 403b30; 406b20–22). This is how the body became a "self-mover."[115] Democritus makes it abundantly clear that soul is responsible for the state of the body (see DK58B159; Laks 1999, 253). Life and death, meanwhile, are associated with the mechanism of respiration, and there are close analogies with the formation of the universe (Aristotle, *On the Soul* 404a9–16). Just as smaller atoms were pushed out by larger atoms in the formation of the universe, the constant pressure from the environment extrudes tiny soul atoms from the body. But the surrounding air contains similar atoms, and during the act of respiration, these atoms enter the body along with the air, preventing extrusion of the other soul, and balancing, so to speak, the pressure from with-out (Aristotle, *On the Soul* 404 a 9–16.) As long as this balance or resistance is maintained, an animal continues to live, but when death does occur, the individual soul atoms are dispersed throughout the universe.

Theophrastus (*On Sensation* 49–83 = DK68A135) provides a detailed account of the atomists' theory of sensation. All sensation is the result of touch, that is, from the contact of atoms. More precisely, sensation is the result of an alteration in our bodies which occurs each time we are struck by atoms from the outside. Sight functions in the same manner. As in the case of Empe-docles, atomists argue that physical objects are constantly emitting atomic effluences from their surface. These effluences form an approximative image of the object. These images themselves do not reach the eye, but what pene-trates the eyes are *tupoi,* or imprints. The eyes have a purely passive role. Once the object is reflected on the pupil, sensation is somehow stimulated.[116] Thought also depends on a physical mechanism. According to Theophrastus (*On Sensation* 58 = DK68A135), thought is produced when soul atoms per-vade the body and agitate the mind with constant movement.[117] The subject must be neither too hot nor too cold; otherwise the thought will be perturbed.

Atoms differ in size and shape. It is only when atoms form compounds through arrangement and position that secondary qualities can be attributed to them. Since secondary qualities (color, hot, cold, bitter, and sweet, etc.) do not exist by nature but are dependent on an observer, Democritus (DK68B9) notes secondary qualities can only exist by convention *(nomōi),* that is, relative to us *(pros hēmas)* (see Taylor 1999a, 176). But, given that Democritus argues that the physical conditions and ages of individuals affect their judgments, that is, how things appear to them (Theophrastus, *On Sensation* 64), there must be a sense in which sensations have an objective reality and a sense that some judgments are truer than others.[118] Similarly, Theophrastus (*On Sensa-tion* 65–67) notes Democritus argued that flavors were contingent on the form of particular atoms (e.g., sweet flavor consists of round atoms; sour consists of many angled atoms, etc.). Although Democritus may simply mean that sen-sible qualities are determined by atoms that predominate, this still suggests objectivity or true judgment is possible.

With this in mind, something must be said about the atomistic theory of knowledge. The evidence on this point (in particular, with regard to the relia-bility of the senses), is inconsistent, contradictory, and highly controversial. Some evidence strongly suggests that atomists were sceptics; other evidence strongly suggests the contrary. Thus, in *Metaphysics* 1009b12 (= DK68A112; see also *On the Soul* 404a27; 405a5 = DK68A101), Aristotle states that since Democritus contends knowledge is sensation and sensation is a physical trans-formation, what appears to the senses is necessarily true. While this position is similar to the position defended by Protagoras (see Taylor 1999a, 189; see also

DK68A101), Sextus Empiricus gives some convincing evidence to the contrary. According to Sextus Empiricus, Democritus contends that sense perception does not conform to truth (DK68B9), whence Democritus' statement that hot and cold, and sweet and sour exist only by convention (B9). The primary reasons for this (as recorded by Sextus), is that both our bodies and surroundings are constantly changing (DK68B9; see also 68B7 and 68A109). Fragment B7, also reported by Sextus, states that "we know nothing about anything" because of the changing world. But this sceptical position is less clear and even contradicted in other evidence. In DK68B11 (= Sextus Empiricus *Against the Mathematicians* 7.138), Democritus clearly distinguishes two kinds of judgment or cognition *(gnōmē);* one illegitimate and associated with the five senses, and a second one legitimate and associated with the mind. In the famous epistemological dialogue between mind and the senses (DK68B125), it is clear that while Democritus makes a distinction between mind and the senses, or sensation and thought, the mind cannot reach the truth about reality without taking perceptual data derived from the senses as its starting point ("wretched mind *[phrēn],* it is from us that you derive your evidence . . ."). In the final analysis, without recourse to experience or sense perception, it is impossible to attain truth about the nature of things visible and invisible.

Thus it is safe to say that the atomists and Democritus were not sceptics and they did not believe in the extreme Aristotelean imputation that sensation is knowledge. Truth, while not impossible, is extremely difficult to attain. Whence Democritus' contention in B117: "In reality we know nothing since the truth *(alētheia)* is in the abyss *(en buthōi)*." This statement could also be a reply to Protagoras. While the equally famous compatriots and contemporaries agreed with each other that perceptual qualities were relative, Democritus believed perceptual qualities had fixed underlying structures, which could be determined if one had the necessary data (Taylor 1999a, 189 and 193; Woodruff 1999, 307; and Guthrie 1965, 455). There is little doubt that the atomists believed the universe was regulated by rigorous atomic laws (natural necessity). From this perspective, truth has many levels and each level depends on the nature of the object under consideration. Thus, in fragment 68B118, Democritus states "he would rather find a single explanation *(aitiologian)* than possess the kingdom of the Persians." Explanations are clearly possible.

While atomistic theory attributes the explanatory principle of all things to necessity, it is at least theoretically possible to discover the laws of the atomic composition of the universe and human behaviour, since human beings as well as the universe are composed of the same elements, and function according to the same laws. It may be true that reality (and knowledge thereof) is only accessible to the mind but the fact remains that sensation in general, and observation in particular constitute (as with Plato) the first step in the acquisition of this knowledge.[119] There is clearly a sense in which physical and epistemological theory can be incorporated into the political and ethical framework of the atomists.

Fragment B33 is particularily revealing in this regard. Here Democritus notes: "nature *(phusis)* and teaching *(didachē)* are similar, for education reshapes *(metarusmoi)* the human being, and in reshaping *(metarusmousa)* creates a second nature *(phusiopoiei)*." See also B184, 242, which states one becomes virtuous by performing virtuous acts and, therefore, like Aristotle, through habituation. There is some consensus that the verb *metaruthmizei* is employed in the sense of reshaping.[120] The meaning here is thus that teaching can cause a reshaping or reconfiguration *(rusmos)* of the soul atoms and thus produce a different or proper relationship between the body and the soul.[121] In sum, in modifying the natural dispositions with which every human is born, teaching makes a second nature. Virtue itself can thus become a second nature through teaching (see DK68B242).[122] In conjunction with this, Democritus (DK68A1 = Diogenes Laertius 9.45) contends that the ultimate aim in life is cheerfulness *(telos d'einai tēn euthumian)*. He associates cheerfulness with a state in which the soul (soul atoms) is without emotional distress, including fear of gods and death (68B189). This is gained, in large part, through prudence and moderation with particular regard to physical pleasures (DK68B191).[123] Again, the observation of nature and the animal kingdom comes to our aid. And so in B198, Democritus suggests that animals are wiser than humans because they know how much they need when they are in need. What animals unconsciously teach us in this instance is the principle of moderation *(sōphrosunē)*, the sine qua non of wisdom. They only use what they need, whereas humans, if unchecked, are moved by an insatiable desire for excess, for *ploutos,* or wealth (DK68B191, 218–222, 224, 282–284). Just as animals taught humans the necessary arts for the satisfaction of their primary needs (B154), the observation of animals can once again instruct humans in the fundamental questions with regard to a virtuous life in society.

Democritus suggests that wealth is the source of evil things since it leads to social unbalance between the rich and the poor (B281). As with Plato's city of pigs in the *Republic,* before the age of abundance humans lived with "moderation," in keeping with their primary nature (B144). Like the animals, they used only what they needed. This does not mean wealth *(ploutos/chrēmata)* is invariably bad, as suggested in fragment B281 (the analogy seems to be between cancer and wealth). It is good to have wealth as long as its possession is accompanied by reflection, moderation, compassion, and fraternity (DK68B255, 191). Indeed, if wealth is used intelligently, it promotes the public good (B282). Otherwise, wealth is the source of grave political unrest, of *stasis,* for it creates envy, the kind of envy that leads to devising new tricks and wicked deeds forbidden by the laws (B191).[124]

Meanwhile, wealth *(ploutos/chrēmata)* provides the necessary leisure to pursue theoretical and practical sciences, which is what Democritus did (at least in part) with his wealth (DK68B279). But how can one seriously exercise any profession that seeks to improve the human condition in an atmosphere of *stasis* or civil strife? Democritus is clear on the importance of participating in public life (B252–253, 263, 265–266). This consideration must have seriously influenced Democritus' preference for a democratic constitution—even an impoverished one (B251). He chose this regime because it avoids extremes (DK68B255, 261, 191). The necessary condition for such a state is respect for law *(nomos)* since "law proposes to improve the human condition" (DK68B248; see also B47) while leaving everyone free to cultivate their own tastes (DK68B245).

It is not surprising to see law *(nomos)* given such an elevated status by Democritus. Law can educate and thus transform human nature into a virtuous second nature. As a result, despite their differences (B245), humans can form a *kosmos,* a well-ordered social *kosmos* (DK68B258, 259) in the image of the universe.[125] If human communities formed under the force of necessity, they also tended to flourish under the force of necessity, the necessity of avoiding civil strife and fostering virtues conducive to social cohesion, goodwill, moderation, and compassion. In the final analysis, humans can consciously control their own fate or *tuchē,* and as Farrar (1988, 245) correctly notes, create their own future.

Conclusion

As I note in the introduction, the impetus behind this investigation was a detailed analysis of Book 10 of Plato's *Laws*. While I believe this volume can stand on its own, it must be supplemented with a second volume to complete this investigation. The natural theology and the society premised on it that Plato presents in *Laws,* is a reaction to those who wrote works of the *peri phuseōs* type and also to the sophists. The subject of a second volume will be the sophists and their movement and Plato's reaction to both the pre-Socratics and the sophists in the form of his own *historia* of the *peri phuseōs* type: the first "creationist" schema.

Of course, there is nothing to indicate that any pre-Socratics were impious. Indeed, the contrary position is closer to the truth. But the situation is more complex. Although the notion of divinity is inherent in the concept of *phusis* from the very first Greek cosmogonies (thus Anaximander and Heraclitus did not hesitate to use a vocabulary with moral connotations to describe the order that governs the universe), the fact remains that for the *phusiologoi* in general, the order that makes our world a *cosmos* is natural, that is, immanent in nature *(phusis).* It could thus be interpreted that for pre-Socratics in general, the destiny of the universe and the destiny of humanity (and even the destiny of society) can only be determined by *phusis; phusis* understood as blind necessity *(anankē),* without any recourse to intentional cause. This explains why natural theology and its arguments are, in certain measure, a reaction to pre-Socratic writings of the *peri phuseōs* type. The comic poet Aristophanes (*Clouds* 376f; 1036–82) aptly captures their influence on the moral, political, and religious thinking of his time in his parody of the jargon of the "physicists" in *Clouds* (ca. 424 BCE). He introduces the notion of *anankē* (blind necessity identified with *phusis* itself) to trivialize the importance of Zeus *and* to show Zeus does not care for us. And in the famous exchange between Just and Unjust Reasoning, Aristophanes gives an example of the antilogical method of the Sophists and the moral problems that it raises (the weaker argument aptly defeats the stronger). Plato, in his analysis of the accusations raised against Socrates in *Apology* (18b, 19b), does not miss the intimate relation between the Sophistic method and pre-Socratic physics.

Criticism of the gods on moral grounds emerged very early. Xenophanes reproached Homer and Hesiod for attributing to the gods all that which in mortals is blameworthy and shameful. Aeschylus (ca. 525–456), for his part, employed all of his genius to transform the ancient conception of an unjust, impetuous and violent Zeus, that is, Zeus the tyrant, into a Zeus who assures the democratic ideal of justice on which the new Greek state was built. On the other hand, Euripides (480–406) asserted in his *Heracles* (339–46) that even the most exalted god was morally inferior to a human in an analogous situation. And in the *Ion* (436–51), Euripides rebuked the gods for holding humans to a standard they themselves failed to live up to. Euripides went even further. In a fit of rage in *Bellerophon* (frag. 286), he exclaims:

> There are no gods in heaven. To believe in such old wives' tales is folly. You have only to look around you. Tyrants murder, rob, cheat and ravage, and are happier than the pious and peaceful. Small god-fearing states are quickly overwhelmed by the military might of those larger and more wicked. (trans. Guthrie)[1]

The fact that Euripides linked poets with the origin of most of the stories *(muthoi)* that are neither true, nor worthy of the gods is one thing (see *Heracles,* 1341–46), but his refusal to believe in the existence of gods in the face of the prosperity of the wicked and the suffering of the just, indicates a profound and troubling change, which is in stark contrast with Aeschylus' time. The Athens of Aeschylus was marked by deep optimism. Its citizens had just experienced the favor of the gods of the city who defended them from the Barbarians (Aeschylus, *Suppliant Women,* 1018f). Furthermore, the gods were the guardians of human laws and there was a belief in providence and in the traditional values whose principle was the justice of gods. In contrast, Euripides' Athens was the Athens of the Peloponnesian war (431–404 BCE) one of the most sinister and absurd conflicts to have afflicted the world. That war demonstrated that the traditional civil or cosmic gods did not defend the righteous who suffered as much as or more than others. The providence of the gods and the existence of a *nomos* capable of governing with true justice began to be doubted. Under these circumstances, it is hardly surprising that critics contested the existence of gods and asserted that gods were indifferent to human affairs or they were not worthy of worship. Plato, who cites these three forms of impiety in *Republic* 2.365d–e, thought, at least initially, that they could be resolved by reforming traditional education.

However, the *phusiologoi* and their *peri phuseōs* writings represented a far graver problem in his eyes. The Sophists, who argued that the law and morality guaranteed by the gods did not truly exist by nature but derived from convention, found real and effective support in the works of the *peri phuseōs* type. Whereas a rational explanation of the origin and evolution of society reduced the civil and traditional gods to human conventions, the theories of Anaxagoras and Democritus even stripped heavenly bodies of the divinity that had been attributed to them. For Sophists, or more precisely, the second generation of Sophists, the *paradeigmata aretēs* designated anything found to be contemptible in the behaviour of the gods of traditional religion. What remained was a *phusis* stripped of divine attributes and transformed in accordance with the beliefs of the Sophists—notably their beliefs that might is right and that one's egoistic passions should not be restricted.

According to Plato, atheism is a disease that periodically afflicts a certain number of minds (*Laws* 10.888b). The cause of atheism is not the inability to master pleasures and desires (*Laws* 10.886a–b) but rather the ancient and modern theories to which atheists appeal. Therefore, it is necessary to persuade and teach *(peithein kai didaskein)* atheists by means of sufficient proofs *(tekmēria ikana)* that gods exist *(hōs eisi theisi: Laws* 10.885d2–3). Clearly Plato is not addressing the average citizen but powerful and penetrating minds (*Laws* 10.908c3), who will only be satisfied with proof that nature offers divine intelligence and providence. This will be the subject of the second volume.

Notes

INTRODUCTION

1. I concur with Kahn (1979, 105) that this is a direct quote from Clement of Alexandria (see also Guthrie 1962, 204). As T.M. Robinson (1987, 104) notes, following Marcovich (1967, 26), many others contest that the expression *philosophoi andres* was employed by Heraclitus himself (see also Brisson, 1996, 21 and Hadot 2002, 15). The term is also found in Herodotus (1.30), but the sense in which he employs the word is debated (see following note). Heraclides of Pontus, a disciple of Plato, relates in a famous anecdote that Pythagoras coined the word *philosophos* (Heraclides fragment 87 Wehrli = Diogenes Laertius 1.12). Again, there are pros and cons with some like Guthrie (1962, 204) that argue that the term actually antedates Pythagoras or more precisely, that it was employed in an Ionian sense before it was employed in an Italian sense with Pythagoras (again, see below). Heraclitus (DK22B129) actually reproached Pythagoras for his type of *historia* and thus *philosophia*. This at least suggests that both terms could have more than one general meaning.

2. Herodotus (1.30) describes Solon's many travels in pursuit of information as concerned with wisdom *(philosopheon)*. Hadot (2002, 16–17) notes in his popular *What is Ancient Philosophy* that the word *philosophia* is associated here with "general culture" and the "wisdom" derived from it, rather then "a way of life" in which the philosopher engaged in an "exercise of wisdom," an exercise which consisted in a desire to progress toward an almost unattainable ideal (see also Brisson 1996, 23–25 who has a similar position).

Hadot (2002, 180) contends that even if this definition of a philosopher first appears in Plato's *Symposium,* the notion of "spiritual exercises" *(askēsis, meletē)* has a prehistory that goes back to the pre-Socratic thinkers. What interests me here is not techniques to control thoughts, which are an essential component in the exercise, but the practice of *historia/philosophia* for the pre-Socratics. For Hadot (2002, 5), the philosopher's choice of life determines his discourse. This choice is never made in solitude, but in a community or philosophical school and "this existential option, in turn, implies a certain vision of the world, and the task of philosophical discourse will therefore be to reveal and rationally justify this existential option, as well as this representation of the world." (2002, 3). Guthrie (1961, 204), referring to the same context in which *philosophia* was employed for the first time, notes that the word has far deeper meaning for Pythagoras than for the Ionians (see also KRS 1983, 218–19). In the later case, it is close to 'curiosity', whereas in the former case it is associated with a 'purification' and the means of escaping from the 'wheel' (which may explain Heraclitus reproach above). Guthrie (1961, 205) then goes on to say that the word *philosophia* "then as now, meant using the powers of reason and observation in order to gain insight." It is unclear what this insight refers to for Guthrie. But one could say (following Hadot) that it is a way of life based on a representation of the world. This will be implicit rather than explicit in our analysis of the pre-Socratics.

CHAPTER ONE

1. Benveniste (1948, 78–79). For another brief and stimulating point of view, see Howard Jones, (1973, 7–29).

2. Chantraine (1968–1980, 4.1233). It appears, moreover, only one time in Homer (*Iliad* 6.149), in the active intransitive sense of to be born. Nevertheless, it can still be translated as in the active transitive sense of "to grow": *hōs andrōn geneē hē men phuei hē d'apolēgei:* "such is the generation of men: one grows, the other comes to its end." I owe this observation to V. Magnien and M. Lacroix, *Dictionnaire Grec-Français,* Paris, 1969, 2068 who translate the Greek as: "telle la génération des hommes: l'une croît, l'autre vient à sa fin."

3. Chantraine (1968–1980, 4.1235). It is essential to note that the root **bhū-* served to complete the system of the root **es-,* "to exist," in a large number of the Indo-European languages, and in no way indicates that the original meaning of the root **bhū-* is "to exist," "to become." Nevertheless, this is the thesis held by Holwerda (1955), and Kirk (1954). According to the latter, "No one denies that *phuomai* means 'grow'—but *this* may be a derivative meaning. Rather, the truth is that, at the 'primitive' stage of language, there is no firm distinction between 'become' and 'be.' The root *phu-* simply means existence" (1954, 228). However, from the point of view of comparative linguistics, the primary and fundamental meaning of the root **bhū-* is "to grow" rather than "to become" or "to exist." See also Burger (1925.1).

4. Burger (1925, 89). Heidegger (1976, 221), for his part, associates the word *phusis* with the root **gen-:* "The Romans translate *phusis* by the word *natura. Natura* comes from *nasci,* 'to be born, to originate . . .' as in the Greek root **gen-*. Natura means "that which lets something originate from itself." *("was aus sich entstammen lässt").* Pierre Aubenque (1968, 8) appears to understand the same thing: "the unity of meanings of the Greek *phusis* is best understood by considering the etymology of the word: *phusis* comes from *phuesthai* 'to be born,' 'to grow' just as *natura* comes from *nasci,* 'to be born'."

However, as we saw, *phusis* comes from the verb *phuesthai* the root of which is **bhū-* and the primordial meaning of which is "to grow," especially when speaking of vegetation. By contrast, the original meaning of the root **gen-* is "to be born" (which is attested in the majority of Indo-European languages: Greek *gignomai;* skr. *janati,* etc.). Latin derived two groups from this root: *gignō, gēns, genius, ingenuus, ingenium,* etc.; and *nāscor* (old **gnāscor*), *nātus, nātiō, nātūra* (A. Ernout and A. Meillet, 1979, 272). While the idea of "descendence" persists in the first group, it is the meaning of "birth" which persists in the second group (272–273). In this regard, the Greek verb *gignomai*, both by its etymology (it is derived from the same root as *gignō* and *nāscor*) and by its evolution (although *gignomai* almost became a substitute for the verb "to be," the nominal forms retained the original meaning of birth, generation, and race), seems to be much closer than *phuomai* to the two Latin groups derived from the root **gen-*. Indeed, despite the evolution of the family of *phuō* in ancient Greek, the original meaning of "to grow" always persisted.

5. It suffices to consult a Greek dictionary. Nevertheless, for more developments, see Burger (1925). Furthermore, it is interesting to note that this is evidently not an isolated phenomenon. We find the same thing in another family of words that is equally important and which is frequently paired with that of *phuomai*, namely, *gignomai*. As Chantraine (1968–1980, 1.224) notes: "The history of this family of Greek words is dominated by the fact that the original meaning of birth, generation and race deteriorated in the present *gignomai*, which can signify 'becoming' and becomes almost a substitute for the verb "to be." In fact, this meaning is the only one found in modern Greek. All the other forms, notably the nominal ones, have retained the original meaning."

6. If this is the case then how can we explain that the term *phusis*, as well as the present verbal group from which it is derived: *phuō-phuomai*, seems to stem from the root **bhŭ-* and not from the root **bhū-* which clearly reveals their primary and original meaning? Although the answer to that question remains uncertain, the solution proposed by Holt seems at least plausible. According to Holt (1941, 46), what is certain is that in the system of Indo-European alternations **ū* is the degree zero as much as **r, *l, *n* (cf. sanskrit *prabhūtih:* source, origin). Now since there is nothing to indicate that **ū* can become *ŭ*, then it is clear that *phusis* does not present an inherited alternation, but a new Greek alternation: long vowel/short vowel. Moreover, since the nominal *phusis* was created from the present group *phuō-phuomai*, and since the group composed of the old aorist *ephun* and the perfect *pephuka* (both of which are attested in Sanskrit) do not have corresponding middle voices, one can infer, on the one hand, that the opposition between the transitive/factitive *phuō* and the intransitive *phuomai* is relatively recent in ancient Greek and, on the other hand, that their respective meanings are based on the ancient root **bhū-*.

7. In Hesiod's *Theogony* (956–62), Oceanus is a Titan and thus one of the six sons of Gaia and Uranos, Earth and Sky. In Homer, Oceanus is actually the source *(genesis)* of all things (see below).

8. According to Irad Malkin (1998, 41), there is a scene on a late eighth century oinochoe from Ithaca depicting a male and a female each holding a curious plant and this may very well be a reference to Odysseus and Circe.

9. The word *phuē* (growth, stature) is quite common in Homer. As noted in the Liddel Scott and Jones *Greek-English Lexicon,* the word is always employed in Homer of "human form" and never to refer to the "the natural form of a plant." As such, it is often closely connected, if not synonymous, with *eidos* (form) and *demas* (bodily frame). See, for example, *Odyssey* 5.212–213; 6.152.

10. "L'accomplissement (effectué) d'un devenir" et donc "la nature en tant qu'elle est réalisée, avec toutes ses propriétés." Benveniste (1948, 78–79).

11. Thus Kahn (1960/1993, 201,n.1) argues that *phusis* here designates only "its bodily form at maturity" and that therefore there is no reference to "growth" here; but assuredly there is more to it than this; not to mention the fact that the object in question is a "plant." H. Jones (1973, 16–17) puts the accent precisely on the "process of growing" rather than the "result of the growth." He argues "that what Odysseus was actually shown was the way in which the plant was grown as manifested by its outward appearance," that is, its black root and white flower. But I fail to see why the way the plant was growing would be relevant in the current context. Why not say that Odysseus was shown the whole process of growth of the moly plant, that is, the complete properties of the plant as they were realized from the beginning to the end of the plants creation.

12. A. Heubeck (1988, 2: 60). In fact, Heubeck provides a stimulating discussion of this passage here. However, his conclusion that the word *Phusis* means "hidden power"—a position endorsed by Mansfeld (1997, 757n1)—appears, in my view, far to restrictive.

13. The black root only becomes visible after it has been withdrawn from the ground. See my comment on Jones in note 11.

14. See in particular Heraclitus' famous phrase: *phusis kruptesthai philei* ("nature loves to hide," DK22B123); to compare with DK22B54.

15. "The gods for whom all things are possible *(dunantai)* call it moly" *Od.* 10.305–6. For an interesting discussion of this passage in the present context, see Jenny Clay (1972, 127–131). She correctly notes its correlation with Plato's *Cratylus* where the gods, as opposed to mortals, are said to know names *phusei*. Divine speech and revelation are also closely connected with Heraclitus' concept of *phusis* as we shall see below.

16. As Jenny Clay notes: "Only after the plant has been described in detail is its name revealed" (1972,130).

17. This is what provides the "magical power" in the context of an origin myth. For a succinct summary of this position, see Burkert (1992, 124–127). See also below note 19.

18. There is an interesting plant analogy in the *Epic of Gilgamish:* "Gilgamish, I will reveal unto thee a hidden thing, namely a secret of the gods will I tell thee; there is a plant like a thorn; like a rose its thorns will prick thy hands; if thy hands will obtain that plant, thou wilt find new life" (Tablet 11. 266f trad. Heidel).

19. There is an interesting passage in *The Homeric Hymn to Demeter* (ca. 650–550 BCE) in which the verb *phuō* is employed in a similar sense and context. While Persephone was gathering flowers in a lush meadow the Earth grew *(phuse,* 8) as a snare "a flower wonderous and bright, awesome for all to see" (10). From its root *(apo rhizēs,* 12) sprang up *(exe pepukei,* 12) an exceptionally fertile and sweet smelling flower. At 428, we learn that the flower in question was a narcissus that "the wide earth bore

(ephuse) like a crocus." In these passages the verb *phuō* comprises the whole process of growth of the narcissus from beginning to end. Moreover, the story is presented as a truthful account (*nēmertea*, 406; *alēthea*, 435). The *Hymn*, of course, refers to the mythical origins of the Eleusian Mysteries and when Persephone repeats the true story of her abduction by Hades and its aftermath (414–33), the initial scene with the narcissus serves as a sort of catalyst for the origin myth in general and a hope of rebirth for the future initiates. It is also worth noting for the case at hand that Demeter or Mother-Earth is described as life-giving (*pheresbion*, 450, 469). Indeed, she is presented as the *archē* or principle of life (306–312) and thus the prototype of *phusis*. The story therefore contains a wealth of information relative to the early history of the word *phusis*. For a recent analysis of this myth (albeit not in this context), see Foley (1994).

20. According to Svenbro (1993, 15f) *phazein* which is connected with *phrēn* (thought) has a nonacoustic nature and he translates it thus as "showing"or "indicating" with signs; whence my own translation as "explaining" (see also LSJ). This fits in well with the Homeric occurrence of *phusis* noted above.

21. The best discussion of this fragment is still in Kirk (1954, 33–47; 227–231).

22. Kahn (1960/ 1993, 201–2). See also Kahn's commentary in (1979, 99) where he connects *phusis* in Heraclitus with both *historia* (inquiry) and *kosmos* (world order). Huffman (1993, 96) appears to agree.

23. In the case of Heraclitus, this would hold whether or not one argues that he held that the universe had a beginning in time. Notwithstanding the fact that for Heraclitus fire always was, is, and will be (a typical *archē*). What is important is that he believes that the world exhibits an objective structure that can be revealed through *logos*.

24. McKirahan (1994, 392) also puts the accent on the essential characteristics when defining the term *phusis,* but his idea of *phusis* is too static.

25. Thus Kirk (1954, 220) has said, "If we look outside Heraclitus we find that all the uses of the word *(phusis)* by Parmenides and Empedocles, except the notable usage in Empedocles fragment 8, probably involve the meaning 'nature' or 'real constitution' of individual things." The same thesis is well illustrated by D. Holwerda (1955).

26. See Pohlenz (1953, 426). It is perhaps not surprising that in the unique Homeric example of the word, as G.E.R. Lloyd correctly notes, the accent is on magic (1991, 418f). See also Lloyd (1979, 31 n106).

27. Thus McKirahan (1994, 75 n7) following Cherniss (1951, 319 n1). They argue that there was no single word for nature before the end of the fifth century. This also appears to be the position taken by G.S. Kirk (1954, 229f).

28. J. Burnet (1930/1945, 10–11) although he doesn't say exactly when this practise began.

29. KRS (1983, 102–103), appears also to concur with this.

30. Kahn also argues that Aristole's use of *peri phuseōs* in *Generation and Corruption* 333b18 certainly gives the impression that the phrase was employed as a title for Empedocles' poem.

31. The whole book in the case of Schmalzriedt (1970) is dedicated to this subject. There is still a good and valuable discussion in J.W. Beardslee Jr (1918, ch. 11, *peri phuseōs,* 54–67).

32. As for Kahn's argument to support his thesis, see his note (240) in this same work. For a recent discussion, see Naddaf (1998b) and most recently (2003).

33. In reality, a case could also perhaps be made for *phusis* as result, that is, if the accent is placed on the structure, strictly speaking, of the thing, and, for the case at hand, the structure of all things, in sum, the universe or *kosmos.* Thus the expression *peri phuseōs* would be synonymous with *peri kosmou.* Indeed, many scholars, if not the majority, have a tendency to put the accent on the "structure" of a thing when referring to the "true" meaning of *phusis.* Further, the *kosmos* is after all a "starting point" for the inquiry.

34. E. Gilson (1972, 24), for his part, follows the interpretation of Burnet.

35. The same seems to hold for L. Robin. See his corresponding note to this passage in his Pléiade translation.

36. Burnet does mention Plato's *Laws* 10.891c, which is obviously a more proper example than the previous one (1914, 21 n1).

37. See notably H. Cherniss (1935).

38. *Metaphysics* 1.983b9–14. At best this may be considered as one of the definitions of the word *phusis.* In fact, this appears to be the fourth definition of the term *phusis* at *Metaphysics* 5.1014b26–28.

39. The word *archē,* a fundamental concept in Greek philosophy, comes from the verb *archō,* which has the meaning of "to begin" and "to command" and it reflects the two uses of this verb (see, Chantraine 1968–1980, 1.119).

40. Guthrie supports the same thesis: "By nature *(phusis)* is meant an actual material substance—that of which the world is made—which is assumed to be alive and so capable of initiating the changes to which it is itself subject, a fact which the Milesians expressed by referring to it not only as water or air or the boundless, but also as god or divine." (1962.142).

41. English translation: "The fundamental meaning [of the word *phusis*] is the idea of an existence which is self-produced or at least self-determined, in whole or in part, without the need of an external cause."

42. W.A. Heidel (1910, 129); C. Kahn (1960/1993, 201–202); J. Barnes (1982, 19–20). However, the thesis that I am presenting here has not (at least to my knowledge) been developed before.

43. This is precisely what Hesiod attempts to do in the *Theogony.* The *Theogony* is a cosmogonical myth that describes *ex archēs* ("from the beginning," 45), the origin of the world and of the gods and the events which lead to the establishment of the present order. It has both a logical starting point: the natural and social world over which Zeus presides and a chronological starting point: the primordial or precosmic chaos.

44. For a definition of the term *gonē,* see Aristotle, *Generation of Animals* 1.724b12–21.

45. This theory is severely criticized by Aristotle in the same treatise, *Generation of Animals* 724b34f.

46. *Parts of Animals* 1.640a11.

47. *On the Soul* 2.415a29. Moreover, for Aristotle it is the soul, already potentially in the seed and fulfilling a nutritive and generative role, which fills this natural function, *Generation of Animals* 2.735a4f.

48. According to Aristotle, the natural philosophers (those who write *peri phuseōs*) must have a clear idea of the principles of health and sickness in order to complete their investigations on the causes of life and death. Indeed, they do not work on inanimate things. As for physicians, and, in particular, those who study their art in a philosophical matter, they investigate the principles of nature for they believe that the principles of medicine are derived from these (*Sense and Sensabilia* 436a17f., and *Respiration* 480b26–30). In fact, Aristotle states that "the most accomplished investigators into nature generally push their studies as far as to conclude with an account of medical principles." *Respiration* 480b 29–30.

49. This subject is treated in more detail in the Hippocratic treatise *Air, Water, and Places*.

50. The Greek word is *sophistai,* but in the present context, the author is referring to philosophers rather than sophists—albeit the word *sophistai* appears to be employed in a prejorative sense.

51. The author of the treatise *Ancient Medicine* wants to demonstrate that the art of medicine *(technē iētrikē)* is not based on an hypothesis, but that it has a historical origin. He retraces this origin to show that it is the fruit of a long progress and a progress that is far from being finished because there are still "discoveries" to be made (ch. 3). This text (whose date is contested—running from the second half of the fifth century to the second half of the fourth century) is extremely rich in terms of a vocabulary of research and discovery which, as I will argue in more detail further on, is an integral part of the third stage of an investigation of the *peri phuseōs* type. Indeed, the verbs signifying "to discover," *heuriskō* and *exeuriskō,* are employed twenty-three and five times respectively and that of *zēteō,* to investigate, is used sixteen times in this treatise. Consider, for example, the following text: "Medicine has for a long time possessed its own means. It has discovered *(heurēmenē)* both a starting point and method through which many valuable discoveries *(ta heurēmena)* have been made over a long period of time. By such a method, too, the rest of the science will be discovered *(heurethēsetai)* if anyone who is clever enough is versed in the discoveries *(ta heurēmena)* of the past and makes these the starting point of his research *(zētēi)*." (Trad. J. Chadwick & W. Mann, with revisions)

The vocabulary in question is certainly not necessary to express the idea of progress. The context of a passage can be equally important. For example, in a well known passage in *Laws* 10, as we will see, such a vocabulary is absent although the context leaves no doubt with regard to the meaning. This does not mean Plato ignores such a vocabulary for he employs these terms (as well as certain equivalents) numerous times in *Laws* 3 when discussing the origins of civilization. Further, Aeschylus employs these terms numerous times in the famous passage of the *Prometheus* (442–506), which describes man's progress from a negative to a positive state (first half of the fifth century), while Sophocles in a no less famous passage of the *Antigone* (332–371) on human progress does not employ them. These texts will be examined in volume two. Finally, it is worth noting that a vocabulary expressing the idea of progress is attested well before the fifth century. We find the verbs *epheuriskō* and *zēteō* in Xenophanes' famous fragment 21B18 as well as in many of Heraclitus' fragments (see below). Pre-Socratics wrote both of these in the sixth century. Their texts will be examined in chapter 4. It is difficult to determine exactly when such a vocabulary first expressed the idea of progress. I will attempt to show that such a concept is at least in germination in Hesiod. And in any event, it is clearly attested in several of the *Homeric Hymns,* including the *Hymn to Hermes* (ca. 550–500 BCE). For an interesting discussion see J. Jouanna's preface to his new edition of *De l'ancienne médecine,* 34–49.

52. It is obvious that Heraclitus is at least an inspiration.

53. Alcmaeon, DK24A13–17; Parmenides, DK28B17,18; Anaxagoras, DK59A107 to 111; Empedocles, DK31A81–84. This is analyzed in more detail in subsequent chapters.

54. This is the psychology behind the Homeric example of *phusis.* For an interesting correlation with Empedocles, see Burkert (1992, 126). I will, of course, return to this idea further on.

55. As Lloyd notes in his introduction to *Hippocratic Writings,* 43 the word *hupothesis* is employed here in the sense of an unverified assumption. For a more detailed analysis see Lloyd (1991, 49–69).

56. See in particular the treatise *Prognosis.*

57. There is a great deal of controversy on precisely whom the author of *Ancient Medicine* is attacking. For a more detailed analysis see Lloyd (1991, 49–69).

58. DK24B4. On the importance of political metaphors (see chapter three).

59. G.E.R Lloyd, *Hippocratic Writings* Introduction, p. 28.

60. For a more recent study, see G. Plambock (1964). For the case at hand, Souilhé's study remains by far the most instructive treatment to date.

61. Thus, in the Hippocratic treatise *The Nature of Man,* the four humours (blood, phlegm, yellow bile, and black bile) are distinguished by convention *(kata nomon),* that is, recognized as such by language), and equally by nature *(kata phusin)* since their forms *(ideai)* are distinct: phlegm does not resemble *(eoikenai)* blood, nor does blood ressemble bile; they differ in colour and in their tangible qualities, the hot, the cold, the dry and the wet. Things that are so different in form and in *dunamis (tēn ideēn te kai tēn dunamin)* cannot be the same thing. "Each thing has its own *dunamis* and nature *(hekaston auteōn echei dunamin te kai phusin tē heōutou).* If a man is given a medication that withdraws the phlegm, he will vomit the phlegm; if he is administered one which withdraws the bile, he will vomit the bile" (ch. 5). Here is an interesting parallel in Plato's *Protagoras* 349b: "I believe that the first question was this: Wisdom,

temperance, courage, justice, and piety—are these five names for the same thing, or is there underlying each of these names a unique thing *(tis idios ousia)*, a thing which has its own power or function *(pragma echon heautou dunamin hekaston)*, each one unlike any of the others."

62. Edition Nauck = DK59A30. This passage could be compared with Euripides *Troades* (884–888) where nature *(phusis)* is also seen as taking on the attributes of divinity and becoming an object of piety. But the accent in the *Troades* is put on the current laws of nature. Indeed the expression is *anankē phuseōs*.

63. Although *pē te* is corrupt, the general meaning is not in doubt.

64. See Aristotle, *Metaphysics* 1.984b9–22 where Anaxagoras is explicitly mentioned in this context.

65. See also *The Homeric Hymn to Demeter,* 242, 260. Although it is not surprising in Euripides' fragment to see *athanatos* (immortal) employed to qualify *phusis* (since whatever the stage in the universe's evolution: *phusis* as *archē, phusis* as process, or *phusis* as result, it is always immortal), *agērōs* (unageing), by contrast, with *kosmos* is somewhat surprising unless this order itself is meant to evoke a certain reverence on the part of the observer.

66. DK12B2–3.

67. See forward to the Budé edition (Les Belles Lettres), 183. For a perfect parallel with this passage, see also the Hippocratic treatise *Regimen* 1.2.1.

68. For Anaximander, see DK12A10–11,30. See also, Xenophanes DK21B29,33; Heraclitus DK22B36 (and the Hippocratic treatise *Regimen* 1.10.1); Parmenides DK28B11; Empedocles DK31B62; Anaxagoras DK59B4, A1,42; Democritus DK68B5,34, A139.

69. Empedocles employs corporeal attributes to describe his moving principles: Love and Strife (see, DK31B17). Indeed, even Parmenides conception of Being is not devoid of this phenomenon.

70. See the first definition of this term Aristotle gives at *Metaphysics* 5.1023b26–27.

71. The origin of this theory is the topic of much discussion but I will not enter into the debate here. My own position is that this theory does not belong to a single author but to Plato's critic of the present state of theories of the *peri phuseōs* type. For an interesting analysis of this passage, see Ada Neschke-Hentschke (1995, 137–164).

72. Although E.R. Dodds (1973, 1) seems to be correct (in opposition to L. Edelstein, 1967, 92–93) on the use of the term *epidosis* (which was generally not employed in the fourth century to reflect the idea of progress), in the context in question there is little doubt that Plato employs this term to mean progress. And for all those who are unconvinced, I would like to refer them to *Laws* 6.781e–782d where Plato summarizes the position he outlined on human progress in book 3. This rarely cited passage is interesting in many respects. First, it shows Plato's ambiguity with regard to the origin of man, that is, he does not seem certain that man, and consequently the universe (at least from a teleological perspective) had a beginning in time (781e5–782a3). More-

over, he appears to insist, like the pre-Socratics, that it was the changes of the seasons, that is, climatic conditions (*strophas hōrōn pantoias,* 782a9), which stimulated the numerous transformations (*pamplētheis metabolas,* 782b1) in living things, including human (*ta zōia,* 782a9). These are not physical transformations strictly speaking, as with Empedocles, but they are rather the transformations of animal regimens due to the effect of climatic variations on the environment. In the case of human beings, this also helps to explain the diversity of cultures. Indeed, Plato states that before the appearance (and thus the discovery) of agriculture, men behaved like animals (782b3–8) and he associates this with the origin of human sacrifice (782c1). In sum, these passages leave clearly understood that Plato developed a theory of human progress.

73. The author of the Hippocratic treatise *Ancient Medicine* (ca. 450–400 BCE) employs these verbs on numerous occasions (notably in ch. 3) in his claim that the art of medicine is the fruit of a long progress and a progress that is far from being finished because there are still discoveries to be made (see above note 51). Aeschylus (525–455 BCE) also employs them in his famous ode to progress in the *Prometheus* (442–506). The vocabulary of research and discovery is already evident in Xenophanes (ca. 570–470 BCE). He thus employs the verbs *zēteō* and *epheuriskō* in his contention that human progress entails research and discovery (DK21B18).

CHAPTER TWO

1. The basic meaning of the word *muthos* seems to have been "something one says," whence *muthos* has the sense of "word," "saying," "advice," or "story," in Homer. The word *muthos* designates the content of the speech rather that the form, which is designated by *epos.* For example, see Homer, *Odyssey* 11.561, "to hear my word and speech" *(epos kai muthon akouseis); Iliad* 9.443, "to be both a speaker of words" *(muthōn)* and "a doer of deeds" *(ergōn).* See Chantraine (1968–80, 3:718–19); Martin (1989,12); Kirk (1970,7); Naddaf and Brisson (1998c, vii–x).

2. The word cosmogony includes the connotation that the existing world order has implications for understanding the present human condition (see Lovin and Reynolds 1985, 5).

3. For what follows, see Eliade (1963, ch. 3; and 1965, ch. 2).

4. A perfect example of this is the cult of Tammuz. See Eliade 1978, 1:66–67. For the analogy with Demeter, see Burkert 1992, 159–61, 276–89. Hesiod alludes to this in the *Theogony,* as we will see below. On the corn king, see Gordon Chide 1954, 72.

5. As Jean Bottéro notes in the conclusion of his section on "The Monarchical Principle and the Organization of the Divine World": " it should become increasingly clear that the system of the organization of the pantheon, vis-à-vis the world in itself, was in all aspects nothing but the magnified reflection of the political system" (1992, 214).

6. For dating, see Dalley (1988, 228–230) for whom the text goes back at least to the twelfth century BCE. This also appears to be Jean Bottéro's position (1992, 214).

R. Labat (1970, 36) places it in eleventh century BCE. I follow Dalley's translation in this chapter. For a succinct summary of the poem, see E. Cassin (1991, 155–62).

7. For an interesting summary of this development and its relation to the geographic milieu, see T. Jocobsen in Frankfort (1949, 184–87).

8. R. Labat (1970, 38, n5). According to Jacobson (1949, 186) in Frankfort, Anshar and Kinshar represent the upper and lower sides of the gigantic ring which resulted as the silt deposits continued to grow. Therefore, the sky and the earth should be associated with Anu and Nudimmund respectively. This entails, for Jacobson, that the origin of the world for the Mesopotamians is closely connected with the geological observations of their own country (1949, 187).

9. According to Jacobson, this indicates that the magic in the spell and the authoritative command associated with it thus supplants pure physical force (1949, 189). This appears to be corroborated in Bottéro's remark that divine commands were likened to destinies (1992, 224).

10. According to Eliade (1965, 15), the *apsu* designates the waters of chaos before the Creation.

11. Karen Rhea Nemet-Nejat notes that "the Mesopotamians believed that what happened in the heavens was mirrored on earth and thus that the movements of the heavenly bodies could be connected with gods, kings and countries in order to make predictions" (1998, 90).

12. Thus from the eyes of Tiamat flow the Euphrates and the Tigris (V.40). See Bottéro (1992, 220 and n9).

13. This was the standard account of humanity's creation in ancient Mesopotamia. However, there is another version in which the human race emergd from the ground like plants. See Nemet-Nejat (1998, 177) and Walcot (1966, 55–57).

14. According to Burkert (1996, 96), this demonstrates the degree to which the king is in need of Marduk's favor and appears to be his slave.

15. Karen Rhea Nemet-Nejat (1998, 178f) gives a succint summary of the evolution of kingship from a temporary position to a permanent one. She explains the movement from the initial belief in mysterious and impersonal supernatural forces as controlling the universe through the progressive humanization of these forces (in particular, the powers of fertility) in order to have a constructive relation with them: "eventually this lead to a growing preference for the human form over the older, non human forms *(numina)* and a preference for organizing the gods according to human patterns of family and profession." The third millenium ushered in a period of war. Kingship was at first a temporary office during times of danger. When the danger passed the king no longer held power. Once war became chronic, the office of king became a permanent position and, once in office, the kings tried to find ways to maintain their position, hence a type of primitive democracy. It was only after the gods were no longer associated with natural phenomena that they became anthropomorphized; they were then regarded as an aristocracy of landowners like the country's most powerful upper class. It is therefore not surprising that gods created mankind to serve them.

This explains why the pantheon included various administrators and divine artisans. In this way, man's world was reflected in the heavenly world of the gods. See also Bottéro (1992, 223–24).

16. However, the story is somewhat more complex, as Eliade notes (1978, 1:63). See also Jacobsen in Frankfort (1949, 214–15).

17. According to LSJ there are only three occurrences of the word *theogonia* in Greek literature: two in Herodotus (1.132; 2.53) and one in Plato (*Laws* 10.886c5). The word does not appear in Hesiod's poem. It is encountered for the first time in Herodotus. The meaning Herodotus employs *theogonia* at 1.132 is particularly interesting; it is employed in the context of the ritual followed by the Persians when they sacrifice to the gods. On the one hand, the one who makes the sacrifice must wish well-being solely not only for himself, but for all Persians. On the other hand, once the offering is deposited, a magus *(magos anēr)* must chant an incantation *(epaoidēi)* in the form of a theogony *(epaeidei theogoniēn)*. According to P. E. Legrand (1932), in a note which accompanies his translation of this passage, Herodotus was mistaken to think that nature of this chant followed the genre of Hesiod's work. For Legrand it was a species of litany with an enumeration of divine characters, as well as their attributes and their qualities. However, there is no reason to believe that Herodotus was not well informed on the nature of this chant. If the magus chanted an incantation in the form of a theogony, it was to return to the origins in order to assure control over the origin of the thing. For the case at hand, what was desired was the well-being of all the world. The use of the word at 2.53 summarizes the meaning of the word in the context of Hesiod's *Theogony:* "for Homer and Hesiod are the poets who composed our theogonies and described the gods for us, giving them all their appropriate titles, offices, and powers" (2.53). I say "summarizes rather well" because just before this (2.52), Herodotus states that the gods were so named because "they disposed all things in order" (2.52.1) and established the physical and moral/social order of the universe. In other words, a theogony explains how the present order of things was established.

When Plato employs the word *theogonia* in *Laws* 10.886c5 in reference to "the most ancient accounts" *(hoi palaiotatoi* 886c3) about the gods (in particular, Hesiod's account), he puts the accent on its etymology: "The most ancient accounts [about the gods] first relate how the original generation *(hē prōtē phusis)* of the sky and so forth occurred and then, shortly after, relate how the gods were born *(theogonian)* and how, once born, they behaved toward one another" (886c3–6). Plato is primarily preoccupied with the fact that these works emphasize that the genesis of the universe *antecedes* the birth of the gods *(theogonia)*; in other words, the gods have nothing to do with the creation, strictly speaking, of the physical universe. There is little doubt that Plato is thinking in particular of Hesiod. As we shall see, the bard gives at least two versions of the generation of the universe in his *Theogony*. However, whatever the role attributed to the gods in Hesiod's theogonic poem, both Herodotus and Plato concur that a *theogonia* explains how the present order of things was established. And if one were to synthesize the observations of both Herodotus and Plato, one could say that Hesiod's *Theogony* describes the origin of the world and the gods as well as the events which led to the establishment of the present order. In sum, the word theogony cannot be understood in its etymological sense in the context of Hesiod's *Theogony*. To get a proper idea of its meaning, the content of the whole poem must be taken into consideration. Thus West writes, "I use 'theogonic' not in a strictly etymological sense, but to describe that which treats of the same subject as Hesiod's *Theogony,* to wit: the origin of the world and the gods, and the events which led up to the establishment of the present order" (1966, 1) From this perpective, the adjective theogonic becomes synonymous with cosmogonic. On this point, see A.W.H. Adkins (1985, 39).

18. See West (1966); Kirk (1960, 63); Lamberton (1988); Nagy (1982); Rosen (1997); Janko (1982). Janko, for his part, places Hesiod's work in the first half of the seventh century. He argues that Hesiod is thus a contemporary of Archilochus and Semonides (94–98).

19. The steady stream of inscriptions around or after 750 BCE point to this period for the adoption of the alphabet into Greece. For some recent discussions, see, Snodgrass (1971, 351); Coldstream (1977, 342); Powell (1997, 18–20); Burkert (1992, 25–26). According to Walter Burkert, the inscription already reflects a practice of writing books—something that would have been learned from the Phoenicians.

20. Indeed, the interaction with the audience can directly affect the form and the content of both the composition and the performance.

21. Gregory Nagy (1982, 45). Furthermore, according to Robert Lamberton, "we are not in a position to explain clearly the relationship between the composition of these poems and their recording in writing, nor do we know how closely these poems we have resemble the ones recorded in the early centuries of Greek literacy" because, as Parry demonstrated, "they were born in an oral rather than a literate context" (1988, 14).

22. As L. H. Jeffrey notes, because of the similarities between the Boeotian and Chalcidic scripts, "it is . . . almost certain that Boeotia received her alphabet from Chalcis" (1990, 90). This is also West's position: "it was probably from Chalcis that the Boeotians got their alphabet . . . they must have had it by Hesiod's time or else we would not have his poems" (1978, 29). Moreover, West contends that "Hesiod must have been one of the first Greek poets to take the momentous step of writing his poems down, or more likely of dictating them to someone who knew how to write. He was no professional singer. He acquired the ability to compose by listening, as people often do in countries where oral poetry is education and entertainment in one. But in competition he could not stake his chance on the inspiration of the moment: he prepared his poem beforehand with labourious care" (1966, 48). On Euboea's role in the introduction of the alphabet, see Powell 1997, 22 and note 39 for other references. Robb, for his part, contends that Hesiod composed not in a local dialect, Boeotian, but in a panhellenic *koinē* of epical speech, with its heavy component of Ionic (1994, 257).

23. Of course, there are those who would argue that oral poetry cannot be learned by rote—at least not verbatim—because oral poetry entails performance and therefore improvisation. The question here is also to what degree writing influences the performance.

24. This is Albert Lord's (1960) general thesis. He argues that since an orally composed poem cannot be transmitted without major changes, and since the powers of

poets are destroyed if and when they write, then oral poems must have been *dictated* (124f). Lord is referring in particular to Homer, but I assume that it would also hold for Hesiod. See West (1966, 47 n8). Lord's thesis on dictation has been championed most recently by Janko (1990).

25. For a more detailed discussion, see Murray (1993, 77f) and Coldstream (1977, 200f).

26. See Murray (1993, 79). As Jeffery notes (1976, 65), if the column was indeed his memorial, then this is a sure sign that Cleomachos was accorded heroic status.

27. The pottery is mainly Corinthian from 700 to 600 BCE.

28. Of course, this may only suggest that the Eretrians lost the city.

29. Janko (1982, 94) argues that Hesiod is a contemporary of Archilochus and Semonides. However, if we place the *floruits* of Archilochus and Semonides *circa* 680–660 (a date with which Janko would concur), I see no good reason to contest the dates in question for Hesiod. Indeed, Janko's closing paragraph on the issue (after a critical analysis of the scholarly literature on the subject) seems to reinforce this dating: "Thus *Th* may best be placed after the outbreak of the Lelantine war in the closing years of the eighth century, and certainly not after *c.* 660, so as to allow imitation of Semonides, while *Erga* will date from later in Hesiod's career" (1982, 98).

30. Murray (1993, 79) sees the future tense as looking back; West (1966, 43) as an indication that slings and bows were no longer used—but otherwise their respective interpretations are the same. Jeffery (1976, 66), for her part, contends that the "slings and arrows" were simply "the weapons of outsiders."

31. It would not be extraordinary, according to Coldstream (1977, 350) if Amphidamas received similar honors in Chalcis. This point is also made by Murray (1993, 79).

32. The main eulogy is at *Theogony* 98–103; but see also 80, 430, 434. I do not believe that Hesiod makes a clear distinction between kings and nobles. In the *Works and Days,* he employs *basileus* in the plural (e.g., 38, 248, 261, 263) when addressing or referring to the leaders of Thespies. Since it is doubtful that there could be many kings, I prefer kings/nobles.

33. I prefer to translate *themistes* as "settlements" because of the context. The context implies that the settlements in question are themselves based on custom or precedent, as Robb notes (1994, 80). The fact that *dikē* is employed almost synonymously with *themis* enables a number of possible translations. However, the general meaning is not in doubt, that is, *dikai* are passed down according to *themis,* that is, oral precedent.

34. For a detailed analysis of the different approaches to and interpretations of these verses, see Robb (1994, 77–78); Gagarin (1986, 24, 107).

35. That the judgments or decisions *(dikai)* are based on *themis,* that is, custom or precedent, suggests a body of oral law which has been passed down orally over the generations (see Jeffery 1976). Since Hesiod puts the accent on the power of poetry, this would entail that the "oral precedents/customs" had to be poetized, that is, put into

verse and set to music (and therefore performed) in order to be conveyed. This conforms well with the aim of the *Theogony*: how Zeus, the father of the Muses, established a new socio-political order for gods and humans. Let us remember that the Muses will speak the truth *(alēthea)* about Zeus (*Theogony* 34–52), a truth which holds for the past, present, and future (32) and which is based on sacred conventions and ways *(nomoi* and *ēthē)* (65–67). This does not entail, from my own perspective, as some contend, that there was already a body of oral law that formed the background for a written law code. See, for example, Roth (1976).

36. At *Theogony* 65–67 we are told that the Muses sing *(melpontai)* the *nomoi* (laws or sacred conventions) and *ēthē* (customs or ways) of the immortals. This strongly suggests that the king's pronouncements would be set to music. As Jesper Svenbro (1993, 113) has noted, *nomos* and *dikē* are always orally dispensated, that is, intended for the ear (e.g., *akoue dikēs,* listen to justice, Hesiod tells Perses at *Works and Days* 213).

37. *Theogony* 30. The *skēptron* is the symbol that they are the gods' representatives. However, it denotes the staff carried not only by kings (*Il.* 1.279) but also by priests (*Il.* 1.15) and prophets (*Od.* 11.90). This is also the case, at least temporarily, for anyone who stands up for the assembly of leaders (*Il.* 1.245). See West (1966, 163).

38. See Eliade (1963, 149).

39. *Gignesthai* is most often employed in the sense of "to be born," and to be born from a mother in sexual or asexual reproduction. Although Hesiod recounts a process of genesis *(geneto),* the first cosmogenesis strongly suggests he is not only "inviting us to relive a birth," as J. P. Vernant contends (1983, 370), but that he is also responding to a preexisting problem. The Spartan lyricist Alcman (ca. 600 BCE) certainly appears engaged with a preexisting theoretical problem: "For when matter *(hulē)* began to be arranged there came into being a kind of way *(poros),* as it were a beginning *(archē)*" (frag. 3; trans. Kirk). For a discussion of Alcman's theogonical cosmogony, see Kirk (1983, 47–49). Given that Hesiod antecedes Alcman by a couple of generations, his own theogonical cosmogony must have influenced Alcman. Hesiod's work was certainly widespread.

40. Akin, one could say, to Anaximander's *apeiron,* as we will see further on.

41. This also appears to be the meaning (in LSJ) *to chaos* "the first state of the universe." *Chaos* has also been interpreted to be a dark and boundless waste (e.g., Hölscher 1953/1970). This would fit in better with the initial state prior to the cosmogonical process, although it is somewhat consistent with the description of Chaos as a gap between Earth and Tartaros at *Theogony* 736–45. But again, this is a description of the nature of the gap itself *after* the cosmogonical process began rather than the precosmic stuff at point zero. For a discussion of this, see KRS (1983, 41). For more on the etymology, see West (1966, 192–93).

42. Cornford (1950, 95f), and (1952, 194f). The idea goes back to Wilamowitz; see West, 1966; KRS (1983, 38); D. Clay (1992, 140); Vernant (1991, 369–71). This is also suggested in Plato's *Laws* 10.886c 3–6. In Vernant's otherwise brilliant account, Tartaros is hardly mentioned. The focus of his analysis is the relation between Chaos and Gaia.

43. KRS (1983, 42–44); West (1966, 211–13) cites similar sources when discussing the castration of Uranos.

44. Tartaros is said to be enclosed by a high bronze wall (726) and Night, in a triple row, round its neck (727). It is unclear, at least to me, if the three rows of night extend from the bronze wall enclosing Tartaros to the roots of earth. At 811, we are told that the underworld is entered through shining gates but the location is not specified.

45. This is correctly noted by McKirahan (1994,12), who otherwise sees the initial gap as what separates heaven and earth. He sees a similar gap between earth and tartaros. He locates tartaros at the *bottom*.

46. Most renditions give a spherical universe rather than a layered universe; e.g. McKirahan (1994, 12); Hahn (2001, 177–178). It is true that sky is said to cover earth completely round about, but Hesiod's cosmos is hardly spherical.

47. In another passage, Hesiod says that only Earth and Sea have their roots *(rhizai)* in the chasm (728). More precisely, he states that above Tartaros are the roots of Earth and Sea (728). M. Miller Jr. (2001, 263–264) argues the roots in question are in Tartaros itself.

48. Tartaros remains like Chaos itself, undifferentiated. Typhoeus, the monster Zeus challenges and defeats in the final episode (820–80), appears to represent the forces of chaos. The monster that was conceived in Tartaros is properly relegated there after its defeat.

49. From which comes the expression *chaeos zopheroio,* "from the foggy abyss," in *Theogony* 884. For an excellent summary of this aspect of cosmogonic myths, see Eliade (1968, 5:60–64).

50. On the role of Night for Hesiod, see Ramnoux (1959).

51. On Hesiod's use of Tartaros in the neuter plural form at line 119, see Miller Jr. (1983, 138).

52. To make Eros "the" principle of movement rather than "a" principle of movement entails that Eros was also behind the generative force that enabled Chaos and Earth to generate their respective products. What is certain is that Eros has no parents in the *Theogony,* as Plato correctly notes in the *Symposium* 178b.

53. Even Chaos, which is gramatically neuter, is treated as female : *hē chaos.*

54. Theia, Iapetos, Koios, Krios, Rheia, and Kronos are not pesonifications of anything. It is worth noting for what follows that the Titans appear no less as givers of good things than the Olympians. For this perspective, *Theogony* 46 and 110 may refer to either the Titans only or to both Titans and Olympians, as opposed to 633 which refers to only the Olympians.

55. This is at least one of the reasons why Hesiod's *Theogony* appears to lack structure. For an interesting recent analysis, which strongly challenges this view, see Hamilton (1989). Mazon (1928), for his part, argues that Hesiod placed the Prometheus scene here in order to show that the defeat of humans is much easier

than the defeat of Titans. According to Hamilton, mankind's interests are central to the story: not only are they being judged, but fire is stolen for their benefit and withheld to their detriment, not to mention that woman is fabricated as an evil for them (34).

56. However, in the *Works and Days,* there is also a version presented in the so-called "myth of the metals." In this version, mortals in general are said to have been "created" *poiēsan* (110), by the gods.

57. Although these references are taken from Hesiod's description of the golden age in the myth of the metals (*WD* 90–92, 109–125), there is no good reason it would not equally apply to the human condition prior to Prometheus' intervention. What is unclear is the status of women. As we shall see, there is no account of the origin of men in the context of the Prometheus episode in either the *Theogony,* or the *Works and Days,* just women.

58. The Greeks could clearly see that they got the better part of the sacrifice. The Prometheus episode also clearly explains why, and the upshot is that humans must henceforth sacrifice to the gods to reestablish the broken bond (*Theogony* 556–57).

59. In the version of the creation of woman in the *Theogony,* woman is not in fact called Pandora, or any other name. Nor does any god other than Hephaestus (who moulds her from clay, 571) and Athena (who aptly dresses her) contribute to her charms, although she is presented to both men *(anthrōpoi)* and gods (*T* 585–88). In *Works and Days* (which follows the same sequence with respect to the confrontation between Prometheus and Zeus), Pandora is molded by Hephaestus from clay *and* water (61) into a sweet maiden. She is then taught skills, including weaving, by Athena, seduction by Aphrodite, and deception by Hermes, etc. Since each Olympian contributes an attribute at Zeus' command, she is given the name Pandora, a gift to man from all the gods (80–82). There is something additionally perverse in the fact that men initially emerged whole from Mother Earth and enjoyed her bountiful fruits, whereas her natural counterpart, woman, had to be created, albeit from earth itself. Walcot (1966, 65–70) attempts to trace the Pandora figure to Egypt, but given the fact that Egyptian women were treated as the virtual equals of men, it is difficult to account for Hesiod's extreme misogyny there.

60. In an interesting but rarely cited passage in the *Theogony,* describing the battle between Zeus and Typhoeus (820–880), Hesiod compares the flames, which consume Typhoeus after he was struck by Zeus' lightning bolt, to the heat/flames employed by young men or artisans *(aizēōn)* in the art *(technē,* 863) of melting iron (or tin) into crucibles (862–864). This passage suggests Hesiod understood that man managed to civilize himself through the arts of fire. On this point, see Schaerer (1930, 4). More important, there is no suggestion this art is secret, that is, a divinely guarded secret restricted only to the initiated. Indeed, it is unclear whether or not Hesiod sees fire as a gift of the gods. In *Hymn to Hermes* (the date of which is uncertain, but could very well be from the seventh or sixth century, see R. Janko 1982, 133–150), it is Hermes who first invents fire sticks and fire (111), the new *puros technē* (108) that enables mankind to produce and control fire at will. For a discussion, see J. Clay (1989, 95–151).

61. Themis and Mnemosyne are thus Titans. This means that certain Titans were not relegated to Tartaros following their defeat. Of course, what Themis and Mnemosyne represent are indispensable to Zeus' own reform, but it is nonetheless strange that Hesiod fails to prepare us for this. For a more general discussion, see Solmsen (1949).

62. Whether or not Hesiod added it himself, it should be no surprise that at the end of the *Theogony* there is a short heroogony (937f). After all, the heros are the offspring of Zeus and his cohorts. What is surprising and confusing is that Zeus must lie with mortal women and the goddesses with mortal men (963–1018). The ultimate consequence of this is that heroic society could then be considered coeval with, as well as a model of, divine society. How this fits in with the Prometheus story is another question. What is consistent is that procreation is still the natural means of reproduction rather than emerging from the soil whole.

63. Many scholars (e.g., Kirk 1970, 212–22; Eliade 1978, 1:139–61; Murray 1993, 87–90) argue that Hittite/Hurrian and Cannaanite sovereignity are closer to Hesiod's account than is the *Enuma Elish*. I certainly do not get the same picture from my reading of the texts in Pritchard's *ANET* (1969). While there are obvious parallels, I concur with Walcot (1966, 26, 32f) that parallels in the *Enuma Elish* are much closer. Although the *Enuma Elish* (as noted above [note 16]) goes back, in its present form, to the eleventh or twelfth century BCE, it is much older. Moreover, the epic continued well into the Seleucid period, since it is employed by the bilingual priest of Baal, Berossus, in his *Babylonica*. In fact, Laroche (1981/1994, 1:528) forcefully argues that the parallels between Hurrian/Hittite and Canaanite pantheistic organizations and theomachies are so striking that they must all stem from a common source: Babylon (see also Kapelrud 1963, 70). Of course, there is another problem here; Murray (1993, 90) argues there is no evidence in Hesiod for a specific vocabulary, independent of the Homeric epic, that we could say was a well-established theogonic tradition with its own formulaic language. According to Murray, the Mycenean continuity (for which I am arguing here) is not necessary and is indeed improbable. He therefore contends Hesiod must have consciously borrowed the eastern elements from material circulating in Boeotia at the time. However, Burkert (1992, 87–124) has certainly shown a number of obvious parallels between eastern texts and the Homeric epics. Some of these are closely akin to what we find in Hesiod.

64. See Faure (1981, 330–40) for the structure of the pantheon and the city.

65. Paul Faure (1975, 109) certainly takes this for granted.

66. Thus the Hittite sovereignity myth, *Song of Ullikummi*, ends with the bull or symbol of chaos boasting that he will return to take possession of heaven.

67. On the correlation between myth and ritual with respect to these sovereignity myths, see Eliade (1978, 1:139–61); Arvid Kapelrud (1963, 67–81); and Johannes Lehmann (1977, 273–87). The ritual aspect of these sovereignity myths is discussed in the various scholarly articles dedicated to these myths in Bonnefoy 1991, vol. 1.

68. The collapse of Mycenaean civilization was initially thought to be due to foreign invasions, but the evidence now seems to suggest that it was due to internal conflict among the rulers of Mycenaean Greece, albeit augumented by other factors, e.g., major earthquakes.

69. Eliade (1978 1:148–49, 247) insists that the cosmogonic act in the *Theogony* is closer to what we find in Hurrian/Hittite cosmogony than in the Babylonian one, in the sense that neither Zeus nor the storm god create the universe; the cosmogonic act preceded it. Perhaps, but the evidence suggests that it was periodically renewed, as Eliade himself is quick to point out.

70. One could retort that, in all myths of this genre, the supreme gods are not all demiurges like Marduk. Thus, the unfolding of events, which led to the present state of things, can be considered linear. It nevertheless remains true that in Hesiod's *Theogony,* for the first time, the society advocated by Zeus is no longer that in which man effectively lives and, consequently, it cannot be renewed by means of a ritual.

71. The fact that war appears to be a thing of the past in *Works and Days* may indicate that rival cities finally exhausted one another, as the archeological evidence seems to confirm (see Murray 1993, 79). It could also suggest that *Works and Days* was composed some time after *Theogony.*

72. For an analysis of the eastern elements, see West's introduction and commentary (1978).

73. For an interesting correlation between justice and farming in Hesiod, see Nelson (1996).

74. Zeus presides over all atmospheric phenomena: wind, rain, and snow, etc., which directly influence rural life. Zeus prolongs the Indo-european *Dyēus,* which etymologically is the god of the daily sky and more generally the weather god. See Chantraine (1968–1980, 2:399).

75. Thus the famous phrase "And I wish I were not any part of the fifth generation of men, but had died before it came or had died afterward" (174–75, trans. Lattimore), does not attribute a cyclical view of history to Hesiod. The expression only shows Hesiod's revulsion for the present. For an interesting historical analysis of this myth, with which I largely concur, see Rosenmeyer (1957).

76. Many scholars refer to the myth of the metals to show that Hesiod was essentially a pessimist. Their interpretation of the myth is that there is a progressive degeneration of humanity and that the age in which Hesiod is living, the iron age, is the worst of all. It is not possible here to give this myth the place it deserves. My own position on a more optimistic Hesiod should be clear. For a succinct and more optimistic analysis of this myth (one with which I concur), see David Grene (1996, 36–42). See also Rosen (1997, 487), for whom Hesiod is telling us how to live productively and morally in the world, something Homeric poetry does not help us to do. For an analysis of this myth, which makes Hesiod far too ingenious and ahistorical for my liking, see Gregory Nagy (1982, 58), who tends to follow Vernant's overly structural approach.

77. On this point, see West (1978, 30).

78. For an interesting analysis of the estimated size of Hesiod's farm, twenty-five to thirty plus acres, see Neale and Tandy (1996, 27–31). They insist Hesiod was nothing more than a peasant (26–27).

79. *Aretē* in the general sense designates those qualities of human excellence that bring a man success and make him a natural leader in his society. In Homeric society, it was only wealthy males of the social elite who demonstrated qualities that lead to success in war and in times of peace. They also exhibited qualities that protected their subjects. These men could claim the *aretē*-norm and the related titles like *agathos* (good) or *aristos* (best). For the Homeric concept, see Adkins (1997).

80. See Saunders (1991, 43) on hard physical work as a new virtue.

81. I agree with Oswyn Murray—albeit not necessarily for the same reasons— that Hesiod replace the primary social excellence in Homer *(timē)* with something else. Murray calls it *Dikē* or Justice (1993, 61).

82. On the difference between Homer's and Hesiod's conception of justice, see Saunders (1991, 39), who notes there is already an innovation in Hesiod, notably that pure self-interest or injustice does not pay.

83. *Works and Days* 248–250. Moreover, like the Cyclopes, the kings do not appear to fear the gods *(theōn opin ouk alegontes),* 251.

84. See Jeffery 1976, 42; and more recently Murray 1993, 60.

85. Over and above the *dikē* of the nobles is *Dikē* the daughter of Zeus. I disagree with Gagarin (1986) for whom *dikē* is always employed in a judicial sense. In my view Nelson (1996, 23) is correct to argue, contra Gagarin, that *dikē* is also employed in a moral sense, a position that is not uncommon. On the other hand, after she argues convincingly for a correlation between farming and justice, she contends *dikē* has nothing to do with "man's participation in the universal balance of the cosmos" (24), for Hesiod is only preoccupied with the particulars typical of "epic poetry" (25). I find this confusing because Zeus himself is behind the rhythms of nature. Ralph Rosen (1997) defines *dikē* in *Works and Days* as "cosmic justice as it manifests itself in the daily lives of human beings" (485). This is close to my own position. Moreover, Rosen is correct to note that there is a radical difference between Homer's and Hesiod's solution to how humans should coexist: "Hesiod's moralizing, simply put, seeks to promote a world in which humans coexist peacefully, resolve their disputes through law, and regard violence as itself a violation of *dikē*" (485). This may explain why *dikē* is associated with both *metron* and *kairos* ("proportion" or "due measure"). Indeed, not only are these two terms synonymously employed by Hesiod, in particular *Works and Days* (694): "observe due measure: proportion is the best of all things": *(metra phulassesthai, kairos d'epi pasin aristos),* but they are absent in Homer.

86. Could this new concept of justice be applied without a written code of laws? Havelock (1978, 19) sees this newly emerging principle of justice and order in the universe as due to the passage from an oral to a written culture. According to him, oral culture is incapable of conceptualizing justice outside of a pragmatic application of daily procedure. The justice of the nobles is not the justice of Zeus although they themselves may see it as justice and as a question of *timē* or honor. *Dikē* is what nobles have

the right to expect between certain persons in a given situation. Murray (1993, 61), for his part, contends Hesiod also created a political vocabulary.

87. Although most scholars give precedence to Zaleucus and Charondas, Robb (1994, 84) contends that Crete can make the best claim because it "has yielded our earliest inscriptional for the existence of written laws anywhere on Greek soil." He argues that the sources citing Locri and Catana are too late and unreliable (90).

88. For a good discussion, see Willetts (1977, 216–23); and more recently, Robb (1994, 99–124). One interesting feature about the advent of law codes, as Detienne (1988, 41) has noted, is that they were always exposed in a public space for all to see. Seeing was more important than reading.

89. On this point, see Gagarin (1986, 62–66), which includes the corresponding references. See also Detienne (1988, 39). As Detienne notes on a number of occasions throughout this article, writing is a political and public gesture.

90. According to Coldstream (1977), this is the earliest known example of "alphabetic writing being pressed into the service of the *polis*" (302). Gagarin (1986, 81) contends that "the main purpose of the Drerian law is to prevent the judicial proces from being corrupted or otherwise abused for political or financial gain" (86). I largely concur with this. See also Robb 1994, 84. For a very different interpretation, see Osborne (1996, 186), for whom the primary purpose of the law was "to control the distribution of powers within the elite." It is thus an elite "self-regulation."

91. For a detailed analysis of the Gortyn law, see Robb (1994, 102), and Willetts (1977), for whom even "a serf family had real social and legal status on the evidence of the Gortyn Code" (169).

92. Gagarin (1986) notes it is possible that the earliest written laws were already enacted in situations similar to the one described by Hesiod (109). See also Jeffery (1976, 42).

93. Gagarin (1986, 124) appears to agree with her: "it is certainly possible that a concern for justice . . . was an effect rather than a cause of written laws."

94. As Giorgio Camassa correctly notes in Detienne (1988, 131).

95. This may explain why the laws of Charondas and Zaleucus had a great deal to do with regulating commercial transactions. See Gagarin (1986, 65–66). Robb's thesis (1994, 87), that established oral custom was behind the first law codes and that the first laws codes *did not* address the core of communal concerns, strikes me as improbable.

CHAPTER THREE

1. G. E. R. Lloyd is the main proponent of the first line of thought (see, for example, Lloyd 1979, 226–67). However, Lloyd still makes it clear that Anaximander was not only "the first philosophical writer, but one of the very first prose writers." (Lloyd 1991, 131). Indeed, he explicitly states that Greek natural philosophy is

concerned with the explicit justification of a position (Lloyd 1991,125), although he is not always clear on this. For a detailed critical analysis of Lloyd's thesis, see Hahn (2001, 22–39). In a forthcoming paper, "Heraclitus: The First Philosopher?", Richard McKirahan argues that Heraclitus should be considered the first philosopher. He rejects Heraclitus' predecessors for three reasons: wrong field, failure to treat philosophical subjects philosophically, and lack of evidence. He also contends that he finds support for his position in KRS (1983) for whom "philosophy is understood not as a first order inquiry into the nature of things (that is now the province of natural science), but as a second order study of what it means to say that something exists or is in motion or is a plurality" (KRS 1983, 213). KRS makes it clear that what we have here are two very different types of mind, but we can still characterize both as philosophy (1983, 213). Kirk (= KRS) does not doubt, however, that the Milesians were philosophers. This is clearly stated on page 213. The extreme narrow view is held by Jaap Mansfeld (1985, 45–65) for whom, since cosmology and physics no longer count as philosophy, we should not speak of philosophy as beginning with the Milesians.

2. See for example, F. M. Cornford (1952, 249f); W. K. C. Guthrie (1962, 34–38); J.-P. Vernant (1983, 345f); W. Burkert (1963, 97–134); M. L. West (1971, 97f); R. Hahn (2001, 16–20).

3. There is no simple answer as to why philosophy originated in Ancient Greece in general and the city of Miletus in particular. There are a number of competing hypothesis, but no one, to my knowledge, argues that one in particular constitutes a sufficient cause. Among the most often cited explanatory hypotheses are (1) trade and economic growth, (2) the intermingling of beliefs, (3) literacy, (4) technology, and (5) polis (see Lloyd 1979, 234f). Although the political factor is clearly the most important, in my view, the other factors are related to some degree. I have developed these factors in some detail in the context of ancient Greece in general and Miletus in particular in other recent essays (Naddaf 2002, 153–170; 2003, 20–32). They are discussed, sporatically and in less detail, in the second part of chapter 3.

4. Thales (ca. 624–545), of course, may be considered as the first to abandon mythological formulation, but Anaximander was the first about whom we have concrete evidence. In fact, it is unclear if Thales wrote anything. Anaximander and Thales resided in the same city and lived during the same period (for more details, see Guthrie 1962, 45–51) and it is clear that they were close associates (Theophrastus [DKA9,17]). While Anaximander is the primary focus of this chapter, the figure of Thales will clearly emerge from time to time.

5. Kahn (1960/1994, 240). Hahn, for his part, makes a most convincing case for influence of the architects on Anaximander's appeal to prose rather than verse in the composition of his book (2001, 55–95).

6. Indeed, it remained the medium of preference for the so-called Italian as opposed to the Ionian school (see below). More important, without the medium of writing in general, and without the Greek alphabet in particular, speculative thought would not have seen the light of day. Anaximander, as we will see, was clearly aware of this.

7. Diogenes Laertius 2.1–2 (= DK12A1); see also Heidel (1921, 253f). The information on Anaximander seems to have been found by Apollodorus in Anaximander's book and implies that Anaximander would have been sixty-four when he published his book. As Kirk notes, sixty-four is "considerably greater than the average for authorship," but it is not improbable (KRS 1983, 102).

8. I examine some of these conditions below, but explore in more detail the history of Miletus during the archaic period in Naddaf (2003, 19–32).

9. Heidel (1921, 287). See also H. Cherniss (1951, 323), for whom "Anaximander's purpose was to give a description of the inhabited earth, geographical, ethnological and cultural, and the way that it had come to be what it is." E. Havelock (1957, 104–5) also seems to lean in a similar direction. This will be discussed in some detail below.

10. Havelock (1978, 78) is clearly an exception. He doubts if there is even a word of Anaximander remaining in Simplicius's text. For an interesting and useful succinct discussion of the pre-Socratic sources in general, see most recently J. Mansfeld (1999) in A. A. Long (1999). The famous fragment (which will be discussed below) is found in Simplicius's *Commentary on Aristotle's Physics* 24.18–21, which is citing Theophrastus' *Opinions of the Physicists (Phusikōn doxōn)*, frag. 2 = Diels, *Doxographi Graeci* 476, 4–11 = DK12A9, 4–8 and B1. Theophrastus remains the principal source of our information on Anaximander and, of course, the pre-Socratics in general (e.g., KRS 1983, 4; Long 1999, 5), since he was responsible for compiling a history of philosophical ideas from Thales to Plato as his contribution to the encyclopedic activity established by his master Aristotle. In fact, most scholars contend that Aristotle and Theophrastus are our *sole* source of *all* ancient doxographic information (e.g., Paul Tannery 1930, 21; Kahn 1960/1994, 17–24; 25–6; Conche 1993, 51) as if to suggest that no one else independently consulted their works. There are some significant exceptions with regard to this position (e.g., Heidel 1921; Cherniss 1935; McDiarmid 1953, 85–156; Hahn 2001). I concur with the latter.

11. Simplicius states that Anaximander was the first to call the primary principle *archē* (*Commentary on Aristotle's Physics* 24.13–16; 150.23–24). Given that *archē*, in the sense of beginning and origin is quite common in Homer (e.g., *Iliad* 3.100; 22.16), Hesiod (e.g., *Theogony* 115), and Theogonis (lines 607, 739, 1114, 1133), there is no good reason to believe that Anaximander did not employ the word *archē* to qualify his originative substance (see Conche 1993, 55–62 and above 43n, chapter 1). Indeed, it could be seen as a direct challenge to Hesiod.

12. According to R. Eucken (1879, 94), the term hylozoism is encountered for the first time in Cudworth. For the three possible connotations of this word, see KRS (1983, 98).

13. In Homer, the *psuchē* is the undifferentiated life which gives life to all bodies. The functions of the conscience and the soul, which characterize individual personality, are expressed by the word *thumos*. See E. R. Dodds, *The Greeks and the Irrational* (1951). Yet, in the sixth and fifth centuries, the *thumos* was absorbed by the *psuchē*—whence this sentence attributed to Anaximenes: "our *psuchē*, which is air,

holds us together and controls us" *(sugkratei hēmas)* (Aetius 1.3.4 = DK13B2). This last remark is important because if *psuchē* now designates the entire living human personality, this may explain why Anaximander says that his *apeiron* directs all things when it is applied to nature in general. This may also explain why Anaximenes characterized his own primordial substance, that is, air, as divine (see texts in KRS 150; for an excellent discussion, see Onians (1951, 116f).

14. Hippolytus *(Refutation* 1.6.1) employs a similar expression to qualify Anaximander's *apeiron (aidios kai agērōs* in DK12A11 and B2).There is clearly an analogy here with the old Homeric formula to qualify the gods: *athanatos kai agērōs* (see chap. 1). On the *apeiron* as eternal *(aiōn),* see Conche (1991, 148–49), for whom eternal in this case means what retains its vital force.

15. See, for example Heraclitus, "Wisdom consists in a single thing, to know true judgment, how everything is directed/steered *(ekubernēse)* through everything" (DK22B41). In DK22B64 we find the same expression but with the verb *oiakizein,* "governing, directing": "The thunderbolt governs all things." See also Parmenides: "Divinity governs *(kubernai)* all things" (DK28B12.3), and the last monist, Diogenes of Apollonia: "All men are governed *(kubernasthai)* by air and it has power over all things" (DK64B5). For Anaximenes, see KRS (1983, 158–62).

16. See, for example, Aristotle, *Metaphysics* 12.1074b3. One major thing that distinguishes the first philosophers from the poets or *theologoi* is that whereas for the former the great law that governs the universe was inherent in the primordial substance, for the later, as Aristotle clearly noted *(Metaphysics* 12.1091b2–6), it was not the primordial powers but a latecomer on the scene, Zeus, who, as both commander and king, held the true power *(kratos).* In other words, Thales' water, Anaximander's *apeiron,* and Anaximenes' air comprise, as divine elements, the same role Homer and Hesiod reserved for both Zeus and the primordial entities.

17. This is clearly the case for Anaximander's contemporaries, Anaximenes and Xenophanes, for whom intelligence or *nous* is inherent to the original *phusis* and is thus behind the natural processes of the universe.

18. See Chantraine (1968–1980, 1:96) and LSJ. For an excellent discussion and relevent examples of *apeiron* in early Greek literature, see Kahn (1960/1994, 231–39).

19. Burnet (1930/1945, 23); Hussey (1972, 17); Barnes (1982, 28–37). Kahn concludes that Anaximander is the first to have employed the term to mean infinite space: "The Boundless is in fact what we call infinite space, the antecedent for the atomistic void as well as the receptacle or Nurse of generation in Plato's *Timaeus.* But this space is not as yet thought of in the abstraction from the material which fills it. Place and body are here combined in a single idea" (Kahn 1960/1993, 233). See also Conche (1991, 63–67).

20. According to KRS, this recognition probably did not occur "before questions of continuous extension and continuous divisibility were raised by Melissus and Zeno" (1983, 110). See also Guthrie (1962, 85) and certainly Cornford (1952, 172; 1936). Richard McKirahan has most recently argued (and quite convincingly), that even in Zeno the word *apeiron* does not have a technical sense of infinite (1999, 139–41).

21. For numerous examples provided by Cornford, see *The Invention of Space,* (1936, 226f).

22. This meaning was also stressed by Cornford (1952, 177); Guthrie (1962, 85–7); KRS (1983, 111–13).

23. Simplicius, *Commentary on Aristotle's Physics* 24.23–25; 41.17–19; 150.22–25. Aristotle uses the verb *ekkrinesthai* instead of *apokrinesthai* and says that "the opposites are separated or secreted out" *(tas enantiotētas ekkrinesthai)* from the one or *apeiron (Physics* 1.187a20–23). See also Hippolytus, *Refutations* 1.6.2 and Pseudo-Plutarch, *Miscellanies* 2 = DK12A10. For an interesting discussion on *apokrisis* and *ekkrisis,* see Conche (1991, 136–37).

24. Kahn claims that the word *gonimon* may be from Anaximander himself since the text of Pseudo-Plutarch is clearly Theophrastian (1960/1994, 57). Conche leans in the same direction (1991, 153). Pherecydes of Syros, a contemporary of Anaximander (who also wrote in prose), said that Zas, Chronos, and Chthonie (Zeus, Time, and Earth) always existed and "that Chronos made *(poiēsai)* fire, water, and wind from his own seed *(ek tou gonou heautou)*" (= Damascius *On Principles* 124 bis; see KRS 1983, 56). Given the dates, it is quite possible that there is an Egyptian influence both on Pherecydes and Anaximander. It is from the seed of Atum (a god whose name means both "everything and nothing") that the first couple Shu and Tefnut, air and moisture, was formed and which in turn gave rise to Geb and Nut, earth and sky (see Derchain in *Mythologies* 1, 91; and J. A. Wilson in Frankfort 1949, 62–64). On Anaximander's possible travels to Egypt, see below.

25. On the specific problems associated with the tree analogy, see Heidel (1912, 686f); G. E. R. Lloyd (1966, 309–12), and Hahn (2001, 192–96, 216–17). Hahn correctly reminds us that the columns of the earliest temples were made from tree trunks. Moreover, he sees that Anaximander's cosmological model (from a three dimentional pespective) is shaped like a cylinder (see above).

26. Aristotle states that when the Pythagoricians undertake an investigation into the nature of all things *(peri phuseōs panta),* they speak of the effective generation of the universe *(gennōsi to ouranon, Metaphysics* 1.989b34), and the description he gives of their cosmogony is certainly analogous to that of the fetus. Indeed, in *Metaphysics* 14.1091a12–20 Aristotle explains that for the Pythagoricians the universe started from a seed *(ek spermatos)* and managed to grow by drawing in *(heilketo)* the parts of the infinite to which was closest. And this comparison seems to be confirmed by the fifth century Pythagorean Philolaus of Croton (for a discussion, see Guthrie 1962, 1:276–80). We will examine a number of similar analogies in the pre-Socratics in the next chapter.

27. For a similar description and perhaps a reference to Anaximander himself, by Plato, see *Phaedo* 108e–109a and *Timaeus* 62d–63a.

28. *On the Heavens* 2.13, 295a8–15, where Aristotle states that all those who hold that the earth came together at the center, attribute it to a vortex *(dinē)* and its flatness.

29. Simplicius, *Commentary on Aristotle's On the Heavens* 532.13.

30. Hahn's intelligent solution is that Anaximander is working with both two and three dimentional models. From the perspective of a two dimensional model, the contention that the earth is equidistant from all points on the celestial circumference certainly holds, but from the perspective of a three dimentional model it does not hold (2001, 198f).

31. See, in particular Pseudo-Plutarch's *Miscellanies* 2 = DK12A10.33–36.

32. There are a number of doxographies in which these descriptions appear: Pseudo-Plutarch, *Miscellanies* 2 (= DK12A10.37); Hippolytus, *Refutation* 1.6.4–5 (= DK12A11.9–16); Aetius 2.13.7 (= DK12A18.28–29); Aetius 2.20.1 (= DK12A21.11–13), 2.21.1 (= DK12A21.14–15), 2.24.2 (= DK12A21.16–17), 2.25.1 (= DK12A22.19–21), and 2.29.1 (= DK12A22, 23).

33. Anaximander speaks of rings *(kukloi)* in the case of the fixed stars. There are a number of problems associated with these but mostly in conjunction with their position relative to the earth.

34. It is not clear why Anaximander would have placed the fixed stars closest to the earth. Scholars are very much divided on the issue. However, if George Burch (1949/1950, 156) is correct that distance is not discernable with the naked eye, then the order proposed by Anaximander (and this would also hold for the numbers corresponding to the sizes and distances of the heavenly bodies) cannot be based on observation. Ironically, as astronomers assure me, it is not that difficult to discern the occultations of the stars by the moon. This also leads to the conclusion that the order proposed by Anaximander cannot be based on observation.

35. Hippolytus, *Refutation* 1.6.5 (= DK12A11). Some scholars like I. Neuhäuser (1883, 399), and Albert Dreyer (1906, 15 n1) hold that the text is not mutilated and that Anaximander is stating that the circle of the sun is twenty-seven times *that of the moon.* However, this would entail that Anaximander was using a unit of measure other than the earth (it would also make the earth appear many times smaller than it actually appears) and this is highly unlikely. For this reason, I do not discuss the options associated with it below. For a detailed discussion of these options, see Naddaf (2001).

36. For an interesting analysis of speculation prior to Tannery (1887/1930), see O'Brien (1967, 423–424).

37. Tannery (1887/1930, 94ff), followed by Burnet (1930, 68); Diels (1897, 231); and Heath (1913, 37).

38. KRS (1983, 136, n1), followed by Guthrie (1962, 96); Burkert ([1962] 1972, 309, n59); Conche (1991, 209–10).

39. Aetius 2.21.1 (= DK12A21).

40. Although the accent in KRS is put on the sun ring, this is valid for all three rings.

41. In fact, according to O'Brien (1967), as long as we "retain the comparison of the radius of the earth with the thickness or width of the rim of the sun wheel then the figures 'will hold' whether we think of the *distance* (my italics) of the sun wheel from the earth in terms of radius, diameter, or circumference" (425). Since O'Brien holds

that the rings are one half the earth's diameter, his calculations are in halves, with the number 4 being dominant (425).

42. One of the few exceptions to this is Joyce Engmann, "Cosmic Justice in Anaximander," *Phronesis* 36 (1991), 22.

43. O'Brien arrives at units of 4 by halving the diameters of the three rings (which he assumes, like the majority, to be 9, 18 and 27 respectively) and postulating the thickness of the rings themselves as $\frac{1}{2}$ the earth's diameter. Consequently, the distance between each ring is 4 earth diameters, and if we add $\frac{1}{2}$ for the thickness of the star ring and $\frac{1}{2}$ for the thickness of the moon ring, then the distance from the *center* of the earth to the inner circumference of the sun ring is $13\frac{1}{2}$ earth diameters ($\frac{1}{2} + 4 + \frac{1}{2} + 4 + \frac{1}{2} + 4$).

44. There has been a great deal of controversy (and confusion) surrounding these numbers, and much of this is due to the fact that commentators do not seem to agree on just what is being compared and measured: is it the size of the rings? or the distance to the rings? or both? And what is the unit of measure: the radius of the earth? the diameter of the earth? the circumference of the earth? the thickness of the earth? or a combination of two or more? (See O'Brien 1967, 425) There also seems to be a great deal of controversy (and confusion) with respect to the thickness of the ring itself and its role in coming to terms with the numbers. In my view, the dimensions of the earth and the number 3 are the keys to the whole problem, and when put into perspective most if not all of the problems and confusion are abated. I have attempted to do this in two recent articles/studies (Naddaf 1998; 2001). And recent studies (e.g., Couprie 2003), have not changed my view.

45. Although it is generally agreed that the star ring or rings become smaller as the stars are nearer to the poles, this would only be the case for the star ring or rings at the celestial equator. But it seems obvious Anaximander did not give this any thought. Again this seems to entail that observational astronomy was not the inspiration behind his cosmological model.

46. Diels (1897, 232); Heath (1913, 37–38); Burnet (1945, 71); Robin (1923, 62); Jaeger (1943/1945, 1:157); Gomperz (1943, 166–67); Vlastos (1947, 75 n105); Baccou (1951, 77); Burch (1949/1950, 155–56); Cornford (1952, 164); Matson (1954/1955, 445); Sambursky (1956/1987, 15); Rescher (1958/1969, 22–25); Kahn (1960/1994, 88); KRS (1983, 136); Guthrie (1962, 95–96); Burkert (1963, 97–134); (1972, 307); O'Brien (1967, 95–96); Lloyd (1970, 28); West (1971, 86); Furley (1987, 28); Engmann (1991, 22); Conche (1991, 209–10); McKirahan (1993, 38–39); Couprie (1995, 160); Wright (1995, 42); and Hahn (1995, 102; 2001, 181–200).

47. While most scholars agree Anaximander gave the structure of the cosmos a mathematical or geometrical basis, I am not aware of anyone who defends the position that the inspiration is purely and solely *a priori*. Even Cornford, who originally announces that the numbers "are *a priori* and cannot be based on any kind of observation" (1952, 165), he later admits they cannot be devoid of references to observation (170). I will note in passing that KRS (1983), Jaeger (1943), Vlastos (1947), and Wright (1995) appear noncommittal with respect to any type of inspiration.

48. Tannery (1930, 91); Diels (1897, 231); Heath (1913, 38); Burnet (1930, 68); Robin (1923, 62); Cornford (1952, 164); Sambursky (1956, 15–16); Guthrie (1962, 95); Burkert (1963, 97–134); West (1971, 89); Furley (1982, 28).

49. In fact, in conjunction with Egyptian accounts, West goes so far as to add the number 36 to the series to account for the diameter of the "outer ouranos," that is, the *apeiron,* which encompasses the whole (1971, 92).

50. This also holds for the famous passage in Hesiod's *Theogony* (722f) where it is said that it takes the same time for a bronze anvil to fall from sky to earth and from earth to Tartarus (nine day intervals). Indeed, we are not dealing here with equidistant concentric circles established from a common center.

51. See Neugebauer (1957, 25, 107, and 140); Dicks (1970, 4–47); G. E. R. Lloyd (1979, 176–177), and again in (1991, 278–302). In fact, the kind of data Anaximander could have obtained from the Babylonians did not even concern the sizes and distances of the heavenly bodies. Their astronomy, as Lloyd notes (1991, 294–95), was computational and not theoretical or geometrical.

52. Hahn (1995) and most recently (2001), and McEwen (1993). Hahn (1995, 101) claims to get some of his own inspiration from Sambursky and Kahn, for whom there is no doubt mechanical models played an important role in Anaximander's picture of the universe. I concur that Anaximander may very well have employed mechanical models (see also Brumbaugh, 1964, 20–22), but to conclude from this that they were the inspiration behind his cosmological model is rather difficult to imagine. McEwen's contention is that the origins of philosophy are grounded in architecture. This is also Hahn's contention in his recent book (2001), albeit from a very different perspective. In what follows, I discuss Hahn (1995) and (2001).

53. Hahn (1995, 99–101). McEwen (1993) also notes this, in particular, in relation to the proportions (27). However, she then focuses on the importance of models, in general, as sources of inspiration. With this, I concur.

54. Hahn (1995, 111). McEwen (1993), for her part, argues that Greek temple building was structured after their vertical weaving looms—something foreign to Egypt (107–18). Hahn has recently demolished this contention with a number of representations clearly showing the contrary (2001, 91–92).

55. Hahn (1995, 117–18) and (2001, 194–98). For an equally interesting analogy see note 71 on *hestia* below.

56. In other words: "The scientist takes the attitude of an architect about to found a city or to lay out a temple. He feels that certain forms, measures and proportions are called for under the circumstances, and thence he immediately concludes that the facts actually conform to them." (Gomperz 1943, 166)

57. Vernant is inspired by the works of Vlastos (1947/1993, 156–78; 1952/1993, 97–123; 1953/1993, 337–66 and Kahn (1960/1994, 191–93). Both Vlastos and Kahn draw our attention to the importance of the socio-political vocabulary which the pre-Socratics in general and Anaximander in particular employ to explain how the universe works. But they did not observe the relation, as Vernant does, between the cosmolog-

ical law and the structure of the universe. Vernant, for his part, does not mention the series of numbers *or* the three concentric circles.

58. Vernant's thesis is expounded in several articles regrouped in *Myth and Thought Among the Greeks* (1983), Part Three: "The Organisation of Space," 125–234.

59. As we saw in chapter two, there is good reason to believe that this is already changing in Hesiod. See also Naddaf (2002).

60. In fact, the *polis,* a uniquely Greek phenomenon, could be defined as a small independent and self-governing community in which all major activity: political, religious, and social was concentrated in one specific point, the *agora* or public gathering place at the center of the city.

61. There is, I believe, a good deal of textual support for this. When the army assembles in a military formation, they make a circle with the center and what it represents as the primary focal point (e.g., *Iliad* 19.173f). This circle constitutes a space where one can engage in public debate, what the Greeks were to call *is ēgoria,* the equal right of speech. Moreover, there is a direct correlation between the middle *(es meson)* and what is common or in common *(dēmion, xunon, koinon, xunēia).* Thus in book 2 of the *Odyssey,* Telemachus summons the full Ithacan assembly (the word *agorē*—which can mean: assembly or place of assembly—is employed on several occasions in this passage: 2.10, 11, 26, 37). Once the circle is established, Telemachus takes his place among the elders *(gerontes)* who have special seats (see also *Iliad* 18.502–505) and remains seated until it is time to speak. When it is time, "he stands in the middle of the assembly" *(stē de mesēi agorēi* 2.37) with the sacred staff *(skēptron)* in hand and speaks freely. When he is finished, he leaves the circle and another takes his place. It is clear that what Telemachus has to say concerns (or is "common" to) the whole group *(dēmion,* 32, 44). It seems that any time the assembly was addressed on a public or common issue, one would advance to the middle of the group and hold the sacred staff. Thus, the herald of the Trojans goes to the place of assembly *(ein agorēi, Iliad* 7.382) and begins to speak once he is standing in the middle of the group *(stas en messoisin,* 384). Moreover, it appears that whatever is seen as common or public *(xunon* or *koinon)* is placed in the middle, and the spoils of war are considered *xunēia* or "common" and placed in the middle before they are divided (e.g., *Iliad,* 9.328; 19.242f; 23.704; *Odyssey* 24.80–86).

These examples, clearly show not only the origin of the *agora* as a place of public assembly located in the middle of the *polis,* but also how it came to be associated both with what was "common" to the citizens *and* with "free speech." Moreover, some of these examples show that, in Homer, we find the basic forms of Greek political organization are already present: an assembly of all adult members of the community (the *agorē*), a council *(boulē)* of elders *(gerontes)* to which the assembly was subordinate, and, in the form of Agamemnon, an elective or hereditary magistracy. In fact, the importance of public opinion is also recognized. Thus when Telemachus convenes the assembly, his aim is "to stir up public feeling against the suitors" (Heubeck, West, and Hainsworth, 1988/1992, 1:128). In sum, the full assembly is already invoked for major decisions. Finally, decision-making was based on debate, and thus to be an effective debater before the people or in council was perceived as important as being a great warrior for the *basileus* (e.g., *Iliad* 2.273; 18.105, 252, 497–505; 19.303; *Odyssey* 2.502–5). Clearly, many necessary conditions for the advent of philosophy, including freedom of speech in a public forum, have already taken root.

62. According to Vernant, this explains why the political expression *en koinōi*, "to make public, to place in common," has a synonym whose spatial value is evident, that is, *en mesōi*, "to put in the center, to set down in the middle" (1983), 184–85.

63. In conjunction with this, it is important to note that written law codes were perceived as *ta koina*, that is "common" or "public" decisions, and were thus placed in public space for all to see. As Solon notes, laws were written for all, and published and displayed in a public central location, the Prytany (where it ruled over the magistrates of the city), near Hestia, the Common Hearth (Detienne 1988, 31–33; Loraux 1988, 95–129).

64. I understand the term *isonomia* in the sense in which it is employed by Alcmeon of Croton (ca. 500) in the expression health is an *isonomia tōn dunameōn* (DK24B4), that is, a balance of powers (disease, on the other hand, is the result of a *monarchia*). In sum, *isonomia* must be understood as a "balance" or "equilibrium" which results when the constituent powers act as equals. This conception of *isonomia*, and the word itself, is completely compatible with the time in question. On this important point, see Pierre Lévêque and Pierre Vidal–Naquet (1997) and Vlastos (1953/1993, 1–35).

65. For an analysis of the passage in question, see Wycherley (1937, 22). For a diagram and discussion, see also Lévêque and Vidal-Naquet (1997, 129).

66. The *gnōmōn* or set square employed by Meton is also indissociable from the seasonal sundial, a time-telling device identified with Anaximander (DK12A1), which identifies the solstices and equinoxes and is thus a confirmation of both the geometrization of space (celestial events occur in circles) and of the regularity and equilibrium of the forces of nature over Time. This is a central image, as we will see, in the one surviving fragment of Anaximander. Moreover, the report concerning Anaximander and the sundial is in connection with his visit to Sparta where the citizens were known as *homoioi* (Aristotle, *Politics* 5 1306b30 and below).

67. Aristotle's *Politics* 2.8, 1267b22f. Although Hippodamus is considered as the Greek inventor of orthogonal planning, Rykwert (1976, 87) argues that "orthogonal planning was found all over the known world" and its aim was to orient the population with the geometric configuration of the cosmos. The two intersecting coordinates being the axis round which the sun turned (202).

68. The reforms instituted by Cleisthenes of Athens (507–506) may constitute an even better example. His aim was to come to terms with the three factions into which Athenian society (and the territory of Attica) was divided: the *pediakoi* (plainsmen or aristocrats), the *paralioi* (coast men or middle class), and the *diakrioi* (highlanders or commoners) (Aristotle, *Athenian Constitution* 13.4; 21.4). However, contrary to Hippodamus, Cleisthenes wanted to create an homogeneous state in which the social realm took on the form of a centered and circular cosmos. For a succinct description, see Vernant (1983, 207–29). Vidal-Naquet and Lévêque (1997), for their part, draw our

attention to the fact that Cleisthenes tripartition of Attica led to the creation of three more or less concentric zones (128).

69. What I understand here by class is a group of people sharing a similar economic and/or social position. Most scholars agree that before the Archaic period (800–500 BCE), Greek society was consciously divided into two distinct social groups: the aristocracy and the *dēmos*. Further, few scholars contest that this *status quo ante* did not radically change during the Archaic period and that this change was closely linked to the evolution of the *polis*. Although no one factor can explain how this phenomenon occurred, economic expansion appears to have played a fundamental role, for economic expansion was not only responsible for the upheaval of the existing society, but also for the hoplite revolution, which many distinguished scholars identify with a new middle class. It is this middle class to which I am presently referring. For example see Forrest (1966, 94); Mossé (1984, 113–14); Snodgrass (1980, 101–111); Starr (1977, 178–79); Andrewes (1971, 62); Finley, (1981, 101); Naddaf (2003, 20–31).

70. This could explain why Anaximander employed the plural *ouranoi* in a famous testimony ascribed to him (see below n75). The *ouranoi* could designate the three rings which correspond to the three social groups. In order to avoid conferring on anyone ring the unique privilege of being called *ouranos*—which would amount to supporting the idea of *monarchia*—Anaximander gave to each ring this privilege. For a discussion, see Naddaf (1992, 145–52).

71. Vernant notes during the course of his argument that in order to represent the value of the center, a *hearth* was constructed in the middle, which did not belong to one family, but to the whole community: the *Hestia koinē* of the entire political community. And in conjunction with this he states that "the name given by philosophers to the earth, immobile and fixed in the center of the universe, is in fact *hestia* . . . what they were doing was projecting on the world of nature the very same view of human society that resulted from the foundation of the *polis*" (1983, 188–89). This, I believe, is a powerful support for my own thesis. But there is something else which appears just as important. In a more detailed discussion of Hestia (127–75) in another chapter, Vernant discusses the link that Louis Deroy (*Le culte du foyer,* 32 and 43) makes between the hearth *(hestiē-hestia)* and a column *(histiē-histia)*. However, Vernant does not make a connection between Anaximander's earth and a column. The point I want to make here is that since a hearth entails a stone slab of sorts, it may be that the community hearth employed a round one with roughly a 3 to 1 ratio. This, I should note, is also suggested by the related word *omphalos* (navel), which can mean not only the center or middle point but equally a "rounded stone" as in the case of the Delphic temple. If such is the case, Anaximander's model could represent a compromise between rationalism and religion.

72. While I do not exclude a three-dimensional mechanical model of the universe for Anaximander, if he did in effect construct one, it is highly unlikely it was the result of astronomical observation for reasons already mentioned (on how complex the model would have to be, see Couprie, 1995; and more recently Hahn 2001, 217–18). What I do see is a plan model inscribed on wood, stone, or bronze analogous to his famous chart and city plan—in sum, three corresponding models.

73. During Anaximander's lifetime, Miletus was able to forge successfully and successively a *xenia,* or friendly and mutually beneficial pact with several of the major powers in the area, including Lydia (under Alyattes and Croseus), Egypt (under Neco and Amasis), and Persia (under Darius) (see Naddaf 2003, 27–30). It seems that this could also have influenced Anaximander's vision of the nature and the cosmos.

74. Plutarch, *Greek Questions* 32 = *Moralia* 298c and Herodotus 5.29. I discuss this in some detail in Naddaf 2003, 26–31. For another interpretation and a detailed analysis of the relevant texts, see V. Gorman (2001, 102–21). She places the conflict in the seventh century.

75. There is considerable controversy as to where the fragment begins and ends as well as the terminology strictly speaking. Moreover, there are literally hundreds of translations of the fragment. For an excellent discussion and still, in my view, the best to date, see Kahn (1960/1994, 166–96). His linguistic and historical analysis of the language of the fragment/doxography has convinced me of the authenticity of at least the above quotation. For a more recent detailed discussion, see Conche (1991, 157–90). The passage that precedes the fragment reads: "Anaximander said that the *apeiron* is the principle and element of existing things *(tōn ontōn).* He says that it is neither water nor any other of the so-called elements, but some other *apeiron* (boundless) nature, from which all the heavens *(tous ouranous)* and the *kosmoi* within them *(tous en autois kosmous)* come into being." There can be little doubt, in my view, that the reference here is to physical processes. But the fragment has been interpreted in at least two very different ways. The interpretations depend on whether or not one argues that the fragment refers to the *apeiron.* My own interpretation is that the predominance of one of the elements (and/or cycles) is succeeded by the predominance of the other and that this process continues, in the form of a balance, *ad infinitum.* In sum, the physical processes are not related to the *apeiron.*

76. In particular, this is the case in summer and winter when hot and dry appear to rival cold and wet. This is also evidenced in night and day and in the summer and winter solstices et cetera. Of course, the heavenly bodies are also behind meteorological phenomena. While it is true that wind plays a predominate role in the explanation of the meteorological phenomena in Anaximander (DK12A11,23), in the final analysis, it is still the sun that explains the wind (DK12A24,27).

77. I do not see the *apeiron,* as many do, as governing the world order. If this were the case, the *apeiron* would be akin to Hesiod's Zeus, a *monarchia.* Nor is there any need for the universe to have an end or to be reabsorbed into the *apeiron* as an atonement for crimes or injustices to which it has been subjected by its components. However, if one considers the *apeiron* secreted the *gonimon,* which was behind the processes that led to the present order of things, and if one considers that these natural processes (that is, the struggle between the opposites) are subjected to laws that cannot be changed, the *apeiron* continues to govern or control the present order of things.

78. An excellent example of this would be the Laws of Hammurabi, which put an end to much of the social and political injustice in his time and created a new more orderly view of the universe. (See Jacobsen 1949, 223.) What we see in Hesiod's *Theogony* (how Zeus got to rule over the universe and create a new socio-political

order) is more typical of the post-Hammurabi period whereas what we see in *Works and Days* (with the crumbling of the old order) is more typical of the pre-Hammurabi period (see above). For an interesting summary of this for the period in question, see Adkins (1985, 279–309).

79. Of course, this is also suggested by the social and legal terminology of the fragment.

80. In sum, Anaximander could have envisaged a sort of circular city with the dimensions of the *agora* serving as the unit of measure for the other circles or divisions of the city (such that the circular divisions of the city with respect to the diameter of the *agora* would be 1 x 3 x 3, 2 x 3 x 3 and 3 x 3 x 3). For a possible analogy, see Plato's description of the city of Atlantis (*Critias,* 113d–e). No one, to my knowledge, has ever pointed this out. Of course, as I noted above, the idea of a circular city centered on the *agora* was not foreign to the Greeks.

81. In sum, the *isonomia* expressed would be akin to, but different from, the one spoken of by Herodotus at 5.37–38, where he informs us that after the Ionian revolt against Persia (500 BCE), the tyrant Histiaeus and his deputy Aristagoras renounced, at least in appearance, tyranny and proclaimed that all the citizens of Miletus had equal rights *(isonomiēn epoiee tēi Milētōi).* Or again, at 3.142 where he tells us that after the fall of tyranny of Polycrates of Samos (ca. 518 BCE and thus earlier by a generation or so), his successor, Maiandros, to distinguish himself from Polycrates, saw his fellow Samians as equals *(homoioi),* placed the power in the middle *(es meson),* and proclaimed *isonomia* for all (3.142). In both these cases *isonomia* seems analogous with democracy, whereas for Anaximander we are approaching democracy. In this respect, Anaximander can be seen as a sort of mixture of his successors, Hippotamus and Cleisthenes. On the one hand, like Hippotamus of Miletus (ca. 460), Anaximander may be seen as advocating three equal, albeit distinct, classes and a single supreme court composed of elders from all three classes (Aristotle, *Politics* 1267b11). On the other hand, like Cleisthenes, he may be seen as advocating the blending of the three unequal factions of his time (Aristotle, *Athenian Constitution* 21.3–4).

82. According to Emlyn-Jones (1980, 126), Anaximander was more farsighted than Phocylides' "middle way," for he "solves the problem of conflict not by eliminating it but by admitting, regulating and perpetuating it." I must admit that I am not clear on just what Emlyn-Jones means. In the case of Anaximander, it is possible that all three classes could be moderate. For more on the relation between the two, see below.

83. Note that even for Heraclitus, for whom strife is justice, "moderation is the greatest virtue" *(sōphronein aretē megistē,* DK22B112). In the final analysis, Anaximander's political model entails that all three groups appeal to the impartial principle of law and, therefore, moderation. Otherwise, the so-called middle group would have a privileged relation with the center. Given what we saw above, what is common *(to koinon)* must also be closely associated with the notions of moderation and centrality.

84. In the *Laws,* Plato, as Lévêque and Vidal-Naquet point out, makes the microcosm of the city participate in the macrocosm of the universe (1997, 97). For the case

at hand, I don't think each group would have to match up a particular ring (e.g., the middle group for some reason with the moon ring). This would be too extreme.

85. As Jaeger notes (1945, 160–61), the idea of systematic justice in the universe was transferred from the legal and political sphere to that of the physical sphere. However, according to Jaeger: "His [Anaximander's] idea of *diké* is the first stage in the projection of the life of the city-state upon the life of the universe" (161). Jaeger does not believe that this conception of the cosmos was related to human life, as it was later on with Heraclitus, because Anaximander's investigation was not concerned with humanity but with *phusis* (161). Jaeger's position on Heraclitus is, therefore, close to my own position on Anaximander.

86. There is however a sense in which humans may disappear from the surface of the earth. Alexander reports that Anaximander believed that the earth was drying up (DK12A27). But clearly this cannot mean that this was the prelude to the earth (and thus the universe) being reabsorbed into the *apeiron*. As Kirk notes (KRS 1983, 139–40), this is in contradition with the sense of the fragment. If this were the case, Anaximander may have believed there were cycles during which humanity was destroyed, but regenerated in a new cycle. There is clearly evidence for this in Anaximander's younger contemporary Xenophanes. I will attempt to show that Xenophanes may very well have derived his inspiration from Anaximander. Moreover, the notion that humanity was periodically destroyed by floods and other natural catastrophes was actually quite prevalent in ancient Greece.

87. For example, see Hippolytus 12A11; Alexander 12A27; Aetius 12A27, 30; Aristotle 12A27; Censorinus 12A30.

88. For a summary of the various mythical positions on the origin of humanity, see Naddaf (2003, 10–13).

89. Aetius, 12A30. The language as well as the terminology *(phloiois periechomena, perirrēgnumenou tou phloiou)* suggest that Anaximander saw an analogy between the development of the animal and that of the universe—or vice versa.

90. For another reading of *ep'oligon chronon metabiōnai*, see Guthrie (1962, 102). According to his interpretation, animals lived on for a short time. I fail to see how this makes any sense. For an excellent discussion of this passage, see Conche (1991, 223–226).

91. See Hippolytus, *Refutations* 1.6.6 = DK12A11.

92. Barnes (1982, 22); see DK12A27 = Alexander of Aphrodisias; and Aristotle, *Meteorologia* 353b5.

93. For an interesting account which contrasts with Anaximander's, see Lucretius, *On the Nature of Things* 5.222–25; 800f.

94. The passage may, however, be translated as "originally, humans were born *(gegonenai)* like another animal, namely a fish."

95. For an analogy, see Diodorus' description and Kahn's comments (1960/1994, 112–13, 70–71).

96. Plutarch alludes to the *galeoi* or squales, of which one species, called the smooth shark, has the remarkable particularity of the foetus being attached to the mother's stomach by an umbilical cord. This is an organ analogous to the placenta; *Table Talk* 730e.

97. The species in question is the subject of one of Aristotle's most famous descriptions in *History of Animals* 565b1. He notes that the young develop with a navel-string attached to the womb.

98. According to J. Mansfeld (1999, 23), Plutarch and Censorius may only be commenting on Aetius's summary in his *Placita*.

99. Kahn (1960/1994, 112–13 and 70–71) does not share the idea that Anaximander believed man was born from or came from another species. Anaximander could very well assign the original human embryo to floating membranes such as we find in Diodorus of Sicily (1.7). In effect (according to Kahn), Anaximander must have believed the origin of man was entirely comparable to that of the other terrestrial animals. In this regard, Pseudo-Plutarch's sentence "man is engendered by animals of another species" does not mean (following Kahn), that these living beings of another species do not distinguish themselves from the original form of the other animals. It simply means they are different from human beings, such as we know them.

100. Agathemeros, *Geographical Information* 1.1 = DK12A6.27–30 and 68B15.

101. Heidel (1937, 132; 1921, 247) argues that the sense of the phrase implies Anaximander's map was accompanied with a written treatise. Kirk (1983, 104) and Conche (1991, 25 n3) contest this. In my view, the ancient testimony clearly implies the map was accompanied with a written treatise explaining its function.

102. Strabo, *Geography* 1.1.11 = DK12A6.30–34. On Anaximander, see also Strabo's opening remarks at 1.1.1: "Geography, which I have now chosen to consider, I hold as much the pursuit of the philosopher as any other science. That my opinion is sound is clear from many considerations. For not only were the first who boldly essayed the subject men of this sort—Homer, Anaximander, and Hecataeus, (as Eratosthenes also says) . . . this task belongs peculiarly to the man who contemplates all things divine and human, the science of which we call philosophy."

103. On this see Christian Jacob, *"Inscrire la terre habitée sur une tablette,"* in Detienne (1988, 276–77). Jacob argues that the map was only a theoretical object and that its construction was not based on empirical data (281). This is a rather extreme position.

104. Cicero, *On Divination* 1.50.112 = DK12A5a. Cicero does not say how Anaximander did this, although he explicitly says that it was not an act of divination (indeed, he calls him the 'physicus'). Anaximander could have based his prediction on the observation of abnormal animal behavior.

105. Favorinus of Arles, *Universal History,* frag. 27; see Diogenes Laertius 2.2 (= DK12A1); see also Eusebius 10.14.11 = DK12A4 who adds times and seasons to the solstices and equinoxes. I will discuss this in more detail below.

106. Although Croesus was successful in convincing the Spartans, it was not for the same reason given by Herodotus. According to Herodotus, the Spartans agreed to

help Croesus because of a gift of gold he had given to Sparta a generation before to use for a statue for Apollo (1.69).

107. See for example, Jucker (1977, 195–96); Gelzer (1979, 170–76); Yalouris (1980, 85–89); Hurwit (1985, 207–208); Conche (1991, 38–41).

108. At least it is strongly suggested by such epithets as *apsorros* or "backward-flowing" to qualify Oceanus (e.g., 18.399; see also *Iliad* 14.200–201). This is also derived from the description of Achilles shield (18.607). This was also clearly Strabo's interpretation (1.1.3). Indeed, he refers to Homer as if he constitued an important authority on the matter (1.1.7).

109. On rationalism, see P. Lévêque and P. Vidal-Naquet (1997, 52–55).

110. See DK12A11.23–24. The impact of Anaximander's rational/natural approach to meteorological phenomena is best described by Aristophanes in *Clouds* 404f.

111. There is no reason to think that Anaximander would not have been aware of the same story that Herodotus relates (4.42) about the pharoah Neco (609–594) sending several Phonecian ships to circumnavigate Africa/Libya.

112. See, for example, P. Lévêque and P. Vidal-Naquet (1997, 80); Couprie (2003, 196)

113. As M. Conche notes (1991, 46, n47, 48). According to P. B. Georges, "Didyma was to archaic Ionia what Delphi was to the Greeks of Europe" (2000, 11).

114. However at 4.110, Herodotus employs *oikeomenē* and not *gē* to refer to the inhabited earth.

115. The Nile, Phasis, and Tanais are explicitly mentioned by Herodotus at 4.45; for the Tanais, see also Hecataeus *FGHI,* frag. 164, 165. Pindar also mentions the Phasis and the Nile as the northern- and southernmost borders of the Greek world at *Isthmia* 2.41f. The Phasis would be seen as flowing from the Caspian Sea, which in turn was seen as a bay of the Ocean. The Ister or Danube also has a strong claim according to Heidel (1937, 31–44); see also Herodotus 5.9; 4.46–50. According to Heidel (21), the Ister and Nile correspond to the tropics.

116. In reality, Herodotus states that this is what the Ionians believe, but it seems from the context that the Egyptians also believed that the Nile Delta was where they originated.

117. This contention is clearly expressed by Diodorus of Sicily 1.10.1. See also Plato, *Timaeus* 22 a–e, Aristotle, *Meteorology* 1.14.352b19–21 and *Politics* 5.10.1329a38–b35. On the north of Egypt as having the ideal climatic conditions, see Hippocrates *Aphorisms* 3.1. Thales' famous contention that life arose from the primordial waters may be of Egyptian origin. Indeed, there is no reason to distrust the doxographical claims that he visited Egypt for reasons discussed below. Aeschylus meanwhile seems to be the exception despite references in *Suppliants* clearly reflecting the Nile's fertility in the context of human origin: "Native stock spawn from the fertile Nile" (281); "the race the Nile breeds" (497–98).

118. One possible allusion to a fabulous past is at *Iliad* 9.181–85, where Thebes is described as a city of a hundred gates and where treasures are in greatest store.

119. On this point, see C. Froidefond (1971, 64–67). According to Froidefond, the only references to Egyptian history in the *Odyssey* date to the last part of the eighth century. Sarah Morris, for her part, argues that a number of episodes reflect the end of the Bronze Age "when foreigners of many lands attacked the Egyptian Delta and engaged the pharaonic forces throughout the Ramesside period" (1997, 614).

120. For a good recent summary of the Greeks in Egypt, see Boardman (1999, 111–59). Egypt's own independence in the seventh and sixth centuries was due in large part, as Austin notes (1970, 410), to Ionian mercenaries. The fact that the Milesian poet, Arkinos, composed a work entitled *Aithiopis* in the late seventh century (see Gorman 2001, 72–73), could attest to the close Milesian relations with Egypt.

121. Alan Gardiner (1961a, 362), notes that in order to appease the native Egyptians, Amasis restricted the merchant activity of the Greeks to Naucratis. On the other hand, as Herodotus notes (1.29), both Croesus and Amasis attempted to attract to their respective courts, the intellectual elite. Given the period, Solon, Anaximander, and many others may have met there.

122. The Saite dynasty included Psammetichus I, Necho (610–595), Psammetichus II (595–89), Apries (589–70), and Amasis (570–26).

123. Froidefond (1971, 71) and Boardman (1999, 141).

124. Boardman (1999, 132). Naucratis fell to the Persians around 525, and archeological evidence indicates that after the Persian invasion of Egypt, the relation between Greece and Naucratis at least until round 500 BCE was severely affected (Boardman 1999, 141). However, there does not seem to have been a decline in the economic fortunes of the Ionian states in general, and Miletus in particular, under the Persian rule of Darius, that is until the Ionian revolt of 500 and its aftermath. It is also worth noting that Darius may have lifted the pharoanic travel restrictions, thus making the rest of Egypt more accessible after 525. On the other hand, given that Miletus maintained a priviledged relation with the Persians, it is unclear why Darius would have surpressed commerce with Naucratis unless Naucratis itself strongly supported the Egyptians during the conflict.

125. J. M. Hurwit (1985, 184); see also Boardman (1999, 143–44). There is evidence Thrasybulus may have already initiated similar temple building (see Naddaf 2003, 29).

126. According to tradition, Deucalion lived only a few generations before the Trojan War; see Gantz (1993, 164f) and Thucydides above.

127. This was certainly Plato's conviction (*Timaeus* 22c–e) and there is no good reason to believe this idea did not have a long history (see Naddaf 1994, 192–95; 1998c, xxiii, xxvi–xxvii).

128. Arrian, *Anabasis* 5.6.5; Strabo 12.2.4; see also Heidel (1943, 264).

129. For a comparision with Anaximander, see Kirk (1983, 140).

130. Guthrie (1962, 1.362–63); Kirk (1983, 163–64); Lesher (1992, 1).

131. Xenophanes recalls the coming of the Mede in fragment 22: "How old were you when the Mede arrived?" (B22). The fact that Apollodorus states that Anaximander was sixty-four in the year 547/46 (= Diogenes Laertius 2.2) suggests he may have been using the fall of Lydia and/or Ionia to the Mede as a reference. Indeed, Anaximander may have made a reference to this in his book.

132. Plutarch suggests he did; see *Isis* 379b and *On Superstition* 171d–e. Heidel (1943, 274) notes that stories of Xenophanes visiting Egypt are probably apocryphal.

133. Naucratis attracted poets such as Sappho and Alcaeus, artists such as Rhoikos, statesman such as Solon, philosophers such as Thales, etc., in addition to get-rich-quick traders. See Boardman (1999, 133).

134. Heidel (1943, 262). In (1921, 243), he states that "Hecataeus was only a trifle over a generation younger than his fellow townsman Anaximander," although the rationale for this on 260 gives a similar date of 560 for his birth. On the other hand, in his book *Hecataeus and the Egyptian Priests in Herodotus, Book 2* (1935, 120), he states that Hecataeus was probably born shortly after Anaximander's death (120). There seems to be a problem. Meanwhile, Hecataeus' dates are similar to those of Heraclitus (555–480). If Anaximenes (580–510) were a pupil of Anaximander (see Diogenes Laertius 2.3), then this suggests Anaximander's wide range of interests.

135. Heidel believes Hecataeus visited Egypt with Cambyses on his expedition of conquest (1943, 263).

136. Heidel (1943, 262). We must remember that the *phusikos* Anaximenes is also said to have been his pupil.

137. This may explain why he wrote his book later in life.

138. The Egyptians contend, according to Diodorus, that this continues to occur for some forms of animal life (see Diodorus 1.10). There is an astonishing similarity between his account in 1.10 and Herodotus' account in 2.13, which may explain the correlation he drew between humans and fish. For an interesting discussion on the reproduction of fish in Egypt, see Herodotus 2.92–94.

139. For a discussion of the importance of chronology for the Egyptians, see Alan Gardiner (1961b, 61–68). He also discusses the famous Palermo Stone.

140. The geological speculation may have been initiated by certain phenomena taking place around Miletus itself (see Kirk 1983, 139). Egyptian phenomena, on the other hand, provided a way of quantifying the hypothesis.

141. DK58C6.19.

142. DK58C6.23–24 = Diogenes Laertius, *Lives* 2.2; see also DK12A1.

143. This is also Delattre's opinion (1988, 589 n2).

144. The doxography is taken from a scholium on the second century BCE grammarian Dionysius Thrax.

145. A number of works are attributed to Dionysius of Miletus including *Description of the Inhabited World* (see Gorman 2001, 82).

146. See, for example, Snodgrass (1971, 351); Coldstream (1977, 342f); Powell (1997, 18–20); Burkert (1992, 25–26).

147. See Coleman (1996, 286); and Tritle (1996, 326), who notes it is somewhat surprising and suspicious.

148. For the genealogical intricacies concerning Io and a reasonable discussion, see Gantz (1993, 198–204). On the Egyptization of the Io story, see M. L. West (1985, 145–46, 150); A. B. Lloyd (1975/1988, 1:125); and E. Hall (1996, 338).

149. Perhaps this is what Plato has in mind in the *Phaedrus* (274e) when he attributes the invention of *grammata* to the Egyptian, Theuth—a story, moreover, which takes place near Naucratis (274c).

150. Page, *PMG* frag. 213.

151. When Aeschylus states, in his ode to progress in *Prometheus Bound* (460–61) that writing *(grammata)* is the memory of all things and thus the productive mother of the arts, the alphabet is clearly not perceived as a relatively new invention as in reality it was.

152. Anaximander, for his part, would have insisted on the fact there would be no room for gods in his genealogical analysis.

153. For a recent discussion on this controversial fragment, see Lesher (1992, 149–55). The fragment is discussed in more detail in our analysis of Xenophanes in chapter 4.

154. See G. L. Huxley (1966, 20); Colophon also has an early Egyptian connection through the travels of Mopsus (20).

155. See Huxley (1966, 20).

156. The popular theme of the fecundity of the Nile is found in Aeschylus' description of it as *phusizoos* (*Suppliants* 584).

157. See R. Thomas (1992, 114) on *kleos* (glory) and writing. Where would Anaximander fit in?

158. On the other hand, he notes at 1.9.5 that the fourth century historian Ephorus (already mentioned above in the context of the alphabet) believed that the barbarians were prior to the Greeks, which suggests that he held a position similar to the one I have attributed to Anaximander.

159. The origins of Diodorus' text provoked a vivid controversy (see Burton 1972). I will discuss certain aspects of the text in more detail in my analysis of Democritus in chapter 4. I recognize that certain features of the account in particular the role of natural necessity (see below), seem traceable to Democritus.

160. The text echoes back to 1.3.4. The text is also concerned with the phenomena of shells that one observes in certain regions of the country.

161. This is also suggested by J. O. Thompson (1948/1965, 97–98). Couprie (2003, 196) is convinced that Hahn and Heidel are correct and attempts a reconstruction of such a map. I attempt a similar rendition below, but using the Nile Delta as the center.

162. R. A. Parker (1974, 67) and Hahn (2001, 207) state the Egyptians were the first to divide the day and night into twelve hours each, and that Egyptians had a very high degree of astronomical knowledge, but this is very much contested by O. Neugebauer (1975, 2:560).

163. As G. E. R. Lloyd notes (1991, 293), the length of the solar year was only determined fairly accurately by Meton and Euctemon in about 430 BCE.

164. J. M. Robinson (1968, 32); Hurwit (1985, 208); Couprie (2003, 196). Although Hurwit and Robinson explicitly state the land was divided into three equal parts with the Nile and Phasis rivers as the dividers, in their reconstruction, Europe appears larger than Asia, and Asia larger than Libya. This is a perfect example of how difficult it is to reconstruct three equal land masses when using the Nile and Phasis as dividers.

165. Brumbaugh (1964, 22); M. Conche (1991, 47, fig. 2); J. O. Thompson (1948/1965, 98, fig. 11).

166. Robinson (1968, 32); Hurwit (1985, 208).

167. Brumbaugh (1964, 22); Vidal-Naquet and Lévêsque (1996, 53); Couprie (2003, 196).

168. Conche (1991, 46); Froidefond (1971, 167).

169. Conche (1991, 47, fig. 2); Thompson (1948/1965, 98, fig. 11).

170. Conche (1991, 46); Heidel (1937, 11–12).

171. Brumbaugh (1964, 22); Robinson (1968, 32); Conche (1991, 47); Hurwit (1985, 208).

172. J. L. Myres (1953, 6, fig. 5); Heidel (1937, 1, fig. 11).

173. J. O. Thompson (1948/1965, 97, fig. 10).

174. These regions could constitute an eternal equilibrium.

175. Couprie (2003, 194–197) gives a lucid explanation of what Anaximander could achieve, with the added, important reminder that for Anaximander, the earth is flat and not spherical.

176. Herodotus informs us (2.32) that it is a four-month march from Elephantine to the Deserters. The Deserters is thought to be Sennar, which is around 150 miles south of Khartoum. Elephantine is approximately the midpoint between the Delta and Khartoum. At this point, Herodotus says the river changes course and no one has gone beyond this point because of the heat.

177. At 2.33 Herodotus mentions the Danube/Ister flowing through the center of Europe (to the Milesian colony of Istria on the Black Sea) and being equal in length to the Nile. More important, he states that Egypt, and thus the Nile Delta, is more or less

in line with the Cilician Mountains, Sinope, and the mouth of the Danube/Ister. At 2.26 he suggests the Danube/Ister and the Nile take rise on the same degree of longitude. For a discussion, see Heidel (1937, 24–25) and Thompson (1948/1965, 98).

178. Of course, no one had ever traveled to the source of the Nile. But there is no reason to believe that Anaximander was not aware of the famous story about the circumnavigation of Libya (Herodotus 4.42). Although Thompson (1948/1965, 72) doubts this story, he does believe that the time it is said to have taken (around three years) would correspond more or less to the reality. If this were the case, given the parameters of Anaximander's map, then there would be no reason to conclude this was evidence that Libya was far smaller than Europe or Asia, as Herodotus appears to contend according to Heidel (1937, 28). Clearly, Herodotus has a very different conception of the size of Europe from his predecessors. Meanwhile, if the circumnavigation did occur, then one would expect the Phoenicians would have also reported that at one point during their southern voyage, the temperature actually got cooler.

179. Miletus is approximately at the midpoint between the mouth of the Nile and the mouth of the Danube/Ister. Of course, Miletus is not on this meridian, but it is a lot closer than Sinope; given the time frame, Anaximander may have thought that it was.

CHAPTER FOUR

1. Jaeger (1947, 40), Burnet (1930/1945, 115) and KRS (1983, 166), Lesher (1992, 7). Deichgräber (1938) has somewhat successively argued for the existence of the poem *On Nature* and Guthrie (1962, 366) and Barnes (1982, 83–84) have followed suit.

2. Aristotle, *Metaphysics* 1.986b10–27 = DK21A30; *On the Heavens* 2.294a21–25 = DK21A47; Simplicius, *Commentary on Aristotle's Physics* 22.22 = DK21A31.

3. Stobaeus (*Physical Selections* 1.10.12 = DK21A36), Crates of Mallus (DK21B30), and Pollux (DK21B39) all mention Xenophanes poem *On Nature*. Moreover, Stobaeus is also the source of the famous fragment B18 on searching for what is better. It will be discussed in context below.

4. As Lesher (1992, 159f) notes, there is no standard interpretation of this fragment. I will discuss it in more detail below.

5. On *Laws* 10.886c, see above chapter 2, note 17.

6. For a discussion of other possible interpretations of these fragments, see Lesher (1992, 89–94). Of course, the gods also had the power, as in Egyptian culture (of which Xenophanes was no doubt aware), to change into other animal forms.

7. Lesher is correct to note that Xenophanes does not fault Homer and Hesiod for saying that there are gods, but only for how they portray the gods (1992, 98). While it is true Xenophanes does not say why he believes there is only one greatest god (Lesher 1992, 99), in my view, one god would appear to follow from the Milesian notion of one primordial substance and the way it is characterized (see below).

8. On *noei*, see Lesher (1992, 104–4); for parallel passages in Plato, see *Laws* 10.901d, 902c, where the same verbs are employed in a similar context with *gignōskō* replacing *noeō*. Moreover, the poet, like Zeus, when properly inspired knows the truth about past, present and future (e.g., Hesiod, *Theogony* 28, 32, 38).

9. Guthrie (1962, 383n) believes that *kradainai* has the same sense as *kubernai* in Anaximander.

10. Given the fact that Xenophanes is trying to undermine the poetic/popular conception of the divinity on the one hand, and the fact that philosophy is still in its nascent stage on the other hand, it is not surprising his conceptual analysis of the greatest god is very much dependent on the poetic conception to make his point.

11. For a list of the products (e.g., fire, air, wind, cloud, water, earth, and stone), see Simplicius, *Commentary on Aristotle's Physics* 24.26–25.1 = DK13A5. For a similar position, see Kahn (1960/1994, 156–57).

12. Aristotle *(On the Heavens* 279b12) notes that all agree the world was generated, but once completed, some state that it is eternal and others that it is destructible, and others again that it alternates. Moreover, as Lesher (1992, 130) notes, the fragment on the roots of the earth extending *es apeiron* (B28) suggests that the shape of the universe is not contingent on the shape of the divinity.

13. The ancient commentators were clearly aware of the confusion; for example, see Theodoretus (in A36), who notes that Xenophanes says that the One/God is ungenerated "and, forgetting this, he has also said that all things grow from the earth" (Lesher 1992, 216).

14. Indeed, the fact that God is by definition and nature ungenerated does not exclude the universe are having a beginning in time anymore then it would exclude humanity as having a beginning in time (contra Aetius A37).

15. For a list of contemporary scholars who argue for an authentic theory of human progress in Xenophanes, see Lesher (1992, 151). Some scholars read this fragment from an epistemological perspective (e.g., KRS 1983, 179–80; McKirahan 1994, 68). Lesher also seems to lean in this direction, although he clearly believes that a theory of progress is not impossible (1992, 151–52). The fact that Xenophanes may not have used the term *thēriōdēs* or "brutish" to characterize the original condition of humanity (M. O'Brien 1985, 264–77) is not, in my view, relevant.

16. 21B35 = "Let these things be accepted as resembling *(eoikota)* the truth." There is an interesting parallel with Hecataeus' opening sentence in his *Genealogies:* "I write these things as they appear to me to be true" (see above chapter 3). For an excellent discussion of the word *eoikota,* see Lesher (1992, 170–76).

17. DK21B38: "if god had not made yellow honey, they [men] would think that figs were much sweeter" clearly reflects the importance of empirical obervation for Xenophanes.

18. This doctrine is already ridiculed by Pythagoras' contemporary Xenophanes (DK21B7).

19. The Orphic and Pythagorean doctrines both appeared in the sixth century BCE. They present many similarities, and it is often difficult to properly distinguish them. For example, both affirm the immortality of the soul, transmigration and metempsychosis, the punishment of the soul in Hades and its final return to paradise, vegetarianism, asceticism, and finally the importance of purifications. One of the major differences between the partisans of the Orphic doctrine and the Pythagoreans relates to the organization of the latter into a closed society proposing to its members a complete formation/training integrating scientific knowledge (including astronomy, mathematics, and music) to a complex of ethical, metaphysical, and religious principles so as to assure salvation. Thinkers have searched in vain for the origin of these doctrines. Pherecydes of Syros (sixth century BCE) is often cited as the first author to have posited the immortality of the soul and its return to earth in successive reincarnations (see M. L. West 1971, 25 and n1–2). Many suppose that Pythagoras was in contact with him. However, according to Eliade (*H.R.I.* 2:199), at the time of Pherecydes, such doctrines had only been clearly formulated in India. As for the Egyptians, they did not have a general theory of transmigration even if they believed in the immortality of the soul and in its capacity to reincarnate itself in different animal forms (contra Herodotus 2.123). Herodotus (4.95) claims that Pythagoras also frequented the Thracian Zalmoxis, which would explain the chamic influences (for Pythagorean chamism, see W. Burkert 1972, 120f). But nothing prevents searching elsewhere for the origins, or at least the influences, of that transformation. For example, it is clear that for the Milesian school, the *nous* and the *psuchē* are no longer two distinct identities, as in Homer, but instead form a single and same thing. Thus for Anaximenes, the *phusis* as *archē,* the air, is both living and intelligent, even if it is not at all supernatural. Since man's *phusis* is similar to that of the universe, it became fairly easy to integrate this view into a general doctrine of transmigration. Another influence, that can be added to the first, relates to the state of the socio-political situation. Ancient Mesopotamia and Egypt shared a conception of life after death whose equivalence can also be found in Homer. As well, as the laws imposed a new arbitration (such as the famous Hammurabi code), putting a brake to the arbitrariness of decision and to the caprices of the nobles and the functionaries, the conception of life after death became clearly more optimistic. In this optimistic view, rewards and punishments were distributed on the basis of conduct here-below. There appears to be a similar phenomenon that developed in Ancient Greece (as evidenced in Hesiod) during the seventh and sixth centuries, which resulted in a change in the conception of life after death. From this perspective, if they did not directly contribute to this transformation, the Elysian mysteries, in conjunction with the belief that there existed certain divinely favored individuals (this fact is mentioned by both Homer and Hesiod), must surely have laid the groundwork. For the relation between Pythagoras and Pherecydes of Syros, see Kahn (2001, 11–12), and the book by H. S. Schibli (1990). M. L. West (1971) must be also understood in this context. For West (75), Pherecydes believed that souls enter a succession of bodies, but there is no evidence that he also had a theory of metempsychosis like Pythagoras, that is, a belief in the interchange of the different animal species (1971, 61).

20. As Huffman (1999, 72) correctly notes, "the way of life must have been designed at least in part to ensure the best possible sequence of rebirths."

21. On Pythagoras' swift rise to power, see also Guthrie (1962, 174) and Kahn (2001, 7–8). There is actually evidence that Croton began to flourish shortly after his arrival (T. J. Dunbabin 1948, 359–60).

22. Von Fritz (1950, 87). According to him, there were probaly two uprisings against the Pythagoreans, with the first being restricted to Croton in the early fifth century (and which was due to the secrecy of the meetings) and the second, which was much more widespread around the middle, due to democratic opposition to the oligarchic policy of the Pythagoreans. On the rebellions, see also Guthrie (1962, 178–179).

23. The expression *tropos tou biou* to qualify the Pythagoreans is found in Plato's *Republic* 10.600b4.

24. Aristotle, who appears uncertain, does not limit the speculation to a seed, but also mentions planes or surfaces as other possibilities. On the importance of the seed and the seed analogy, see Philolaus DK44B13. The fact that Aristotle (*Metaphysics* 1091a15) states that the One itself was constituted from more basic principles (e.g., a seed) is confirmed somewhat by Philolaus (see below). For other Pythagorean texts on the seed and an excellent discussion, see Guthrie (1962, 276–77). As Guthrie correctly notes, it is hard to miss the connection with Anaximander's contention that the universe emerged from a seed *(gonimon)*, but that the seed, in turn, emerged from something more basic.

25. *Metaphysics* 14.1091a12–20; see also *Physics* 4.213b22 = DK58B30 and Kahn (2001, 29).

26. There is no doubt that Alcmaeon of Croton is earlier than Philolaus. Indeed, he appears to be a younger contemporary of Pythagoras. However, although Alcmaeon was clearly influenced by Pythagoras, he is not considered a Pythagorean. Given the influence of the Pythagoreans at the time (he believed in the immortality of the soul and its kinship with nature) and the fact that he and Pythagoras resided in the same city, this is quite extraordinary. Alcmaeon, as we saw, appeared to be a proponent of democracy. Moreover, he was the first to argue that thought or intellect is what distinguishes humans from animals. For a good discussion, see Guthrie (1962, 341–59).

27. Kahn (2001, 24) begins Philolaus's account in *On the Nature of Things (Peri phuseōs)* with fragment 1. On the idea of *phusis* in Philolaus, see Huffman (1993, 96–7); he also stresses the importance of a cosmogony. On *Peri phuseōs* as a book title in Philolaus, see Huffman (1993, 94).

28. Although Philolaus himself does not state that all things are numbers, because of Aristotle's testimony this is commonly assumed to be the case. Aristotle may have simply meant that the *kosmos* exhibits order and structure because of number. This is clearly the spirit behind Philolaus, fragment 5. In the final analysis, as Huffman notes (1993, 71): "The study of number is the equivalant to the study of the structure of the cosmos in so far as it can be expressed in mathematical relations."

29. At DK44B8, we are informed that the One itself is the first principle of all things *(archē pantōn)*. For a discussion, see Huffman (1993, 345–46) who contests the authenticity of this fragment.

30. On the role of the seed in Philolaus, and the embryological analogy, see DK44A27 and Huffman's commentary (1993, 290f).

31. On the other hand, the text suggests (in conjunction with Aristotle's testimony above) that the One, or the central fire, is a combination of a limiting or form-giving element and an unlimited or amorphous element. Huffman (1999, 82), for his part, sees the "central fire" as a combination of an unlimited (fire) with a limiter (center). It is only after this, according to Huffman, that the central fire draws in the unlimiteds of breath, time and void (contra Kahn 2001).

32. For a detailed analysis of the astronomical system of Philolaus, see Huffman (1993, 240–61).

33. Aristotle, *Metaphysics* 986a2; Philolaus DK44A16–17, 19 = Eudemus on the authority of Aristotle and Theophrastus.

34. On the soul as an attunement for the Pythagoreans, see Plato, *Phaedo* 86b5; for a complete list of the relevant texts, see Huffman (1993, 324–26).

35. In the famous Pythagorean doctrine of the tetractys, the tetractys that corresponds to society has unsurprisingly man as its principle: Society: man, family, city (See Theo Smyrnaeus, *Exposition des connaissances mathématiques* (ed. Hiller, 160–161).

36. According to Boardman (1999, 100), one of Ephesus' rulers is reported to have married a daughter of Alyattes.

37. I concur with Kahn (1979, 3) on this point. See also Gorman (2001, 132), where Ephesus seems to have been a city that remained free of tyranny "suggesting that the Persian king did not change the government of subject cities arbitrarily."

38. I am paraphrasing here and following, to some degree, Kahn's punctuation of the fragment (1979, 120–21).

39. See also DK22B106: "the nature *(phusis)* of every day is one and the same."

40. Clement of Alexandria, *Miscellanies* 1.65 = DK22A3; the story is related by Diogenes Laertius, *Lives* 9.14. We are told that Darius admired Heraclitus' cosmology and wanted some clarifications. Heraclitus was not as admiring of Persian culture as we see in his apparent scorning of the Persian *magoi* in DK22B14 (see Kahn 1979, 2), but he was no more tolerant of Greek traditional religion.

41. For example, Strabo, *Geography* 14.25, 624 = DK22A3a; see also Aristotle, *Rhetoric* 3.5, 1407b11.

42. See also Glenn Most (1999, 357). In a recent paper ("On the Nature of Heraclitus' Book," SAGP, Chicago 2002, 2), Herb Granger has actually called this the orthodox view. He contrasts this with the view that Heraclitus' book falls into the tradition of Ionian *historia* (see below).

43. In chapter 1, we saw the author of the Hippocratic treatise *Regimen* I, using Heraclitus as an inspiration/source for his own cosmogony and anthropogny.

44. J. Barnes (1982, 60–64) also leans in this direction. Given fragment B30 he thinks Heraclitus could support a cosmogony only with great difficulty. However,

unlike Kirk and Guthrie, he believes Heraclitus is a strict monist, that is, he argues that for Heraclitus, fire is the principle of all things in the same way that air is for Anaximenes. T. M. Robinson (1987, 186) contends both interpretations can be equally defended.

45. E. Hussey (1972 50), for his part, emphasizes fragment B 51, that famous fragment of the arc and the lyre. According to him, the key is to know whether one should read the text to say *palintropos harmonië* (a structure which turns in the opposite sense) or *palintonos harmonië* (a structure which is hung in the opposite sense). According to Hussey, if one opts for the first meaning (as he does) there is an *ekpurosis* for Heraclitus. If one opts for the second, there is not an *ekpurōsis*. By contrast, T. M. Robinson (1987, 115–16) who also opts for *palintropos,* argues the inverse, namely that there is a conflagration. This shows to what extent Heraclitus' fragments are open to discussion and disagreement.

46. At *Metaphysics* 1.984a7, Aristotle also explicitly states that Heraclitus declared that fire was his first principle or *archë*.

47. On the possible length of this Great Year, see G. Vlastos (1955/1993, 311f).

48. See Kahn (1979, 138–144); in any event, it is something hot and wet: a hot atmospheric component of the *kosmos;* see Hussey (1972, 53). This may be analogous to the condition that preceded the explosion in Anaximander's cosmogonical account that gave rise to the heavenly bodies.

49. This is not the only possible interpretation of this fragment. For a full discussion, see Kahn (1979, 238–40).

50. As Hussey (1999, 106) notes, there is also the notion of participating "in the inner and cosmic struggle."

51. For Heraclitus, Zeus alone is wise because he plays the game perfectly. Otherwise, to be wise "is to understand the cosmic plan and to get it put into action." (Hussey 1999, 108). Is this why Heraclitus considered Hermodorus to be the best among the Ephesians?

52. Hermodorus could also be seen as the incarnation of the cosmic principle insofar as he would dispose of enough force to assure that the opposing forces would adhere to the law all in being himself subject to the law. As Vlastos (1947/1993, 74) notes in echoing Heraclitus' contention that "it is law, too, to obey the counsel of the one" (22B33): "the will of the one is law only when it expresses the common to which all (including the 'one') are subject."

53. Apollodorus (DK28A1) contends that Parmenides was born around 540 BCE. The date seems to be based on the foundation of Elea. Plato, for his part, gives a date of around 515 BCE. This date can be deduced from information that Plato provides at the beginning of the *Parmenides* (127 a–c). For more detail, see Guthrie (1965, 1–2) and KRS (1983, 240–41).

54. Parmenides' most famous student and fellow citizen, Zeno, is described by Diogenes Laertius as also being very active in politics. He relates his encounter with and resistance to a tyrant named Nearchus (DK29A1.26–28; 29A2.6–9). Unless this

occurred after the death of Parmenides, it would suggest that Elea was ruled by a tyrant during at least part of Parmenides' lifetime. Minar Jr. (1949), for his part, argues that the fact that Zeno apparently murdered a tyrant supports his position since tyrants were generally supported by the democrtic tradition contra the aristocrats.

55. Aristotle also includes Parmenides among those who did not recognize realities beyond sensible ones (*Metaphysics* 12. 1075b24–7; see also *Metaphysics* 1009b12–1010a30).

56. Diogenes Laertius 1.16 = DK28A13; for other references to the title see above.

57. Heraclitus apears to make a similar distinction, as Lafrance notes (1999, 296–7).

58. This is clearly the interpretation of Theophrastus according to Alexander of Aphrodisia, *Commentary on Aristotle's Metaphysics* 31.12.150 = DK28A7.

59. Lafrance notes (1999, 300f) that the Greek word *hodos* means not only "way" or "path," but also the journey toward an end and thus a method. In sum, Parmenides is proposing two methods of research.

60. There are several references to generation and growth (or the exclusion of generation and growth) at DK28B8.6–8 with respect to the *phusis* as *archē* of Parmenides' predecessors. This suggests again that the universe is the primary topic of discussion.

61. As Sedley notes (1999, 121), the sphere is the only shape that can be conceived as a single whole without distinction of parts.

62. There are a number of important similarities between the Ionian and Eleatic monisms. Both argue that the unity was primary and unengendered on the one hand and eternal and divine on the other; indeed both argue that it was/is identical with the sum of existing things (see Sedley 1999, 120).

63. On the three possible approaches in Parmenides' poem, namely the one practiced by Parmenides, the one which is impossible, and the one which is intermediary, see Tarán (1965, chap. 2, "Aletheia and Doxa"), where he reviews the different possibilities. For my part, I follow Aristotle (*Metaphysics* 1.986b27) for whom Parmenides was constrained by the phenomena in the second part of his poem. For a summary of the diverse interpretations regarding Parmenides' cosmogony, see A. A. Long (1963/1975, 82–101 and Curd 1998).

64. In sum, Parmenides holds a discourse similar to Plato's in the *Timaeus.* For another interpretation, see Gallop (1986, 23). According to Gallop, the goddess does not claim a greater truth for Parmenides' cosmogony in relation to those of his rivals.

65. A case could also be made for the center of the mixed rings, but it is unimportant for the case at hand, see Tarán (1965, 249). Note that at 28B8.44, being is also described in analogy with the body [sic] of a well-rounded sphere from the middle *(messothen),* it is everywhere of equal strength.

66. Several doxographies portray Parmenides as a student of Xenophanes, of the Pythagoreans, and of Anaximander. While Anaximander must be rejected outright

because of the dates, given the geographical proximity and the facility of travel by sea (Parmenides' trip to Athens is taken for granted), he may very well have been a pupil of Xenophanes and/or the Pythagoreans. Their philosophical sensibilities are evident in Parmenides' poem. Of course, one does not have to encounter someone to be influenced by them. Heraclitus (Tarán, 1965, 64–72 and more important Lafrance 1999, 296–8) and Anaximander (W. Jaeger 1939, 215; Vlastos 1947/1993, 65–66) appear to be both well represented in his poem.

67. E. L. Minar Jr. (1949, 41–55) argues that Parmenides' philosophical conception of being and seeming are more in line with the aristocratic tradition. This aristocratic temper, according to Minar (1949, 47), explains "the strenuous opposition to change, or the denial of change, which we saw in the first part of his poem." He argues that Parmenides was involved with the Pythagoreans and their idea of "proportional justice," which is seen as grounded in nature. Just as the dominant features of the One (Being) is harmony, order, and hierarchy (1949, 46), justice should be based on a man's worth. In sum, hierarchical political theory is grounded in their idea of nature. While Minar Jr. once again shows the relevance of contemporary socio-political conditions on Parmenides' thought, the vocabulary lends more support to Vlastos' position.

68. For a more detailed account of the history of Acragas, see Dunbabin (1948, 315).

69. I take two poems to be a fact since ancient sources attribute two different titles to his works: *Peri Phuseōs*, and *Katharmoi*, and also that they were addressed to two different audiences (e.g., Diogenes Laertius 8.54, 60). Of course, there is no consensus on this among contemporary scholars. For a recent discussion in favor of two distinct poems, see Kingsley (1995, 359–370); for arguments in favor of one poem, see Inwood (2001, 8–19).

70. It is unclear why he chose these exact ratios, but Empedocles may have based his general hypothesis on the practice or technique of metallurgy.

71. It is ironic that separation occurs through attraction, and that Strife is associated with similar groups of entities coming together. Is there a political allusion? For example, is there an allusion here to aristocrats banning together so naturally (or blindly!) that the result is strife, that is, strife with the other social groups? Love, we will recall, is the force that tends to bring the divergent elements together in one heterogenous mass.

72. Diogenes (8.77) and Aetius (2.6.3 = A49) both claim the sun is composed of fire.

73. The heat of the sun caused the earth's surface to sweat, thus creating the salty sea.

74. As we saw in chapter one, Empedocles was also a physician with a strong following. This may explain why one of the longest surviving fragments is on respiration, which is connected with the movement of blood within the body (DK31B100).

75. Since we are composed of the same elements as the world, when these elements are blended in the same ratios, consciousness and awareness result.

76. This explains the possibility of transmigration from one form of existence to another (B117). For Empedocles' idea of immortality, see. M. R. Wright (1981, 63–76) and more recently Inwood (2001, 52–62). According to Wright, the exile or the "fall" for Empedocles has nothing to do with an original sin but is related to a spillage of blood or a perjury made by his daimon under the impulsion of Strife. In conjunction with this, she argues that there is no personal immortality for Empedocles since immortality is only achieved after one's personal identity is reintegrated into the basic elements. Inwood, for his part, argues that Empedocles doctrine of reincarnation does not imply that the soul is immortal, but only that the soul can survive many bodies as we see in Plato's *Phaedo* 86e–88b. Moreover, he contends that whatever one's mode of existence, the cosmic cycle will continue according to necessity.

77. It is unclear if this fall, or "original sin," is associated with the spillage of blood or a perjury of sorts. What is clear is that every act of killing is considered murder since all living beings are related through reincarnation (B137). This may also be a way of advocating democracy since we can all thus be seen as equal before the law.

78. In fact, numerous analogies borrowed from the trades also attest to his keen interest in technical know-how: bakery (B34); metallurgy (B96); weaving (B92, 93); and dyeing (B93).

79. This is the case not only for Love and Strife, but also for the four elements, which albeit equal, dominate in turn as time revolves (B17.27–29) .

80. For an attempt to date Anaxagoras much earlier, see Cleve (1949/1973, 1–5). He argues that Anaxagoras may have been born as early as 534 BCE, came to Athens after the fall of Miletus in 494 (see Cleve 1949/1973, 2–3 referring to nineteenth century German scholars Hermann and Unger), and died around 461. This seems plausible if one considers the number of references to the great Milesian cosmologist Anaximenes, of whom Anaxagoras is invariably considered a pupil and associate. On the other hand, it is very difficult to reconcile these references to the clear references to Parmenides and Zeno, to whom Anaxagoras is clearly responding. The consensus is that Parmenides was born circa 515 BCE.

81. For a good discussion, see O'Brien (1968, 235–54) who argues that Empedocles composed after Anaxagoras and was influenced by him; Guthrie (1965, 266) takes the opposite view. Capizzi (1990, 390–91) contends that, while Empedocles composed before Anaxagoras, "after having kept company with him," he rewrote many parts of his own treatise.

82. Sider (1981, 1–8); for other interpretations, see Cleve (1949/1973, 1–5). Sider (1981, 5–6) contends that Anaxagoras' book must have been written before he arrived in Athens—whence his fame. Guthrie's observation (1965, 266) that the fall of the meteorite at Aegospotamie (467 BCE) to which Anaxagoras refers, should be taken as the earliest date for the composition of his book. Although it could be argued that Anaxagoras may have composed different versions of his book.

83. For a more detailed account of the entities and principles of Anaxagoras' system, see McKirahan (1994, 203–23). It is worth noting that Anaxagoras' DK59B3 strongly suggests an exchange with Zeno.

84. It is unclear why *nous* initiated the original movement when it did, but it is clear that it must have permeated the original mixture to do so (at first in a small area and then in an ever increasing area = B12). It is also clear that *nous* caused the original mixture to rotate. This movement initially affected only a small portion of the primordial matter, but it subsequently affected a larger and larger area (connected with the speed of the rotation) and continues to do so (DK59B12, 13).

85. On seeds and the origin of life, see Schofield (1980, 124–133).

86. There is thus a clear analogy here with Xenophanes' conception of the divinity and by extension the Milesian conception of a first principle (see above). It is the lack of details in Anaxagoras' description that may have prompted Plato to add the descriptive details as he does in his description of the Demiuge in the *Timaeus*.

87. In this, there is a crucial difference with Plato for whom the celestial bodies were not only created by the demiurge, but according to a mathematical model.

88. On all accounts, the formation of the sea is indissociable from how it became salted (DK59A90).

89. See Aristotle *On the Soul* 404b1. In DK59B12, Anaxagoras contends that Mind controls (or animates) all things that have soul or life. In reality, Mind controls all things, that is, animate and inanimate (see below).

90. Furthermore, his interest in the floods of the Nile (DK59A91) suggests he visited the country of "spontaneous generation." In fact, the passages relating to men who have cities and who cultivate fields "like us" (DK59B4) could imply travels in certain countries and notably in Egypt much more than in an infinite number of worlds (e.g., Kahn 1960/1994, 52–53), although I am also sympathetic to the interpretation of Vlastos (1975) and Schofield (1980, 103), for whom Anaxagoras is stating that if Mind were to cause another cosmogony, "it would result in a world exactly the same as ours, right down to the specific institutions of farming and city life" (Schofield 1980, 103). See also McKirahan (1994, 230), for whom Anaxagoras is referring "to different regions of this world," albeit regions not known to the Greeks. All these interpretations seem to suggest Anaxagoras believed in some sort of divine plan, that is, the present order of things could not have unfolded otherwise than it has.

91. This position is held by a number of distinguished scholars, e.g., Vlastos (1946/1993, 56–57), Lämmli (1962, 92–96), Edelstein (1967, 54), and Dodds (1973, 11).

92. Euripides, a close associate of Anaxagoras, expounds a similar position in the *Supplices* (203–14), although he contends that it was a god behind this human progress. The three most famous Athenian tragedians all developed explicit and detailed odes to human progress (e.g., Aeschylus, *Prometheus Bound* 442–68; 478–506; Sophocles, *Antigone* 332–71). Anaxagoras' position also has analogies with his contemporary Protagoras, at least Plato's version (see *Protagoras* 321d–322d). Indeed, the texts are strongly reminiscent of the famous texts by Aeschylus, Sophocles, and Euripides and their respective odes to progress. It is also worth noting that Anaxagoras' student, Archelaus, after giving an account of the origin of the universe and living beings, continues his *historia* with a genetic account of the origin and development of civilization (Hippolytus 1.9.5–6 = DK60A4; see Farrar 1988, 87–88).

Archelaus notes that while *all* animals have *nous,* humans were quicker to use it and this led to the gradual development of human societies, laws, and arts.

93. To be sure, we can see the correlation between the cosmic *logos* and the human *logos* in Heraclitus, but Anaxagoras goes further than this. He explains the causal origin of human *nous.*

94. Vlastos (1947/1993, 174/85) strongly suggests that Anaxagoras' doctrine of *nous* is antidemocratic.

95. There is also, of course, the opposition between the Athenian or democratic paradigm and the Spartan or aristocratic paradigm.

96. Diogenes Laertius (9.34 = DK68A1) contends that Democritus states in his *Great World-System* that he was young in the old age of Anaxagoras, whence 460, since it is assumed that Anaxagoras was born ca. 500 BCE. The *Great World-System* is generally attributed to Leucippus (see below). According to Guthrie (1965, 384), he influenced Diogenes of Apollonia whose treatise was satirized by Aristophanes in 423. Capizzi (1988, 449) gives a date of 490 for the birth of Democritus.

97. A number of doxographies contend that Leucippus was a pupil of Zeno of Elea (see DK67A1, 4, 5), which is not improbable. Meanwhile, if Zeno was born around 490–85 BCE (the conventional date) and if one assumes the traditional gap of twenty years between master and student, one could conjecture that Leucippus was born around 470–65 BCE.

98. Democritus may also have edited this work, whence the contention that he was young in the old age of Anaxagoras in the *Great World-System.*

99. Diogenes Laertius (9.48 = DK68A33) credits Democritus with two treatises on the military art. As with Plato (e.g., *Republic, Timaeus, Laws*) and the Platonic Protagoras (*Protagoras* 322b), military art and political art are intimately (and realistically) connected.

100. Other fragments suggest a certain reservation toward democracy (e.g., DK68B254, 49) as some scholars note (C. C. W. Taylor 1999a, 230; Proscopé 1989/1990, 314). However, nothing excludes a penchant for democracy and the notion that those who would best further the "common" good should rule. Thucydides (2.37.1) attributes these two fundamental principles to Periclean democracy: power should reside with the people as a whole; high offices should be entrusted to the most able. See also below.

101. A decree introduced by Diopeithes ca. 433, that is, if Anaxagoras were a victim of this decree and not an earlier prosecution as some argue. For a discussion see KRS (1983, 354); for the details, see Derenne (1930). That Democritus believed that the images of the gods that appear to humans and sometimes speak to them could predict the future (68B166) is some indication that he tried to accommodate popular belief. Indeed, he also spoke of the gods as givers of good and not evil; of loving only those who hate injustice (DK68B175, 217). Whether this would have saved him from prosecution for impiety is difficult to say.

102. The fact that Plato never mentions Democritus by name although there are numerous references to Protagoras, including a dialogue named after him, is disconcerting. Did Plato feel more threatened by Democritus than Protagoras or the contrary?

103. This was also the case with Protagoras, who attacked Parmenides' theory on political grounds.

104. Zeno argued that one could not distinguish two existing things as being two unities without taking recourse in a third intermediary thing between them; also this intermediary had to exist. According to Aristotle, that is the reason Leucippus took a draconian measure. He proposed to introduce "that which is not" *(to me on)* as a factor in the explanation of the world and thus affirm it existed in a certain manner.

105. Aristotle, *On the Heavens* 300b11; and also *Generation of Animals* 789b2–3 where there is no recourse to final causation. For Aristotle, the elements have natural places.

106. For a good discussion of this fragment, see Taylor (1999b, 185f); see also McKirahan (1994, 321–22); Guthrie (1965, 414–419).

107. According to Aristotle, Democritus identified soul with fire (see Aristotle *On the Soul* 403b25–404a31; *The Parts of Animals* 625b8–15; *On Respiration* 471b30–472a18; on the identification of soul and mind in Democritus, see *On the Soul* 405a8–13).

108. Several doxographies suggest that hook-shaped atoms form the membrane: see Taylor (1999a, 94–96).

109. For the cosmogony, see also Hippolytus and Pseudo-Plutarch (in Taylor 1999a, 95–96). Pseudo Plutarch (*Epinome* 1.4 = Aetius 1.4) gives a good description of how the earth was formed: the material initially contained in the earth was compressed by the winds and exhalations of the stars and this compression caused moisture to rise and flow into hollowed and low lying places.

110. See, for example, Aristotle, *Physics* 250b18–20; 203b24–7; Simplicius, *Commentary on Aristotle's Physics* 1121.5–9; Philoponus, *Commentary on Aristotle's Physics* 405.23–7.

111. While C. C. W. Taylor does not contest that Democritus accounted for the development of human society (1999b, 181), it is conspicuously absent in his recent book (1999a). Indeed, contrary to other scholars, Diodorus' account (DK68B5) is not included in the fragments.

112. There were probably a number of different and competing theories on the origin of speech or *phōnē* (see, for example, Sophocles and Euripides in their own odes to progress; and Guthrie (1971, 204). Democritus' account, as related by Diodorus, seems to put the accent on the political function of speech. Thus, as Vlastos (1946/1993, 54/355) notes ethnic differences are conceived as essentially linguistic in origin.

113. Democritus supports his thesis in 68B26 with arguments such as: different things are sometimes called by different names; different names are applied to one and the same thing; and the name of a thing or of a person is sometimes changed at will.

114. Aristotle contends the ancients in general maintained that sensation and thought were the same thing (*On the Soul* 427a21–22 and also *Metaphysics* 1009b12–15).

115. The spherical shape of the soul atoms is the sine qua non of their essence since all atoms are in motion. It is the shape proper to other atoms (or certain other atoms) that causes them to become entangled (as we saw in the formation of the uni-

verse) and thus form a composite body. Because of their shape, once the soul atoms pervade the body, they become trapped within its framework, but since the soul atoms continue to move, they communicate their motion to the other atoms thus making the whole body a self-mover. Aristotle was correct to point out the naivety of this particular explanation (*On the Soul* 406b16–25 = DK68A104).

116. Theophrastus, *On the Senses* 50–53 = DK68A135. In the case of Leucippus images actually enter the eye, whereas for Democritus images themselves do not actually enter the eye but appear as reflections in a purely passive pupil. In *Sense and Sensibilia* 438a5–12, Aristotle observes that if sight is only a case of reflection, as in the case of Democritus, one would expect any reflecting surfaces to see. This criticism of Aristotle suggests Democritus' theory of sight was indeed simplistic.

117. The atomists seem to have made an exception for the mind, or the thinking part of the soul. The doxographies state that the mind is composed of a concentration of soul atoms which are located in the head (Aetius 4.5.1 = DK68A105).

118. As Theophrastus himself notes in *On Sensation* 70–71.

119. Anaxagoras suggests the same thing when he states: "what is visible (appearances), opens our eyes to what is invisible" (DK59B21a).

120. See Taylor (1999b, 200–201) and (1999a, 233); McKirahan (1994, 339); Vlastos (1945/1993, 54/342); Farrar (1988, 229); and McKirahan (1994, 339).

121. And not, of course, the physical shape of the individual person (See Farrar 1988, 229).

122. This may be Democritus' reply to (or way of mediating) the darker side of the *nomos/phusis* antithesis.

123. Democritus' sense of living in conformity with nature or *phusis* was quite different from the view of many of his contemporaries. They associated living in conformity with nature as involving the pursuit of one's egoistic passions. This will be developed in the next volume.

124. From Hesiod on, wealth is the driving force behind social unrest and the source of arrogance and resentment. Its antidote was invariably seen as moderation.

125. The analogy here with the formation of the universe is clearer if we consider that the atoms behind the initial formation of the universe were different. The *kosmos* only becomes ordered when similar atoms move toward one another according to the mechanical law expressed in the famous fragment 68B164, where both animate and inanimate things of the same kind have a natural tendency to congregate together.

CONCLUSION

1. I owe this quote to Guthrie (1971), 229. I am also using his translation. This passage is also cited by Festugière (1949/1983, 162) in the same context.

Bibliography

Adkins, Arthur W. H. (1985). "Ethics and the Breakdown of the Cosmogony in Ancient Greece." In Lovin and Reynolds (1985):279–309.

———. (1985). "Cosmogony and Order in Ancient Greece." In Lovin and Reynolds (1985):39–66.

———. (1997). "Homeric Ethics." In Morris and Powell (1997):694–714.

Allen, R. E., and Furley, D. J., ed. (1970, 1975). *Studies in Presocratic Philosophy*. London: Routledge and Kegan Paul.

Andrewes, Anthony. (1971). *Greek Society*. London: Penguin.

Aubenque, P. (1968). "Physis." In *Encyclopaedia Universalis*. Paris: Press Universitaire de France, vol. 8, 8–10.

Austin. M. (1970). *Greece and Egypt in the Archaic Age*. Cambridge: Cambridge Philological Society.

Baccou, R. (1951). *Histoire de la Science Grecque de Thalès à Socrate*. Paris: Aubier.

Baldry, H. C. (1932). "Embryological Analogies in Presocratic Cosmogony." *Classical Quarterly* 26:27–34.

Barnes. J. (1982). *The Presocratic Philosophers*. London: Routledge and Kegan Paul.

Beardslee, J. W., Jr. (1918). *The use of "phusis" in fifth century Greek Literature*. Chicago: University of Chicago Press.

Benveniste, Emile .(1948). *Noms d'agents et noms d'action en indo-europeens*. Paris: Klincksieck.

Bernal, Martin. (1987). *Black Athena*. Vol. 1. *The Afroasiatic Roots of Classical Civilization*. New Brunswick: Rutgers University Press.

———. (1991). *Black Athena*. Vol. 2. *The Archaeological and Documentary Evidence*. New Brunswick: Rutgers University Press.

Boardman, John. (1999). *The Greeks Overseas*. 4th ed. London: Thames and Hudson.

Bonnefoy, Y., and Doniger, W., ed. (1991). *Mythologies*. Chicago: University of Chicago Press.

Bottéro, Jean. (1992). *Mesopotamia: Writing Reasoning and the Gods*. Chicago: University of Chicago Press.

Brisson, L. (1996). *Introduction à la philosophie du mythe*. Paris: Vrin.

——. (1994). *Platon. Parménide*. Paris: GF-Flammarion.

Broadie, Sarah. (1999). "Rational theology." In Long (1999):205–224.

Brumbaugh, Robert. (1964). *The Philosophers of Greece*. New York: Thomas Crowell.

Burch, George. (1949/1950). "Anaximander, The First Metaphysician." *Review of Metaphysics* 3:137–160.

Burger, A. (1925). *Les mots de la famille de "phusis" en grec ancien*. Paris

Burkert, Walter. (1963). "Iranisches bei Anaximander." *Rheinisches Museum für Philologie* 106:97–134.

——. (1972). *Lore and Science in Ancient Pythagoreanism*. Trans. E. L. Minar. Cambridge: Harvard University Press.

——. (1985). *Greek Religion*. Trans. J. Raffan. Cambridge: Harvard University Press.

——. (1992). *The Orientalizing Revolution: Near Eastern Influence on Greek Culture in Early Archaic Age*. Trans. M. Pindar and W. Burkert. Cambridge: Harvard University Press.

——. (1996). *The Creation of the Sacred: Tracks of Biology in Early Religions*. Cambridge, MA: Cambridge University Press.

Burnet, John. (1930/1945). *Early Greek Philosophy*. 4th ed. London: Adam and Charles Black.

——. (1914). *Greek Philosophy. Thales to Plato*. London: Macmillan.

Burton, A. (1972). *Diodorus Sicilus: Book I*. Leiden: Brill.

Calame-Griaule, G. (1970). "Pour une étude ethnolinguistique des littérateures orales africaines." *Languages* 18:22–45.

Camassa, Giorgio. (1981). "Aux origines de la codification écrite des lois en Grèce." In Detienne (1981):130–155.

Capelle, W. (1912). "Meteoros-Meteorologia." *Philologus* 71:414–427.

Capizzi, A. (1990). *The Cosmic Republic*. Amsterdam: Brill.

Cassin, E. (1991). "Mesopotamian Cosmogony." In Bonnefoy and Donigen (1991):228–235.

Chadwick, J. (1976). *The Mycenean World*. Cambridge: Cambridge University Press.

Chantraine, P. (1968–1980). *Dictionnaire étymologique de la langue grecque*. 4 vols. Paris: Klincksieck.

Cherniss, Harold. (1935). *Aristotle's Criticism of Presocratic Philosophy*. Baltimore: Johns Hopkins University Press.

———. (1951). "The Characteristics and Effects of Presocratic Philosophy." *Journal of the History of Ideas* 12:319–345.

Chide, Gordon. (1954). *What Happened in History*. Harmmondsworth: Penguin.

Clay, Diskin. (1992). "The World of Hesiod." In *Essays on Hesiod II*. Ed. A. N. Athanassakis, *Ramus* 21:131–155.

Clay, Jenny. (1972). "The Planktai and Moly: Divine Naming and Knowing in Homer." *Hermes* 100:127–131.

———. (1989). *The Politics of Olympus*. Princeton: Princeton University Press.

Cleve, F. M. (1949/1973). *The Philosophy of Anaxagoras*. The Hague: Nijhoff.

Coldstream, J. N. (1977). *Geometric Greece*. New York: St. Martin's Press.

Colemen, J. E. (1996). "Did Egypt Shape the Glory That Was Greece?" In Lefkowitz and MacLean (1996):280–302.

Collingwood, R. G. (1945). *The Idea of Nature*. Oxford: Oxford University Press.

Conche, Marcel. (1991). *Anaximandre: Fragments et Témoignages*. Paris: Presses Universitaires de France.

Cornford, Francis M. (1934). "Innumerable Worlds in Presocratic Philosophy." *Classical Quarterly* 28:1–16.

———. (1936). "The Invention of Space." In *Essays in Honour of Gilbert Murray*. Ed. H. A. L. Fisher. London: Allen and Unwin, 215–235.

———. (1950). *The Unwritten Philosophy and Other Essays*. Cambridge: Cambridge University Press.

———. (1952). *Principium Sapientiae: The Origins of Greek Philosophical Thought*. Cambridge: Cambridge University Press.

Couprie, Dirk. (2001). "Anaximander's Discovery of Space." In Preus (2001):23–48.

———. (1995). "The Visulaization of Anaximander's Astronomy." *Apeiron* 23:159–181.

———, with Hahn, R., and Naddaf, G. (2003). *Anaximander in Context. New Studies in the Origins of Greek Philosophy*. Albany: State University of New York Press.

Curd, P. (1998). *The Legacy of Parmenides*. Princeton: Princeton University Press.

Dalley, Stephanie. (1988). *Myths of Mesopotamia*. Oxford: Oxford University Press.

Deichgräber, K. (1938). "Xenophanes *peri phuseos*." *Rheinisches Museum* 87:1–31.

Delattre, A. (1988). *Les Présocratiques*. Paris: Gallimard.

Derchain, P. (1991). "Egyptian Cosmogony." In Bonnefoy and Doniger (1991):91–95.

Derenne, E. (1930). *Les procès d'impiété intentés aux philosophes à Athènes au Ve et au IVe siècles av. J. C.* Liège: Vaillant-Carmanne.

Deroy, Louis. (1950). "Le culte du foyer dans la Grèce mycénienne." *Revue de l'histoire des religions* 167:17–41.

Detienne, Marcel. (1996). *The Masters of Truth in Archaic Greece*. New York: Zone Books.

————, ed. (1988). *Les Savoirs de l'écriture en Grèce ancienne*. Lille: Presses Universitaires de Lille.

————. (1988). "L'espace de la publicité: ses opérateurs intellectuels dans la cité." In Detienne (1988): 29–81.

Dicks, D. R. (1970). *Early Greek Astronomy to Aristotle*. Ithaca, NY: Cornell University Press.

Diels, Hermann. (1897). *"Ueber Anaximanders Kosmos." Archiv für Geschichte der Philosophie* 10:228–237.

————, and Kranz, W. (1954). *Die Fragmente der Vorsokratiker*. 6th ed. Berlin: Weidmann.

Dillon, M., and Garland, L. (1994). *Ancient Greece: Social and Historical Documents from Archaic Times to the Death of Socrates*. London and New York: Routledge.

Dodds, E. R. (1951). *The Greeks and the Irrational*. Berkeley: University of California Press.

————. (1973). *The Ancient Concept of Progress: And Other Essays on Greek Literature and Belief*. Oxford: Clarendon Press.

Dreyer, J. L. E. (1906). *A History of Astronomy from Thales to Kepler*. Cambridge: Cambridge University Press.

Dumont, J.-P. (1988). *Les Présocratiques*. Paris: Gallimard.

Dunbabin, T. J. (1948). *The Western Greeks*. Oxford: Clarendon Press.

Edelstein, L. (1967). *The Idea of Progress in Classical Antiquity*. Baltimore: John Hopkins University Press.

Eliade, M. (1963). *Aspects du Mythe*. Paris: Gallimard.

————. (1965). *Myth of the Eternal Return*. Trans. W. R. Trask. Princeton: Princeton University Press.

————. (1968). "Création: Les mythes de la création." *Encyclopeadia Universalis*. Vol. 5. Paris: Presses Universitaires de France, 60–64.

————. (1978). *A History of Religious Ideas*. 3 vols. Trans. W. R. Trask. Chicago: University of Chicago Press.

Emlyn-Jones, C. J. (1980). *The Ionians and Hellenism: A Study of the Cultural Achievement of Early Greek Inhabitants of Asia Minor*. London: Routledge and Kegan Paul.

Engmann, Joyce. (1991). "Cosmic Justice in Anaximander." *Phronesis* 36:1–25.

Ernout, A., and Meillet, A. (1979). *Dictionnaire étymologique de la langue latine*. 4th ed. Paris: Hachette.

Eucken, R. (1879). *Geschichte des philosophischen Terminologie.* Leipzig: Hildesheim G. Olm.

Farrar, C. (1988). *The Origins of Democratic Thinking: The Invention of Politics in Classical Greece.* Cambridge: Cambridge University Press.

Faure, Paul. (1975). *La vie quotidienne en Grèce au temps de la guerre de Troie 1250 av J.C.* Paris: Hachette.

———. (1991). "Crete and Mycenae." In Bonnefoy and Doniger (1991):330–340.

Festugière, A. (1949/1983). *La révélation de Hermès Tristmégiste II. Le dieu cosmique.* Paris: Les Belles Lettres.

Finley, Moses. (1981). *Early Greece: The Bronze and Archaic Ages.* 2nd ed. New York and London: W. W. Norton.

Foley, H. (1994). *The Homeric Hymn to Demeter. Translation. Commentary and Interpretative Essay.* Princeton: University of Princeton Press.

Forrest, George. (1986). "Greece: The History of the Archaic Period." In *Greece and the Hellenistic World.* Ed. J. Boardman, J. Griffin, and O. Murray. Oxford and New York: Oxford University Press.

———. (1966). *The Emergence of Greek Democracy.* London: McGraw-Hill.

Fränkel, H. (1973). *Early Greek Poetry and Philosophy.* Trans. Hadas and Willis. New York and London: Harcourt Brace & Jonovich.

———. (1974). "Xenophanes' empiricism and his critique of knowledge (B34)." In Mourelatos (1974):118–131.

Frankfort, H., ed. (1949). *Before Philosophy: The Intellectual Adventure of Ancient Man.* Harmondsworth: Penguin Books.

Fritz, K. Von. (1943). *"Nous, noein* and their derivatives in Homer." *Classical Philology,* 38:79–93.

———. (1950). *Pythagorean Politics in South Italy: an analysis of the sources.* New York: Columbia University Press.

Froidefond, C. (1971). *La Mirage Egyptienne dans la littérateure grecque d'Homère à Aristote.* Aix-en-Provence: Publications Universitaires des lettres et Sciences humaines d'Aix-en-Provence.

Furley, David. (1987). *The Greek Cosmologists.* Vol. 1. Cambridge: Cambridge University Press.

———, and Allen, R. E., eds. (1970). *Studies in Presocratic Philosophy.* Vol. 1: *The Beginnings of Philosophy.* New York: Humanities Press.

Gagarin, Michael. (1986). *Early Greek Law.* Berkeley: University of California Press.

Gallop, D. (1986). *Parmenides of Elea.* Toronto: University of Toronto Press.

Gantz, Timothy. (1993). *Early Greek Myth: A Guide to Literary and Artistic Sources.* Baltimore: John Hopkins University Press.

Gardiner, Alan. (1961a). *A History of Ancient Egypt*. Oxford: Oxford University Press.

———. (1961b). *Egypt of the Pharoahs*. Oxford: Oxford University Press.

Gelzer, Th. (1979). *"Zur Darstellung von Himmel und Erde auf einer Schale des Arkesilas Malers in Rom." Museum Helvetium* 36:170–176.

Georges, P. B. (2000). "Persian Ionia Under Darius." *Historia* 49:1–39.

Gigon, O. (1935). *Untersuchungen zu Heraklit*. Leipzig: Dieterich.

Gilson, E. (1972). *L' Etre et l' Essence*. Paris: Vrin.

Gomperz, Heinrich. (1943). "Problems and Method in Early Greek Science." *Journal of the History of Ideas* 4:161–176.

Gorman, V. (2001). *Miletos, the Ornament of Ionia. A History of the City to 400 B.C.E.* Ann Arbor, MI: University of Michigan Press.

Graham, D. W., ed. (1993). *Studies in Greek Philosophy, by Gregory Vlastos*. Vol. 1. *The Presocratics*. Princeton: Princeton University Press.

Granger, H. (2002). "On the Nature of Heraclitus' Book." *Society for Ancient Greek Philosophy*. Chicago.

Grant, Michael. (1987). *The Rise of the Greeks*. New York: Macmillan.

Greenhalgh, P. A. L. (1973). *Early Greek Warfare. Horsemen and Chariots in the Homeric and Archaic Ages*. Cambridge: Cambridge University Press.

Grene, David. (1996). "Response to Nelson." In *The Greeks and Us*. Ed. R. B. Louden and P. Schollimeier. Chicago: University of Chicago Press. 36–42.

Guthrie, W. K. C. (1950). *The Greek Philosophers from Thales to Aristotle*. London: Methuen.

———. (1957). *In the Beginning: Some Greek Views on the Origins of Life and the Early State of Man*. London: Methuen.

———. (1962). *A History of Greek Philosophy*. Vol. 1. *The Earlier Presocratics and the Pythagoreans*. Cambridge: Cambridge University Press.

———. (1965). *A History of Greek Philosophy*. Vol. 2. *The Presocratic Tradition from Parmenides to Democritus*. Cambridge: Cambridge University Press.

———. (1971). *The Sophists*. Cambridge: Cambridge University Press.

Hadot, P. (2002). *What is Ancient Philosophy*. Trans. M. Chase. Cambridge: Harvard University Press.

Hahn, Robert. (1995). "Technology and Anaximander's Cosmical Imagination: A Case Study for the Influence of Monumental Architecture on the Origins of Western Philosophy/Science." In *New Directions in the Philosophy of Technology,* ed. Joseph C. Pitt. The Netherlands: Kluwer Academic Publishers. 93–136.

———. (2001). *Anaximander and the Architects*. Albany, NY: State University of New York Press.

———, Couprie, D., and Naddaf, G. (2003). *Anaximander in Context. New Studies in the Origins of Greek Philosophy*. Albany, NY: State University of New York Press.

Hall, Edith. (1996). "When Is Myth Not a Myth?" In Lefkowitz and MacLean (1996):333–348.

Hamilton, Richard. (1989). *The Architecture of Hesiodic Poetry*. Baltimore: John Hopkins University Press.

Havelock, Eric. (1957). *The Liberal Temper*. New Haven: Yale University Press.

———. (1978). *The Greek Concept of Justice: From Its Shadow in Homer to Its Substance in Plato*. Cambridge, MA: Harvard University Press.

———. (1963). *A Preface to Plato*. Cambridge, MA: Harvard University Press.

Heath, T. L. (1913). *Aristarchus of Samos*. Oxford: Clarendon Press.

Heidegger, Martin. (1976). "On the Being and Conception of φύσις in Aristotle's *Physics* B1." In *Man and the World*. Trans. J. Sheehan. New York: Harper and Row, 1976.

Heidel, W. A. (1910). "Peri phuseos." *Proceedings of the American Academy of Arts and Sciences* 45:77–133.

———. (1912). "On Certain Fragments of the Pre-Socratics: Critical Notes and Elucidations." *Proceedings of the American Academy of Arts and Sciences* 48.

———. (1921). "Anaximander's Book: The Earliest Known Geographical Treatise." *Proceedings of the American Academy of the Arts and Sciences* 56:239–288.

———. (1935). *Hecataeus and the Egyptian Priests in Herodotus,* Book 2. New York: Garland.

———. (1937). *The Frame of Ancient Greek Maps*. New York: American Geographical Society.

———. (1943). "Hecataeus and Xenophanes." *American Journal of Philology* 64:257–277.

Heubeck, A., West, S., and Hainsworth, J. B. (1988/1992). *A Commentary on Homer's Odyssey*. 3 vols. Oxford: Oxford University Press.

Hölscher, U. (1953/1970). "Anaximander and the Beginnings of Greek Philosophy." In Furley and Allen (1970):281–322.

Holt, J. (1941). *Les noms d' action en -sis (-tis). Études de linguistique grecque (Acta Jutlandica XIII, 1)*. Cophenhagen.

Holwerda, D. (1955). *Commentatio de vocis quae est "phusis" vi atque usu*. Groningen: J. B. Wolters.

Huffmann. C. (1993). *Philolaus of Croton*. Cambridge: Cambridge University Press.

———. (1999). "The Pythagorean Tradition." In Long (1999):66–87.

Hurwit, J. M. (1985). *The Art and Culture of Early Greece, 1100–480 B.C*. Ithaca, NY: Cornell University Press.

Hussey, Edward. (1972). *The Presocratics*. London: Duckworth.

———. (1999). "Heraclitus." In Long (1999):88–112.

——. (1995). "Ionian Inquiries." In Powell (1995):530–549.

Huxley, G. L. (1966). *The Early Ionians*. New York: Faber and Faber.

Inwood, B. (2001). *The Poem of Empedocles* (rev. ed.). Toronto: University of Toronto Press.

Jacob, Christian. (1988). *"Inscrire la terre habité sur une tablette."* In Detienne (1988):273–304.

Jacobsen, Thorkild. (1949). "Mesopotamia." In Frankfort (1949):137–234.

Jacoby, F. (1912). "Hekataios." In *Realencyclopädie der Klassischen Altertumswissenschaft*. Ed. G. Wissowa, W. Kroll et al. Stuttgart: Metzler. 2702–2707.

——. (1923/1958). *Die Fragmente der griechischen Historiker*. Leiden: Brill.

Jaeger, Werner. (1939/1945). *Paideia: The Ideals of Greek Culture*. 3 vols. Trans. G. Highet. Oxford: Blackwell.

——. (1947). *The Theology of the Early Greek Philosophers*. Oxford: Clarendon Press.

Janko, Richard. (1982). *Homer, Hesiod and the Hymns: Diachronic Development in Epic Diction*. Cambridge: Cambridge University Press.

——. 1990. "The *Iliad* and its Editors: Dictation and Redaction." *Classical Antiquity* 9:326–334.

Jeffery, L. H. (1976). *Archaic Greece: The City States c. 700–500 B. C.* New York: St. Martin's Press.

——. (1990). *The Local Scripts of Archaic Greece*. Revised ed. with supplement by A. W. Johnson. Oxford: Oxford University Press.

Jones, H. (1973). "Homeric Nouns in *-sis*," *Glotta* 51:7–29.

Jouanna, J. (1990). *De l'ancienne medecine*. Paris: Les Belles Lettres.

Jucker, H. (1977). *Festschrift für Franck Brommer*. Mainz am Rhein: Von Zabern.

Kahn, Charles. (1960/1993). *Anaximander and the Origins of Greek Cosmology*. Indianapolis, IN: Hackett. Reprint.

——. (1979). *The Art and Thought of Heraclitus*. Cambridge: Cambridge University Press.

——. (2001). *Pythagoras and the Pythagoreans: A Brief History*. Indianapolis and Cambridge: Hackett.

Kapelrud, Arvid. (1963). *The Ras Shamra Discoveries and the Old Testament*. Norman: University of Oklahoma Press.

Kerferd, G. B. (1981). *The Sophistic Movement*. Cambridge: Cambridge University Press.

Kingsley, P. (1995). *Ancient Philosophy, Mystery and Magic*. Oxford: Oxford University Press.

Kirk, G. S. (1954). *Heraclitus: The Cosmic Fragments*. Cambridge: Cambridge University Press.

———. (1960). "The Structure and Aim of the Theogony." In *Hésiode et son influence; Entretiens sur l'antiquité classique. Tome V.* Geneva: Fondation Hart.

———. (1974). *Greek Myths.* Harmondworth Penguin.

———. (1970). *Myth, Its Meaning and Function in Ancient and Other Cultures.* Cambridge: Cambridge Universty Press.

———. Raven, J. E., and Schofield, M. (1983). *The Presocratic Philosophers.* 2nd ed. Cambridge: Cambridge University Press.

Labat, R. (1970). *Les religions du proche orient.* Paris: Fayard-Denoël.

Lachier, L. (1972). "Nature." In *Vocabulaire Technique et Critique de la Philosophie.* 11th ed. A. Lalande. Paris: Presses Universitaires de France.

Lafrance, Yvon. (1999). *"Le sujet du poème de Parménide: l'être ou l'univers?"* *Elenchos* 20:265–308.

Laks, A. (1999). "Soul, Sensation and Thought." In Long (1999):250–270.

Lamberton, Robert. (1988). *Hesiod.* New Haven: Yale University Press.

———, and Lombardo, S. (1993). *Hesiod. Works and Days, Theogony.* Indianapolis, IN: Hackett.

Lämmli, F. (1962). *Vom Chaos zum Kosmos: zur Geschichte einer Idee.* Basel: F. Reinhardt.

Laroche, E. (1946). "Les noms de l'astronomie." *Revue de philologie* 20:118–123.

———. (1991). "Hurrian Borrowings from the Babylonian System." In Bonnefoy and Doniger (1991):225–227.

Lattimore, R. (1959). *Hesiod: The Works and Days, The Shield of Heracles* (trans.). Ann Arbor: University of Michigan Press.

Lefkowitz, M. R., and MacLean Rogers, G., ed. (1996). *Black Athena Revisited.* Chapel Hill: University of North Carolina Press.

Legrand, P. E. (1932). *Hésiode. Théogonie, Travaux et les Jours.* Paris: Les Belles Lettres.

Lehmann, Johannes. (1977). *The Hittites.* London: William Collins.

Leisegang. H. (1941). "Physis," *Realencyclopädie der klassischen Altertumswissenschaft* 39, eds. G. Wissowa, W. Kroll et al. Stuttgart: Metzler. 1130–1164.

Lesher, J. H. (1992). *Xenophanes of Colophon: Fragments.* Toronto: University of Toronto Press.

Lévêque, P., and Vidal-Naquet, P. (1997). *Cleisthenes the Athenian: An Essay on the Representation of Space and Time in Greek Political Thought from the End of the Sixth Century to the Death of Plato.* Trans. and ed. D. Ames Curtis. New Jersey: Humanities Press.

Lévi-Strauss, Claude. (1958). *Anthropologie Structurale.* Paris: Gallimard.

Lewis, David. (1990). "The Political Background of Democritus." In *'Owls to Athens': Essays on Classical Subjects for Kenneth Dover.* Ed. E. M. Craik. Oxford: Oxford University Press. 151–154.

Lloyd, A. B. (1975–1988). *Herodotus. Book I.* 3 vols. Leiden.

Lloyd, G. E. R. (1966). *Polarity and Analogy: Two Types of Argumentation in Early Greek Thought.* Cambridge: Cambridge University Press.

———. (1970). *Early Greek Science.* London: Chatto & Windus.

———. (1979). *Magic, Reason and Experience. Studies in the Origins and Development of Greek Science.* Cambridge: Cambridge University Press.

———. (1983). *Science, Folklore and Ideology. Studies in the Life Sciences in Ancient Greece.* Cambridge: Cambridge University Press.

———. (1991). *Methods and Problems in Greek Science.* Cambridge: Cambridge University Press.

———. (1986). *Hippocratic Writings.* Harmondsworth: Penguin.

Long, A. A., ed. (1999). *The Cambridge Companion to Early Greek Philosophy.* Cambridge: Cambridge University Press.

———. (1999). "The Scope of Early Greek Philosophy." In Long (1999):1–21.

———. (1963–1975). "The Principles of Parmenides' Cosmogony." In Furley and Allen, vol. 2 (1975):82–101.

Loraux, Nicole. (1988). "Solon et la voix de l'écrit." In Detienne (1988):95–129.

———. (1991)."Origins of Mankind in Greek Myths: Born to Die." In Bonnefoy and Doniger (1991):390–395.

Lord, Albert. (1960). *Singer of Tales.* Cambridge, MA: Harvard University Press.

Lovin, R. W., and Reynolds, F. E., eds. (1985). *Cosmogony and Ethical Order.* Chicago: University of Chicago Press.

Malkin, Irad. (1998). *The Return of Odysseus.* Berkeley: University of California Press.

Mansfeld, Jaap. (1985). "Myth, science, philosophy: a question of origins." In W. M. Calder III, U. K. Goldsmith, and P. B. Kenevan, ed. *Hypatia. Festschrift Hazel E. Barnes.* Boulder, CO. 45–65.

———. (1997). Review of Naddaf 1992. *Mnemosyne* 50:754–758.

———. (1999). "Sources." In Long (1999):22–44.

Marcovich, M. (1967). *Heraclitus.* Merida, Venezuela: Los Andes University Press.

Martin, Richard. (1989). *The Language of Heroes. Speech and Performance in the Iliad.* Ithaca, NY and London: Cornell University Press.

Matson, Wallace, I. (1954–1955). "Cornford on the Birth of Metaphysics." *Review of Metaphysics* 8:443–454.

Mazon, P. (1928). *Hésiode.* Paris: Les Belles Lettres.

McDiarmid, J. B. (1953). "Theophrastos on the Presocratic Causes." *Harvard Studies in Classical Philology* 61:85–156.

McEwen, Indra, K. (1993). *Socrates' Ancestor. An Essay on Architectural Beginnings.* Cambridge, MA: MIT Press.

McKirahan, Richard, D. (1994). *Philosophy before Socrates.* Indianapolis and Cambridge: Hackett.

———. (1999). "Zeno." In Long (1999):134–158.

Miller, M. Jr. (1983). "The Implicit Logic of Hesiod's Cosmogony: An Examination of *Theogony,* 116–133." *Independent Journal of Philosophy* 4:131–142.

———. (2001). "'First of all': On the Semantics and Ethics of Hesiod's Cosmogony." *Ancient Philosophy* 21:251–276.

Minar, Jr. E. L. (1949). "Parmenides and the World of Seeming." *American Journal of Philology:*44–53

Mondolfo, R. (1958). "The evidence of Plato and Aristotle relating to the ekpyrosis in Heraclitus." *Phronesis,* 3:75–82.

Morris, Ian. (1986). "The Use and Abuse of Homer." *Classical Antiquity* 5:129–141.

———, and Powell, B., ed. (1997). *A New Companion to Homer.* Leiden: Brill.

Morris, Sarah. (1997). "Homer and the Near East." In Morris and Powell (1997):614–63.

Mosse, Claude. (1984). *La Grèce archaïque d'Homère à Eschyle.* Paris: Maspéro.

Most, G. W. (1999). "The poetics of early Greek philosophy." In Long, ed. 1999:332–362.

Mourelatos, A., ed. (1973). *The Presocratics.* Garden City, NY: Anchor Press-Doubleday.

Mueller, I. (1997). "Greek arithmatic, geometry and harmonics: Thales to Plato." In Taylor (1997):271–322.

Murray, Oswyn. (1993). *Early Greece.* 2nd ed. London: Fontana Press.

Myres, J. L. (1953). *Herodotus, Father of History.* Oxford: Clarendon Press.

Naddaf, Gerard. (1992). *L'Origine et l'évolution du concept grec de phusis.* Lewiston: Edwin Mellen Press.

———. (1994). "The Atlantis Myth: An Introduction to Plato's Later Philosophy of History." *Phoenix* 4:189–209.

———. (1996). "Plato's Theologia Revisited." *Méthexis* 9:5–18.

———. (1998a). "Lefkowitz and the Afrocentric Question." *Philosophy of the Social Sciences* 28:451–470.

———. (1998b). "On the Origin of Anaximander's Cosmological Model." *Journal of the History of Ideas* 59:1–28.

———, and Brisson, Luc. (1998c). *Plato the Myth Maker.* Trans., ed., and with an Introduction by Gerard Naddaf. Chicago: University of Chicago Press.

———. (2001). "Anaximander's Measurements Revisited." In Preus (2001):5–21.

———. (2002). "Hesiod as a Catalyst for Western Political *Paideia.*" *The European Legacy* 7:343–361.

————, with Couprie, D., and Hahn, R. (2003). *Anaximander in Context. New Studies in the Origins of Greek Philosophy.* Albany: State University of New York Press.

Nagy, Gregory. (1982). "Hesiod." In *Ancient Writers.* Ed. T. J. Luce. New York: Scribner.

————. (1990). *Greek Mythology and Poetics.* Ithaca, NY: Cornell Universirty Press.

Neale, W. C., and Tandy, D. W. (1996). *Hesiod Works and Days.* Berkeley: University of California Press.

Nelson, Stephanie. (1996). "Justice and Farming in Works and Days." In *The Greeks and Us.* Ed. R. B. Louden and P. Schollimeier. Chicago: University of Chicago Press. 17–36.

Nemet-Nejat, Karen Rhea. (1998). *Daily Life in Ancient Mesopotamia.* Westport, CT: Greenwood Press.

Neschke-Hentschke, Ada. (1995). *Platonisme Politique et Théorie du Droit Naturel.* Paris-Louvain: Editions Peeters

Nestle, W. (1942). *Vom Mythos zum Logos.* Stuttgart: Alfred Kröner.

Neugebauer, Otto. (1957). *The Exact Sciences in Antiquity.* 2nd ed. Providence, RI: Brown University Press.

————. (1975). *A History of Ancient Mathematical Astronomy.* 3 vols. New York and Berlin: Springer-Verlag.

Neuhäuser, I. (1883). *Dissertatio de Anaximandri Milesius sive vetustissima quaedam rerum universitatis conceptio resituta.* Bonnae: Max Cohen et Filius.

Nilsson, M. P. (1932/1963). *The Mycenean Origin of Greek Mythology.* New York: Norton.

O'Brien, D. (1967). "Anaximander's Measurements." *The Classical Quarterly* 17:423–432.

————. (1968). "The Relation of Empedocles and Anaxagoras." *Journal of Hellenic Studies* 88:93–113.

O'Brien, M. (1985). "Xenophanes, Aeschylus, and the Doctrine of Primeval Brutishness." *Classical Quarterly* 35:264–277.

Onians, R. B. (1951). *The Origins of European Thought.* Cambridge: Cambridge University Press.

Osborne, Robin. (1996). *Greece in the Making 1200–479 B.C.* London and New York: Routledge.

Parker, R. A. (1974). "Ancient Greek Astronomy." In *The Place of Astronomy in the Ancient World.* Ed. F. R. Hobson. Oxford: Oxford University Press.

Plambock, G. (1964). *Dunamis im Corpus Hippocratium.* Mainz: F. Steiner.

Pohlenz, M. (1953). "Nomos und Physis." *Hermes,* 418–438.

Powell, Barry. (1997). "Homer and Writing." In Morris and Powell (1997):3–32.

Preus, A., ed. (2001). *Before Plato*. Albany, NY: State University of New York Press.

Pritchard, J. B. (1969). *Ancient Near Eastern Texts Relating to the Old Testament*. 3rd ed. Princeton: Princeton University Press.

Procopé, J. F. (1989/1990). "Democritus on Politics and the Care of the Soul." *Classical Quarterly* 39:307–331; 40:21–45

Ramnoux, C. (1959/1969). *La Nuit et les enfants de la nuit*. Paris: Flammarion.

Rescher, Nicholas. (1958). "Cosmic Evolution in Anaximander." *Studium Generale* 11:718–731. Reprint in *Essays in Philosophical Analysis*. Pittsburgh, PA: University of Pittsburg Press.

Robb, Kevin. (1994). *Literacy and Paideia in Ancient Greece*. Cambridge: Cambridge University Press.

Robin, Leon. (1921/1963). *La pensee grecque et les origines de l'esprit scientifique*. Paris: Albin Michel.

Robinson, J. M. (1968). *An Introduction to Early Greek Philosophy*. Boston: Houghton Mifflin.

———. "Anaximander and the Problem of the Earth's Immobility." In *Essays in Ancient Greek Philosophy*. Ed. J Anton and G. Kustas. Vol. 1. Albany, NY: State University of New York Press. 111–118.

Robinson, T. M. (1987). *Heraclitus. Fragments. A Text and Translation with a Commentary*. Toronto: University of Toronto Press.

Rosen, Ralph. (1997). "Homer and Hesiod." In Morris and Powell (1997):463–488.

Rosenmeyer, T. (1957). "Hesiod and Historiography." *Hermes* 85:257–283.

Roth, Catherine. (1976). "The Kings and Muses in Hesiod's *Theogony*." *TAPA* 106:331–338.

Rykwert, Joseph. (1976). *The Idea of a Town*. Princeton: Princeton University Press.

Sambursky, Samuel. (1956/1987). *The Physical World of the Greeks*. 3 vols., trans. Merton Dagut. Princeton: Princeton University Press.

Saunders, T. (1991). *Plato's Penal Code*. Oxford: Oxford University Press.

Schaerer, R. (1930). *EPISTEME et TECHNE: Étude sur les notions de connaissance et d'art d'Homère à Platon*. Macon: Protat.

Schibli, H. S. (1990). *Pherecydes of Syros*. Oxford: Oxford University Press

Schmalzriedt, E. (1970). *Peri physeōs: Zur Frühgeschichte der Buchtitel*. Munich: Fink.

Schofield, M. (1980). *An Essay on Anaxagoras*. Cambridge: Cambridge University Press.

Sedley, D. (1999). "Parmenides and Melissus." In Long (1999):113–133.

Severyns, A. (1926). "*Le cycle épique et la légende d'io*." *Le Musée Belge* 29–30:119–130.

Sider, D. (1981). *The Fragments of Anaxagoras*. Meisenheim am Glan: Verlag Anton Hain.

Snodgrass, A. M. (1980). *Archaic Greece: Age of Experiment*. Berkeley and Los Angeles: University of California Press.

———. (1971). *The Dark Age of Greece*. Edinburgh: Edinburgh University Press.

Solmsen, F. (1949). *Hesiod and Aeschylus*. Ithaca, NY: Cornell University Press.

Souilhé, J. (1919). *Etude sur le term "dunamis" dans les dialogues de Platon*. Paris: F. Alcan.

Starr, Chester. (1977). *Economic and Social Growth of Early Greece: 800–500 B.C.* New York: Oxford University Press.

Svenbro, J. (1993). *Phrasikleia*. Ithaca, NY: Cornell University Press.

Tannery, Paul. (1887/1930). *Pour l'histoire de la science hellène: de Thalès a Empédocle*. 2nd ed. Paris: Gauthier-Villars.

Tarán, L. (1965). *Parmenides*. Princeton: Princeton University Press.

Taylor, A. E. (1928). *A Commentary on Plato's "Timaeus."* Oxford: Oxford University Press.

Taylor, C. C. W. (1999a). *The Atomists: Leucippus and Democritus*. Toronto: University of Toronto Press.

———. (1999b). "The Atomists." In Long (1999):181–204.

———, ed. (1997). *Routledge History of Philosophy*. Vol. 1. *From the Beginnings to Plato*. London: Routledge.

Thomas, Carol, and Conant, C. (1999). *Citadel to City-State: The Transformation of Greece 1200–700 B.C.E.* Bloomington: Indiana University Press.

Thomas, Caroline. (1977). "Literacy and the Codification of Law." *Studia et Documenta Historiae et Juris* 43:455–488.

Thomas, Rosalind. (1992). *Literacy and Orality in Ancient Greece*. Cambridge: Cambridge University Press.

Thompson, J. O. (1948/1965). *History of Ancient Geography*. Cambridge: Cambridge University Press.

Tritle, Lawrence. (1996). "Vision or Dream of Greek Origin." In Lefkowitz and MacLean (1996):303–330.

Van Wees, Hans. (1997). "Homeric Warfare." In Morris and Powell (1997):668–693.

Verdenius. (1947). "Notes on the Presocratics." *Mnemosyne* 13:271–289.

Vernant, Jean-Pierre. (1983). *Myth and Thought in Ancient Greece*. London: Routledge and Kegan Paul.

———. (1991). "Greek Cosmogonic Myths." In Bonnefoy and Doniger (1991): 366–378.

———. (1991). "A Theogony and Myths of Sovereignty in Greece." In Bonnefoy and Doniger (1991): 375–378.

Vlastos, Gregory. (1945/1993). "Ethics and Physics in Democritus." In Graham (1993):328–350.

——. (1946/1993). "On the Pre-History in Diodorus." In Graham (1993):351–358.

——. (1947/1993). "Equality and Justice in Early Greek Cosmologies." In Graham (1993):57–88.

——. (1950/1993). "The Physical Theory of Anaxagoras." In Graham (1993):303–327.

——. (1952/1993). "Theology and Philosophy in Early Greek Thought." In Graham (1993):3–31.

——. (1953/1993). "Isonomia." In Graham (1993):89–111.

——. (1955/1993). "On Heraclitus." In Graham (1993):127–150.

——. (1975). "One World or Many in Anaxagoras." In Allen and Furley (1975):99–118.

Walcot, P. (1966). *Hesiod and the Near East.* Cardiff: Wales University Press.

West, Martin. (1966). *Hesiod's Theogony.* Oxford: Oxford University Press.

——. (1971). *Early Greek Philosophy and the Orient.* Oxford: Clarendon Press.

——. (1978). *Hesiod Works and Days.* Oxford: Oxford University Press.

——. (1985). *The Hesiodic Catalogue of Women.* Oxford: Oxford University Press.

Willetts, R. (1977). *The Civilization of Ancient Crete.* New York: Barnes and Noble.

Woodruff, P. (1999). "Rhetoric and relativism: Protagoras and Gorgias." In Long (1999):290–310.

Wright, M. R. (1995). *Cosmology in Antiquity.* London and New York: Routledge.

——. (1981). *Empedocles. The Cosmic Fragments.* New Haven and London.

Wycherley, Richard. (1937). "Aristophanes, the Birds, 995–1009." *Classical Quarterly* 31:18–33.

Yalouris, N. (1980). "Astral Representations in the Archaic and Classical Periods and Their Connection to Literary Sources." *American Journal of Archaeology* 84:85–89.

Index of Concepts and Proper Names

(For ancient authors, see also the Index of Classical Passages Cited.)

237

Index of Classical Passages Cited